Praise for *My Young Life*:

"Highly readable . . . With loving detail, Tuten brings to life the time and place of the creatively exciting, post-WWII decades in New York City. . . . In the end, Tuten's achievement is in telling a story that is at once his own while also being universally familiar."

—*Booklist*

"In writing his early life [Tuten] turns what could be act of narcissism—speaking of himself—into one of sparkling generosity."

—Literary Hub

"[A] beautifully composed, accumulative portrait of Tuten at different stages of his young life."

—*Hyperallergic*

"This is a wonderfully raw story of city boy's transformation into a writer."

—*Publishers Weekly*

"[A] perspicacious generosity colors the entire book . . . Tuten's [story], dry and tender, brings something I don't think I've ever encountered in any other young man's artistic coming of age."

—*Los Angeles Review of Books*

"Tuten's path is fascinatingly tortuous. This is not the story of a boy's imagination or a mature man's, but what Keats called 'a space of life between, in which the soul is in ferment, the character undecided, the way of life uncertain' . . . The reader comes away with a dazzling sense of a time when the arts had fewer guardrails, tremendous change was on the way, and liverwurst sandwiches were available everywhere."

—*BOMB Magazine*

"So thrilling. *My Young Life* describes a specific period, but it also evokes the timeless fascination with the Romantic life. I don't think I've ever read a book so precise in presenting a young man's preoccupation and occupation."

—Steve Martin, actor and author of *Born Standing Up*

"This memoir is about more than what happens, though what happens is quite a lot. It's about a young man in search of a life, in search of himself. It's about love found and lost. It's about all of us. I love it."

—Diane Keaton, actor and author of
Let's Just Say It Wasn't Pretty

"Frederic Tuten has written a sweet, openhearted, guileless, and deeply moving account of his formative years, one that will resonate with anyone who has undergone the process of trying to become an artist. He somehow manages to merge the young and older Frederics so that both are speaking at once, which is quite a feat."

—Luc Sante, author of *Low Life* and *Evidence*

"Tuten's memoir of growing up in the Bronx is passionate and rueful and, at times, hilarious. His bold, unabashed prose rushes beautifully through the decades. A naïf with attitude, Tuten's younger self is a hopeless romantic, an impoverished dreamer who conflates his desire to be an artist with his yearning for love. He idealizes art and women in equal measure, failing at one but succeeding spectacularly at the other. A burning tale of the long journey from Arthur Avenue to the world of art and artists in Alphabet City."

—David Salle, artist and author of *Debris*

"Like Tuten himself, *My Young Life* has an enormous heart. It's the story of a young man in love with art, with New York, and with just about every person who crosses his path. *My Young Life* is an antidote to this cool, anxious century: a reminder that we can feel the most overpowering feelings, and dream the most dizzying dreams."

—Paul La Farge, author of *The Artist of the Missing* and
The Night Ocean

"Sensational. So clearly and movingly written—its sentences so funny and quirky and matter-of-factly Steinian—its tone as lucid as James Baldwin's in *Notes of a Native Son* or Delmore Schwartz's in "In Dreams" or Willa Cather's or Jean Rhys's. A straightforward-shaped American (or French-American) tone. (The best American writing—such as yours—is mostly French in its leanness and succulence.) The feelings behind the words are so full and rich and (I daresay) *pregnant* with meaning, that the language therefore needs to do nothing fancy; it can simply be itself. A stylistic (and visionary) pinnacle."

—Wayne Koestenbaum, author of *Humiliation* and
The Queen's Throat

"A remarkable—and remarkably beautiful—cultural record that is deeply personal, and a personal record that is deeply cultural."

—Tom McCarthy, author of *Satin Island* and
Men in Space

"The memoir got into my head in a very deep way, and for many nights I had dreams that it provoked. What the book seems to be about (and this is what made it so moving and disturbing) is the sadness of getting what you want. You (or 'you') begin by wanting art and sex and you get more sex than you hoped for or imagined, but it leaves you just as lonely as you began. The chance to make art is something hinted at all along and the ending of the book is a wonderfully somersaulting marvel."

—Edward Mendelson, Lionel Trilling Professor
in the Humanities, Columbia University

My Young Life

A Memoir

1944–1964

The Bronx, Manhattan, Mexico, Syracuse, Alphabet City

Frederic Tuten

Simon & Schuster Paperbacks

New York   London   Toronto   Sydney   New Delhi

Simon & Schuster Paperbacks
An Imprint of Simon & Schuster, Inc.
1230 Avenue of the Americas
New York, NY 10020

First Simon & Schuster trade paperback edition March 2020

SIMON & SCHUSTER PAPERBACKS and colophon are
registered trademarks of Simon & Schuster, Inc.

For information about special discounts for bulk purchases, please contact Simon &
Schuster Special Sales at 1-866-506-1949 or business@simonandschuster.com.

The Simon & Schuster Speakers Bureau can bring authors to your live event. For
more information or to book an event, contact the Simon & Schuster Speakers
Bureau at 1-866-248-3049 or visit our website at www.simonspeakers.com.

Interior photos from the Frederic Tuten collection in the Rare Books
& Manuscripts Library of The Ohio State University Libraries

Interior design by Ruth Lee-Mui

Manufactured in the United States of America

10 9 8 7 6 5 4 3 2 1

Library of Congress Cataloging-in-Publication Data is available.

ISBN 978-1-5011-9445-0
ISBN 978-1-5011-9446-7 (pbk)
ISBN 978-1-5011-9447-4 (ebook)

For Gloria De Petriums Colliani Loomis
With love

Contents

About this time, the loneliness of our voyage was relieved by an event worth relating.

—Herman Melville, *Mardi, and a Voyage Thither*

My Young Life

Rex's Visit. The Race

The Bronx, Pelham Parkway North, 1944

Sometimes she brought me a little present she had found on a fruit cart she passed on her way home from work, a pomegranate—my favorite color—or a little cellophane bag of salty roasted soybeans. If it was a Friday night, I could tell if she still had her job the moment she walked in the door. If yes, she was smiling and would kiss me and say, "*Figlio mio, ti voglio bene, bene.*" If no, she'd put on a brave face and, before removing her coat, say with a forced smile, "How was school today?"

Francesca, my grandmother, had dinner ready, and as soon as my mother washed up we three were at the kitchen table. Sometimes there was fish, which I hated and whose spines I dreaded choking on, but mostly there was pasta, prepared the Sicilian way, with little meatballs cooked with parsley and pine nuts. I hated everything my grandmother made. If there was money in the house, we had a dessert of nuts and cheese, but I wanted the apple pie I was sure all real American boys had when they concluded their meals. Sometimes we ate by candlelight. My mother pretended it was for the fun of it, but I knew she had once again forgotten to pay the electricity bill.

My mother was a draper and sometimes a designer in the fabled garment center on Seventh Avenue in faraway Manhattan, and she talked in Sicilian about the cheap bosses, the haughty cutters, her jealous fellow drapers, and the pressers—like tired slaves, she said.

My grandmother listened keenly, wanting news of the outside world where she seldom traveled, wanting, above all, to advise my mother in matters where my mother, born in America and thus naïve and innocent, had no clue. She advised whom to watch out for, whose favor to curry, and whom to run from, like the bosses who offered to fly off with her for a weekend in Florida. "Why don't you go, Mom?" I asked. "It's warm in Florida."

I was ten, and even though my Sicilian was fair, all this talk meant little to me in any language, so I daydreamed that maybe my father would come back soon and bring me the cap gun I wanted. Maybe he would take me to the ball game at Yankee Stadium, as he had promised time after time. Or maybe he would just come home and that in itself would be everything.

My mother was never happy when my father was not home with us. No sooner had we finished dinner and I had washed the dishes than she kissed me good night and went to her room to read in bed. My grandmother opened the screen separating her part of the living room and came to my cot. She was dressed all in black, as she did from the day her husband died, so she always looked like an old thin crow and was a bit frightening as she hovered over to kiss me good night.

I could hear my mother crying in her bedroom, on the other side of the wall. Then silence. I could feel her light go out.

One evening in the middle of dinner, the doorbell rang, and Carl, a giant in coveralls and work boots, came to tell us that Rex, my father, would be home the following week, maybe on Tuesday, or maybe Thursday, or maybe in two weeks. Carl wasn't sure. We still had no phone, so this was the way my father got in touch with us: different giant men, shy at the door, came with Rex's messages. My grandmother was always alarmed by these sudden appearances, and urged my mother not to open the door, not even with the chain attached, and to let the man say his words through the peephole.

My mother, Madelyn, in one of her rare moments of happiness.

With the news that Rex would be coming home, my mother burst alive. Over the weekend she sang, she hugged and kissed me every ten minutes. I helped her wash the windows, bringing her bowls of rinse water and drying the windows with newspapers. My grandmother was sent to do the shopping with a list my mother had scribbled to show the grocer and the butcher. She spoke very little English, so the list was necessary; it also asked to put the bill on our credit, which we had not paid for a long time. My father, from Savannah, Georgia, loved Royal Crown cola, pork sausages, pickled pig knuckles, pork chops, and hominy grits. Where did she find such stuff in our Jewish neighborhood, where we had moved a year after I was born, my mother telling me later that she wanted me to be raised among people who prized education rather than among the southern Italians not too far away on Arthur Avenue, where I would become a truck driver or a Mafia lowlife?

My father was coming: my mother walked with a lilt and lightness—with joy. I was excited, too. I told my friends that my dad was coming home and was sure to bring me a cap gun, caps, and firecrackers, and that we were going to a ball game. It was the same thing I told them each time I expected him home, and I was met with snickers because I had said the same thing countless times before.

"Where's your father?" the kids asked. Their fathers came home from work every day and took the families to dinner every Sunday night at the neighborhood "Chinks." "My dad is in the Seabees and he builds roads and airports in the war against the Nazis," I said, as I was told to say. "And he has to be away a lot."

I half believed it, but I knew from what passed between my mother and my grandmother that there was another story. Rex had another life in Jersey City, New Jersey. I was not sure even what that meant, but when the family met for Sunday dinners at my uncle Umberto's seemingly palatial private home with its garden and fruit trees, this New Jersey life eventually found its way to the table, and with the same consequences. My mother defended Rex, said he was a wonderful man, that she loved him, and that he would soon return home.

Her sister, my aunt Sadie, had warned my mother not to marry a non-Italian. "Anyway, so he left you," she said. And, nodding over to me, she added, "And him, too."

My mother rushed into the bathroom and sobbed behind the door. My uncle and aunt stood there, cajoling her to come out, saying that they loved her and just wanted her to be happy. Eventually she emerged, her mascara running. They all hugged and kissed and brought her back to the table and to the unfinished meal. By the end of the dessert of pears and a plate of cheese and nuts—my uncle cracked the shells for all—and a round or two of golden muscatel, made by my uncle and mellowed in casks in his cellar, all conflict and crying was suspended until we were home again, when my mother went back to her room, and back to her crying. I wanted to hug her and make her not cry. But she did not welcome me into her room and the night ended. I was left alone with my grandmother in the living room, where she went to her cot and I went to mine. I turned off the light and dreaded the morning.

Monday meant school again, and I had not done my homework.

I rarely did, and my mother, who had left grade school to go to work, had no idea what homework was and never asked why I wasn't doing it. I often imagined myself becoming invisible at will and also able to fly whenever I wished, so I could escape a scolding from my teacher and the mockery from the other students, who were obedient and did their homework and kept their hands folded as they were told.

One winter morning, when I was safe in my predawn sleep, when the snow muffled the sounds of passing cars and I could hear, even deep in my dreams, the comforting clinking and rattling of the chained tires as the cars plowed their way in the snow, the buzzer buzzed and kept buzzing, until my frightened mother and I woke up and went to the door. "Damn it, Madelyn, open up." It was an unexpected, welcome voice that I had not heard in months.

My mother checked the peephole before unlocking the door; she was angry and happy at the same time. It was Rex, grinning—his coat covered in snow, his head, too—with two pails brimming with water standing at his feet. He lifted them, bending to kiss my mother, and walked into the narrow kitchen. The wall clock said four. I was still half-asleep and plunked myself down in a kitchen chair. "Hello there, son," he said. I put out my hand, like the little gentleman he had taught me to be.

"How did you ever get here in this storm, Rex?"

When we had last looked, the cars were buried in snow and I dreamed that school would be closed.

"Just a few flakes, sugar, but parking was hell. I think I left the old jalopy in some tree."

"We were expecting you later," my mother said testily. "It's his school night," she added, to give weight to his offense.

"Tried to tell you, honey. I asked Carl to stop over with the news a week ago. Didn't he come by?" He flashed that "Did I do wrong again?" look that I'd often seen him use on her. He gave me a wink,

Rex and Madelyn's soulful wedding photo.

as if to say: See what we men have to go through? I winked back.

She didn't soften right off. But with his kissing and touching her in a way that made me feel shy to watch, she slowly did. She caught herself for a moment and took his hand from her breast. "Rex," she whispered, nodding over to me.

He gave me a big smile. "That's all right, Madelyn," he said. "He's a big boy now." That was wonderful to hear—a big boy, soon grown-up enough to go off on adventures with him wherever he went in the world, wherever men go to get the job of life done.

He gave me a soft punch in the arm—one man to another.

"Isn't that true, son?"

"Yes, sir," I said. I wanted to hug him and have him do the same, but that kind of thing didn't come from him, as it did from the Italian side of the family, who were always kissing and hugging each other whenever they felt like it. Crying, too, even the men.

He was done with me and went to the business at hand.

"Madelyn—and you, too, son—how much money do you have in the house?"

I had a few pennies and three dimes saved in a jar from when my uncle Umberto slipped them to me some Sundays past after church. Mom had part of the rent money, she said, but she couldn't touch that.

"Don't be cheap. Just go and get it, honey." He was beaming.

"It's for the rent," she repeated.

"Oh, don't worry about that," he said. "I'm flush."

When we returned to the kitchen with our savings, Rex was on his knees and peering into the pails and giving each a stir with his hand.

He cleared away the kitchen chairs, bringing them into the living room, where my grandmother usually slept on a fold-up cot. She was at her other daughter's home on Laconia Avenue, farther up in the pastoral area of the Bronx, where my aunt Sadie and my uncle Umberto's home flowed with electricity that was never interrupted by the bill collector.

"Now, Madelyn," Rex said in his most chivalrous manner, "I'm going to be fair about this." He grabbed a lobster from each pail, holding them so that their claws chewed the air. He placed the lobsters side by side on the kitchen floor. "You choose first. They're not for eating right away but for betting on. A lobster race's slower than the ponies, but more fun."

My mother laughed and kissed him for the first time since he arrived. "Oh, Rex," she said. "What am I going to do with you?"

"Trifle with me awhile longer, sugar. Place your bet," he said, pointing to the uneasy lobsters. "And you, too, son."

She chose the one closest to her and I took the other, the one my father would have bet on. He released the racers and let them crawl helter-skelter across the linoleum, putting them back on track from time to time and prodding them when they got lazy or gave out, which they often did. It was a long race and I soon grew bored and very tired. My mother did, too, pleading with Rex to return the lobsters to their pails and come to bed.

"Oh, Madelyn," he said, "why spoil all the fun?"

"Rex," she said, apologetically, "I have to be at work in a few hours."

"Well, let's have some coffee and talk about that later."

"There's no milk in the house."

"No cow juice? I'll run out and get some." Run outside in the early morning Bronx, where the snow was feet high in the streets and sidewalks and ice had already pulled down trolley lines? In Pelham

Parkway, every store and shop usually opened at nine and closed at seven. Then everything was shut down and shuttered, people were at home, everyone except for those glued to the bars, where, my grandmother said, "the desperate live."

"May I have permission to leave the table, sir?" I asked, half-asleep. If I left without asking, my father would blow up.

"See, Madelyn, see! He's being raised like a Yankee without manners." He'd threaten to put me on a train to his sister's in Savannah, where I'd learn to be a gentleman. My mother, so unlike her, would stand up to him until he relented and drifted to another subject, maybe to one of his passions, like the cruelty of Sherman's March to the Sea. "Madelyn, they burned down every damn house and field and they left us nothing to eat."

I was not at the table but propped against the kitchen wall. I did not care about the lobsters anymore, or even about my father, only sleep. Without a word he carried me to my cot, tucked me in, and put his coat over me for extra heat.

"Good night, my little man," he said.

It was still dark when I woke to their laughter in the next room. Rex was speaking in the low, soothing voice of a man calling down a kitten stuck in a tree.

"Now, come over here, honey."

I listened to them for a long time talking and laughing. I wished I could be there with them and, without knocking, I opened the door to their bedroom. They were under the covers. My mother turned red and said angrily, "What are you doing here?" My father, in a most gentle whisper: "This is not a good time, son."

I returned to my cot but I could not sleep in all the excitement of the lobster race, in his being home, in our being men together. But finally, the first thin light of the day carried me swiftly to my dreams.

Illness. Houses Without Windows

The Bronx, Pelham Parkway North, 1946–1947

I was eleven when, after years of his coming and going, Rex finally left us for good. "You're the man of the house now, son. Take good care of your mother," he said. My mother begged him not to leave. She tried to block him from the door, but he stood there wordlessly until she moved aside.

"Don't go, Dad, don't go," I called out from the open window as he walked, cardboard suitcase in hand, to the Pelham Parkway subway station. He did not turn or wave.[1]

A few weeks after Rex left, I developed rheumatic fever and was moved to my mother's big bed, where I convalesced for almost a year. My mother slept in the living room on my old cot behind a moldy brown screen. We had no television; only a few homes in our neighborhood did, but we could not afford one even on the installment plan. When I was strong enough, I sat all bundled up in a chair in my grandmother's side of the room listening to the kids' programs on the radio from five to six: I loved *Jack Armstrong, the All-American Boy*, who always did the right thing, *The Shadow*, who knew what secrets lie in the hearts of men, and, best of all, *The Lone Ranger*, who at the end of each show selflessly rode away from the lures of home and comfort to continue his crusade against injustice. For years, until his death, I thought of my father as a man who had left home to save the world.

I spent my days sleeping and reading books my mother brought me from the local library. I loved Stevenson's *Treasure Island* and *Kidnapped* and Twain's *Huckleberry Finn* and *Tom Sawyer*. Sometimes I fell asleep holding a book, not wanting to leave the adventures I found there. I liked Tom for his troublemaking but preferred Huck because he was the more sincere. I was sorry that Huck had a brutal father who had abandoned him. Mine had done the same, but he raced lobsters.

Antibiotics were not yet in general use, and I was given sulfa drugs with the hope that I would recover without damage to my heart. It took a year to get well but I was left with a heart murmur, restricting me from a fully active physical life. When, finally, I was ready to return to school in the fall, my grandmother walked me there slowly and with many stops along the way. Sometimes, when she left me at the school entrance with all the healthy kids running about while I was slowly mounting the stairs, she rushed up and said, "*Ti voglio assai.*"

She looked so old now and so bent in her black getup that I worried about her all day, and if she was even a few minutes late to take me home, I worried that with her cataracts she had fallen into a pothole or tripped on a crack in the sidewalk, as she had twice before.

I was the tallest in class and was seated in the last row by the huge window facing the street. I had no friends among the students and I did not know this teacher, Mrs. McCarthy, an Irishwoman with red cheeks and a ruler that never left her fist. She was stern and distant.

The teacher called on me and I did not answer.

"Come to the desk," she said, "and explain to everyone why you are so special that you are exempt from doing your homework like everyone else."

To my teacher's amazement, I remained in my seat. The class went silent, waiting for the teacher to erupt. But she did not and said instead, "We'll take care of this later."

When the day was over, she took me aside and said she wanted to phone my father and mother and needed the number—there was none on record.

"We don't have a phone," I said. She turned reddish, slapped me, and said, "Lying is the road to criminality. Now go home and write two hundred times 'I am a liar' and set it on my desk tomorrow morning."

I nodded, my face burning from her injustice. I never told my mother what had happened and I did not write the two hundred lines. Now I was the Fred who let his books stay untouched on the shelf, who stared out the window at home and in school, and who not only did not write but who hardly spoke.

At the first deep snow of the winter, I rose up from my seat and stood by the window. The teacher said nothing and the class continued as if I were not there. I stared at the mounting snow and saw no way that my grandmother could walk through the drifts to bring me home. But then a greater worry: What if my father, should he have missed me, should he have decided to come back to his family, he who had never done so before, suddenly wanted to come pick me up in his old rattling Ford. How would he find me in all the blinding snow? I needed to get my coat so I could stand outside on the school steps so that he would not miss me. I went to the closet and searched for my coat. The teacher came and took me by the arm and marched me back to my seat.

I opened my notebook and started to make drawings. Eyeless men and women. Horses without legs. Houses without windows. I sat in my coat, drawing until the final bell.

I lived in a sleepy haze that nothing could shake. My grandmother was more affectionate to me than ever. When I returned from school, she would have waiting for me a few-days-old chunk of semolina bread to have with *caffè latte*, coffee and hot milk, my favorite thing in the world other than pizza. Afterward, we two sat by the radio and listened to my programs, even if she understood only a few words.

One morning, even before I had my coat off, my teacher sent me upstairs to the principal's office. She was Miss Middleton, a small woman with glasses, fiery red hair, and a soothing, sweet voice. She asked me about my home life and what I enjoyed doing. "Reading," I said, and told her of my love for *Huckleberry Finn* and *Tom Sawyer* and the novels of Robert Louis Stevenson—*Kidnapped*, especially. I told her that I liked to draw with colored pencils.

"Do you like your mother?"

"Sometimes."

"That's all right. We don't have to love everyone all the time." She smiled, and that made me like her.

"Yes," I said.

"I think you are a very bright boy."

I was too embarrassed to say thank you. She came from behind her desk and said, "We shall see each other again."

I put out my hand, as my father had taught me to do. She shook it and held it firmly. Her perfume clung to me all day and I missed its embracing, mysterious aroma when it finally vanished into the ordinary air.

---

¹REX REDUX
Rex Sterling Tuten (1913–1977)

I didn't see Rex again until thirty-one years later, when his brother, my uncle Perry, phoned me from Columbus, Georgia, saying my father was dying in a hospital in Jersey City, New Jersey. He said, "Fred, I think you should go see him and say good-bye."

"He never cared about me or my mother when he had the chance. Why should I care about him now?"

"I think you'll regret not going," he said. "Anyway, I know you're a Catholic, and I think you should practice forgiveness."

"Thank you for calling, Perry. Very thoughtful of you," I said.

Dooley Worth, my girlfriend, urged me to go, saying that whether I forgave Rex or not, I would regret not going. "I'll go with you," she said. And we went.

There were four persons in the ward; all were sleeping and looked half-dead. I recognized Rex immediately. He had not changed a day since he left us, suitcase in hand. I looked at him for a long time, amazed at how youthful he was. He opened his eyes and in his gentle, soft, Southern voice said, "How are you?"

"How are *you*?" I said.

"I'm dying."

"How do you know that?"

"A Catholic priest came this morning to give me last rites."

"But you're not a Catholic. Why would a priest come?"

"I was married to a Catholic woman once."

"Do you know who I am?"

"You're a doctor, aren't you?"

"No, I'm your son from that marriage."

He turned away for a few moments, and when he faced me again, his eyes were swollen with tears. He said, "Anyway, I had a good life."

"I'm glad you did, Rex." I astonished myself by my familiarity, but could not bring myself to say "Dad" or "Father." Calling him by his first name made me feel that we were now somehow equals.

"What have you been doing with yourself?" he asked.

"I'm a writer," I said.

"Uh-huh. Well, you know, if I ever get out of this thing, we should get to know each other." He reached over to the nightstand and took a pack of Camels from the top drawer. "Light one for me, please." I did, with the strike of a wooden match. Immediately, two of the patients in the adjacent beds cried, "Smoke, smoke!" I rushed to put the cigarette out in the bathroom. When I returned, I asked, "Is there anything else I can do for you, Rex?"

"Yes, I would love some Chinese food, but they won't let me have it here."

He looked very tired; his eyes kept fluttering. "I have to go to sleep now, but come again soon," he said. I went downstairs to the waiting room and said, "Dooley, please come upstairs and see him. I need a witness that this really happened."

He seemed deeply asleep, but as we approached his bed, suddenly he opened his eyes.

I said, "Rex, this is my girlfriend, Dooley. She wanted to meet you."

He extended his hand. She took it. He held it, smiling, for a long time. Finally he said, "I'm very pleased to meet you. I'm a bit sleepy now, but come again soon. You hear?" He held on to her hand as if he would never let go, until finally she gently withdrew it.

When we got to the street, Dooley finally spoke to me. "You're sexy, but your father! I understand exactly what your mother felt. I would have gone off with him in a second." That hurt. Even while dying, he has power, I thought.

Years later, I wrote a novel, *Tallien: A Brief Romance*, in which I intercut the history of a young French revolutionary, Jean Lambert Tallien, with my father's story when he was a radical during the Great Depression. In the novel I imagined my father's deathbed scene in a rooming house, where his friends had taken him from the hospital and indulged him in his last wishes.

I wrote in purplish prose: "In the foreground of a room in a rooming house in Jersey City, New Jersey, Rex's corpse, yellowish, mummified, stiff as a laundry brick. In the background, an ashtray of dead Camels, the ashes of dead stars. In the receding lines of infinity, little white paper cartons of Chinese food and gnawed spare ribs sprinkled along an avenue leading toward a sky where hopes take refuge."

First Love and Icarus

The Bronx, P.S. 96, 1948

The following week I took a battery of IQ tests that the principal had ordered. I did so well that I was transferred to a Special Progress class, where I learned about the Greek myths and was taught how to use pastel sticks and watercolors. We numbered only sixteen in the whole class and sat four at a desk, like a life raft on a friendly sea. My classmates were bright and courteous. "May I borrow your pencil?" one asked, instead of grabbing it off my desk. My father would have loved them.

I was seated beside Marilyn, a girl with blond braids and freckles who spoke in paragraphs. She read poetry and recited lines to me like "Life is real, life is earnest, and the grave is not its goal."

"Who is Ernest?" I asked, playing dumb. Marilyn drew with crayons and colored pencils and painted in oil at home, she said, adding, "I'm going to start smoking French cigarettes when I turn thirteen." She was fond of kissing me on the cheek when the teacher's back was turned and she put notes in my hand: "I almost love you." I was twelve but knew already that I was in love with her. "I love you all the time," I wrote back. Everything about her was cheerful, her face always sunny. She told me that her name meant Sunday in German. I said: "You warm me like the sun. You shine like the sun."

Our teacher, Miss Kaplan, was plump and childlike. She spoke to the window and often giggled in the middle of a sentence she never finished. Marilyn said that Miss Kaplan wore wigs.

"Have you not noticed, Freddy, that one week her hair is red and one week black and one week a crazy-looking strawberry blond?" I had not noticed.

"I see no one but you."

"Where do you get that stuff, Fred?"

"My father," I said.

"He sounds great."

"He *is* great."

One morning Miss Kaplan stopped at each table to review our homework. I'd written about Icarus and how he had flown too close to the sun, melting his waxed wings and falling to earth. The moral, I had written, was "Do not aim higher than what is possible." My script, some letters small and some giant, fled the page for no apparent reason.

I was afraid that she would mock my scrambled writing.

"That is very wise, what you wrote, Fred," she said. "But I notice that you write like Icarus himself. All the words flying off the edge of the page."

I had no answer, but I knew she was pleased with me and I was proud. Marilyn said, "He's a genius, Miss Kaplan."

"You all are," she answered, "but that doesn't mean you don't have to work your hardest."

A week later, I was sent to the principal's office. I was afraid I had done something wrong and that I would be returned to the "dummy class," as my classmates called it. Miss Middleton was behind the desk, her hands folded—a bad sign?—but she smiled and said, "Are you happy in your new class?" I saw the ax fall, expecting her next line to be "Maybe you'd be happier where you were?"

"I want to stay here, please."

"Why not, Fred? After all, I hear you are doing so well."

"I hope so."

"I'm told you wrote a little essay about Icarus."

I thought she was going to ask if I had copied it from a book. Instead she said, "And that you thought the moral was to not fly too high in life."

"Yes, not get hurt. Not make people jealous of you."

"Who taught you that?"

"My grandmother."

"Fred, what do you want to do when you are older?"

"I'd like to be a writer or an artist or get a job in the post office."

"You can do or be anything you want," she said.

She walked me to the door. "I'd like to meet your parents one day."

"It's hard for my mother to take time off from work," I said. "And my father works far away."

"Oh? Where?"

"In Greece," I said, imagining the slides of Ionic and Doric columns that Miss Kaplan had shown us.

"Is that why only your mother signs your report card?"

"Yes."

"Try to remember this, Fred: Always be with older people who can help you."

I took the stairs, each step slowly, wanting to keep the warmth of her good-bye.

When I returned to class, Marilyn came right up to my face and asked, "What are you going to do this summer, Freddy?"

I did not want to tell her that my mother had found me a delivery-boy job with Marty, our local butcher. I had known him since childhood, when my grandmother and I shopped there for chopped meat and got free soup bones. My mother and the butcher had arranged to have a portion of my weekly salary deducted from what we owed him on credit. I was excited to have some money on my own to help my mother, and to be the man of the house, as my father had asked.

"I'm not sure yet. Maybe I'll get my seaman's papers and ship out." I liked saying "ship out" for the grown-up sound of the thing. The father of one of my neighborhood pals was a minor official in a seamen's union and had promised us both such papers when we turned eighteen.

"I'm going to Paris. With my parents, of course. Have you been?"

"One day, I'm sure."

"Maybe you can visit us this summer?"

"Yes, maybe."

"Ask your parents. I'm sure they will let you go. And you can stay with us."

"I'll ask," I said.

On the last day of school I walked her home. She lived not far from me but in a better section of the neighborhood, in a large building facing the Bronx Park. It was after three and hot for a June afternoon. We went in the building's cool lobby and sat on a soft blue sofa with not one stain.

"Don't make such a sad face, Freddy."

"And you don't cry," I said.

She kissed me on the lips and rushed to the elevator and waved good-bye before the door closed.

I waited for her letters and soon they came, one after another, sometimes two in a day. Light blue aerograms bearing huge stamps with a beautiful woman's face.

"I feel very grown-up in Paris. Even my parents treat me differently. They send me down to the corner bakery every morning to bring back a baguette and croissant—rolls to you!—and never worry if I'm a bit late. We sit at a wooden kitchen table with a window to a beautiful park and drink coffee with hot milk in big bowls—not in cups like we Americans do. Everything is beautiful in Paris. When we grow up, we will go and live there and be artists together." She asked me to swear on it. I swore, in two letters the same day.

Some of her aerograms had ink drawings of bridges over a river, of cafés with people sitting outside under an awning. "I'm in a café on my corner where my parents let me come alone and I'm drinking *un express*," she wrote. The page was spotted with brownish flecks. "Can you smell it?" Another letter: "The museums here are BEAUTIFUL. Van Gogh, do you know his paintings? He is the best artist in the world. He makes me dizzy with happiness." She ended with: *Tu me manques* and *Bisous*. I had to ask a French neighbor, Mr. Morin, who had fled Paris from the Nazis, to tell me what those words meant. He did, smiled, and added, "You are a lucky young man."

Earning My Keep

The Bronx, Pelham Parkway North, circa 1948–1949

Marty the butcher was a giant with thick leather shoes and a blood-stained apron. "Get rid of those sneakers," he said on my first day at work. "Wear shoes with heavy leather in case a knife falls on your foot. I haven't got time to take you to the hospital." He wheezed all day, his lungs chilled from his goings and comings in and out of the walk-in meat locker.

"Sonny, this is no life," he said.

I washed the display windows with ammonia, wiped and dried them with newspapers. At day's end, I scrubbed down the cutting stalls with a wire brush; I swept the floors and sprinkled them with fresh sawdust. But most of the time I rode the store bike with fat tires and no gears and a huge wire basket on the handlebars; I pedaled fast in the July heat to deliver the packages of lamb chops and steaks while they were still cold from the fridge.

Sometimes I was given a tip of soda bottles in a bag for me to cash in; once I got a whole dollar from an old woman for also bringing the garbage down her five flights. Sometimes I got nothing, and I'd ride home angry and feeling cheated and sorry for myself. Otherwise, I liked the job, the freedom of riding the bike all over the neighborhood all day, and I loved the tips heavy in my pockets.

After a round of deliveries and before returning to the butcher shop, I'd bike to Louie's luncheonette, drop coins down on the counter, and order anything I wanted, a Lime Rickey and a juicy hamburger with greasy fried onions, or a thick chocolate milk shake and a side of sizzling french fries. I felt very American eating this stuff and wished my grandmother would make hamburgers like the Americans did and not embed them with Italian parsley and pine nuts. At the week's end Marty gave me chopped meat to take home and paid me ten dollars, keeping ten for what we had owed on the credit. I could keep all the tips. "You're a good boy," he would say, and called me *tatala* and other Yiddish things, all to say that I was an OK *boychik*.

I gave the money to my mother. Sometimes she would say that I should keep it all but ended up giving me five and taking the other five. She pinched my cheeks and said, "*Figlio mio.*" And "my little man of the house."

Aerograms. *Romeo and Juliet*

The Bronx, Pelham Parkway North, circa 1948–1949

All summer long I thought of Marilyn. I couldn't wait to get home from work to write her. Her letters, in a perfect script that filled the page, told me about the street musicians, about the houseboats along the always-blue river that ran through the center of Paris. "I love speaking French!" she wrote. "You should learn it and we can *parler* together."

Because there was nothing but the routine of my delivery routes to recount—because I felt ashamed of my life as a butcher boy—I wrote about how much I missed her and couldn't wait for her to return. I threw in some other details to make it vivid: "You are my sky and my stars." I regretted how sugary those words were the second I slid the letter into the corner mailbox, but it was too late. In a less syrupy note I said that I was saving money every week so that one day we could live together in Paris. That was not true—there were no such savings—but I wanted to remind her we had a future.

In late August, I dreamed of the quick return of fall. In just a few more weeks it would be Labor Day and, right after, school, when Marilyn would be home and the big, wide, deep, empty space in my heart—so I wrote—would be filled. I heard nothing for nine days and wondered if she was ill or had fallen into that Paris river or, worse, that she did not love me anymore.

An aerogram arrived two weeks before school opened. The

news: Marilyn's parents had gotten jobs teaching at a high school in Los Angeles and they were not coming back to New York. It all happened in a big rush and they were flying to Los Angeles directly from Paris. "I have been crying all week," she wrote, drawing little teardrops along the margins of the page. She loved me and would always love me. "Fred, we will still be in Paris *ensemble* one day."

We continued to write each other, frequently at first, then, on her side, less frequently and less fervently. One rainy November day I received a rather curt letter of four pages. It was filled with descriptions of her trip to the Mojave Desert, where she and her parents and a next-door neighbor, a boy her age named Eugene, camped out under the blackest sky filled with the brightest stars. "You will love the desert, Fred. Maybe you can come out and visit me one day."

She was slipping away. I wrote: "I wish I was there with you instead of Eugene. I will try to come see you one day soon. Is there any hope you can come here?" Then I made a list of what I was reading and of the paintings I loved in art books from the library. I quoted a passage from a letter of Van Gogh to his brother Theo, from another book I got from the library: "I want to paint the heat of the sun." And I ended with a flourish: "I love you more than books and paintings."

Her letters came less frequently and were briefer. Now a week or two would pass before I got even a postcard. I tried not to think of her. But the more I tried, the more she filled my thoughts. After dinner, when my mother went to bed, I spent my evenings at the kitchen table and read books like *The Portrait of a Lady*, books that were beyond my comprehension but that I knew were considered classics and enriching. I drank pots of Earl Grey tea because I liked the way it made my heart race and pound; I believed that drinking tea was sophisticated and that it distinguished me from simple, ordinary coffee drinkers and elevated me into the sphere of genteel high culture and good taste; tea was the elixir for intelligent people. I had learned that from the Sherlock Holmes movies, where the brilliant Holmes and Dr. Watson were always having tea brought to them by their kindly housekeeper, Mrs. Hudson.

I had tuned the radio in the kitchen to WQXR and other classical music radio stations. I was sure that Pyotr Ilyich Tchaikovsky's *Romeo and Juliet* was the most profound music in the world. Competing for depth was Nikolai Rimsky-Korsakov's *Scheherazade*, whose melancholy sweetness enriched my missing of Marilyn, but it also enlarged my sense of my life as very small and eventless. I imagined myself in a vast sea, in a little sailboat riding the swells to the colors of the music and seeing, waiting for me there in the distance, the outlines of a magical island.

With music staging my background, I made colored-pencil drawings of my kitchen with my teapot in the foreground, the rest of the space filled with the stove and the fridge, the window that opened to a small courtyard with untrimmed hedges. One day I would show Marilyn my drawings and she would see in them my yearning for her and for our future life as artists together in Paris.

In the spring of 1949, when I was six months over thirteen, her letters stopped. I wrote again and again with no reply.

One night, my mother walked to the kitchen hours after she had already gone to bed. She was in her fluffy worn nightgown and pink slippers, and I saw that she was distressed.

"What's wrong, Mom? Is the radio on too loud?"

"No."

"Does the smoke bother you?" I had started smoking a pipe, for effect. It went with the tea and the scarf that I wore only in the apartment.

"Not that. I'm worried about you. You are sad all the time."

"It will go away, Mom," I said, not believing it. I did not want it to go away because I knew my love would disappear with the sadness, and what would I be left with then?

"Is it that girl you write to?"

"Yes. But we don't write anymore."

"Maybe you both will write again."

"When, Mom, in heaven?"

"If it is in your and her destiny to be together, one day you will."

I resented her useless good cheer, resented her for invading the house of my sadness. "And what about you and my father, Mom? What is destiny doing for you there?"

"We will be together again. It's in our stars."

"Oh, Mom," I said, my heart hurting for her, for her delusions and her helplessness in life. "I'm sure you're right."

The Last Radio

The Bronx, Pelham Parkway North, circa 1952

My grandmother grew very old very fast. She stayed in her cot all day and barely came to eat with us in the kitchen. She grew weaker and thinner, bones in an old, frayed housecoat. Dr. Marcuccio, who had treated my rheumatic fever, made his weekly house calls and recommended she drink thick Guinness stout to "put some meat on her bones." It didn't.

Francesca slept through her Italian programs. She was too weak to go to Sunday Mass. My mother had to help her go to the bathroom. She slept most of the day, and when awake she wanted me to sit by her and hold her hand; she would hold mine tightly for a moment, then let it go slack. I was frightened she would die and never let go of my hand. One spring afternoon in 1953, I opened the window to bring fresh air into the room which stank of stale sheets and tarry medicines. I put my chair close to her cot.

"Grandma, tell me about Sicily."

"La Sicilia, è molto lontana."

"Yes, I know it is very far."

"Non ti sposare quando sei ancora giovane. Aspetta. Vivi ancora un po."

"I have no plans to marry anyone, Grandma. I love only you."

She smiled, fell asleep. I drew the blinds against the sunlight coating her eyes.

My Sicilian grandmother, Francesca, and me when I was about five, some five years before my world collapsed.

One Saturday, Uncle Umberto and Aunt Sadie arrived. We all sat in the living room watching my grandmother sleeping and wheezing and gasping for air. My mother had called the doctor on our newly installed party-line phone, and he promised to come over right away. He was a northern Italian and, he joked, he liked my mother even though she was a Sicilian. He adored my grandmother and he would talk with her after his official visit. He laughed. They shared a world I would never know. Once I heard her give him a recipe for making codfish with capers.

"It will help your memory," she said.

"You will live forever," he said, winking at me.

"I hope not," she answered. "My husband is getting tired of waiting for me."

My grandmother had her eyes closed. She was breathing in short bursts and sometimes let out a moan. My mother was crying; my aunt, too; my uncle lit his third cigarette. My mother had forgotten she was brewing coffee until we all heard it overflowing on the stove. She rushed into the kitchen. I answered the doorbell.

The doctor pinched me on the cheek like I was still a kid. We huddled in the kitchen while he examined my grandmother, which didn't take long. He still had his stethoscope around his neck when he joined us in the kitchen.

"I'll stay here awhile longer, *finché non è finita.*"

I understood that. Did he think I did not know Italian? He would stay until it was finished, he had said. I wanted to cry.

My mother offered him a glass of Fernet-Branca, which he accepted readily. I heard rattling sounds from the living room and everyone stopped talking. My aunt sobbed.

The doctor turned to me: "Go outside for a half hour. It's too crowded in here."

"I want to see my grandmother."

"When you come back."

My mother said, "Please leave."

I walked to the park playground. Five kids were shooting hoops; two were James and George, the Charon brothers, who lived in a building adjacent to mine. They were in their baseball uniforms; they lived in them, even came to school in them. No one asked me to join in. I watched, but all I was thinking about was when I could go home.

George called out, "Why aren't you home boiling some worms?" It's a line he had used since I was ten, calling the snails we ate "worms." Then James joined in: "Where's your book, little girl?" What they would have liked was another fistfight; another like all the fights since forever, since I was eight. I never won even once.

"Very funny!" I shouted back. I was not sure I'd been away long enough to return and I knew that if I stayed much longer we would fight. The problem was that they'd both attack you at the same time, two against one, and they did not care if you said that was unfair. Finally, I decided I could not wait anymore and ran back home. One of them shouted, "That's right, run home, you fruit."

The doctor had gone. Everyone was in the kitchen weeping. I

was not sure they knew I had come back, and I went into the living room and went behind the screen and pulled back the sheet covering my grandmother's face. She had a beautiful smile. Now I could go to the kitchen and cry with the others.

My mother and I took the long subway ride to Saint Raymond's Cemetery, where the priest and my aunt and uncle were already waiting. Soon a hearse from the funeral parlor drove up and men in black suits drew out a casket. Its golden handles looked plastic. Our parish priest from the church on Gun Hill Road intoned: "Her soul is in heaven now."

I was glad her soul was there. But what did that matter? Francesca was going into the earth forever and I would never see her again.[2]

---

[2]FRANCESCA AND THE FUNERAL
Francesca Scelfo (1874–1952)

An old man appeared just as the casket was being lowered into the grave. I was the only one who seemed to know who he was. I remembered him coming to visit my grandmother years ago, maybe when I was eight. He was very poor, my grandmother later told me, and had come all the way from Brooklyn to tell her about a dream that had haunted him for months. He wore an iron-gray suit that looked like the outfit convicts in 1930s movies were given when they were released from prison. He was even thinner than my grandmother, and frailer. He limped; one shoe needed laces, the other had a raised heel and huge thick sole.

We sat in the kitchen, where my grandmother poured him a full glass of cold water from a pitcher in the fridge. My grandmother was polite but not friendly, which surprised me, since he had come to see her.

He was silent for a few moments, looked about the kitchen.

"*Signora Lepare, mi perdoni, ma posso avere anche un piccolo pezzo di pane?*"

He looked pained, and I felt sorry for him, a grown man asking for a piece of bread. My grandmother went right to work and made fresh coffee and heated the milk and broke two huge chunks of semolina bread we had bought on Arthur Avenue. All the while he ate his eyes grew fat with tears.

They spoke too quickly in Sicilian for me to follow, and I was glad to leave them. I went to sit by the window in the living room to read, but their voices distracted me: my grandmother's steady, firm; the old man's choked. After a long pause, I heard my grandmother say, "Alfonso, I'm sure Giuseppe is glad you came to see me and I'm glad he said he has forgiven you."

"Oh, Francesca, lei è un angela."

Maybe another hour passed when my grandmother brought him to me to say good-bye. I was a good boy, and I should love my grandmother, he said, kissing me on both cheeks. Unlike my uncle Umberto, who smelled of Old Spice, he reeked of old rags kept under the sink.

"It will be too dark to walk back," my grandmother said, giving him a knotted handkerchief. I could see the outline of some coins. He protested; he would not think of taking any gift. It was he who owed her gifts.

"Non viene da me, Alfonso. E da parte di Giuseppe," she said.

We watched from the window as he limped to the subway, and when he was at last out of sight, my grandmother sat in her chair, sighed three times, and shut her eyes.

"Pace, pace," she said, *"finalmente."*

At dinner she told us the story. Alfonso came from the same region where she and my grandfather Giuseppe had lived, some miles from Palermo, in the hills. A year before they fled to America, Alfonzo came to borrow money, which they gave him, even though they themselves had very little. But he was her husband's cousin. She added, "One must feed the sparrows in winter, even if it is your last crust of bread."

"But one day, when we needed every penny to come to America, my husband went to Alfonso who said, '*Certo*, I will bring the money tomorrow.' He did not, and in fact he went into hiding."

"Why did you even let him in the house?" I asked.

"He's a poor devil. And he came all the way from Brooklyn. Also, he brought me a message my husband sent him in a dream from heaven."

"Don't make me die waiting. Tell me," I said.

"Giuseppe said, 'There are no vineyards in heaven.'"

"Was that all?"

"The rest were the special things that pass between a husband and a wife," she said with a youthful smile I had never seen before.

Paint Tubes and an Easel

The Bronx, Pelham Parkway North, 1953

The snow mounted high along the sidewalks and covered the roads; cars crawled and slid and one, a wheezing black Ford, skidded through a red light and crashed into a tree. I didn't mind the storm; I put on my galoshes and bundled up with two sweaters under my coat and went out to give myself a present for my fifteenth birthday. I made it to the shop near the Pelham Parkway subway station that sold greeting cards and stationery and rented, for two cents a day, the bestsellers and the romances that my mother read. It was there that I had bought my colored pencils and drawing pads and where, in the back room behind a blue curtain, like porno, the art supplies were stashed.

Seymour, the owner, looked surprised. "Warm enough for you?"

I had no ready joke answer, focusing on why I had come there.

"Plenty warm enough."

"I was just going to close. No sane person is coming out today."

"I won't stay long," I said, worried he could get rid of me before I had gotten what I wanted.

"Sure, but go outside and brush off your coat: it's dripping snow all over the floor."

We went to the back room, where I chose a few small tubes of oil, the bare essentials, all by Grumbacher: a zinc yellow, medium tube (I liked the French name for it, *jaune zinc*); a large tube of zinc white (I knew this was important because it blended with and toned down all the other colors); a cerulean blue, for the skies I would one day paint *en plein air*, like Van Gogh; a *jaune citron* for the sunflowers I would come across somewhere. A large tube also of *noir d'ivoire* that I would need for outlining, for boldness, as did Gauguin. Because it was the least expensive, I took a red with no name in French; it was simply a Grumbacher Red, with whose purchase I felt I had lessened my artistic credentials.

"You'll need a tube of green."

"I have a few at home," I said, knowing that I could make a green by mixing blue and yellow and save some money.

I also took a bottle of turpentine, a jar of linseed oil, and one of glaze, to protect the colors from aging and fading in the sunlight: I had longevity planned for my paintings. I read in an artist's manual that I would also need a painting knife, but I thought my kitchen butter knife would do just as well.

For the last, I bought a large wooden palette with a thumbhole that I could use to paint while standing up before a sunny hayfield or a grove of cypress trees in a night of hills and moons.

Seymour said, "You're over eighteen, right?"

"Of course," I said. I was tall and looked older and had, I was told, a mature air.

"I guess I can show you, then. If you want a book on how to draw a nude, I'll make you a good price."

I turned the pages. "Another time, maybe." I did not like him to think I wanted the book for dirty reasons, though I was disappointed that the black-and-white photos of the models, obscured in artistic shadow, showed little frontal nudity.

As I was leaving, Seymour said, "Look at this," and pulled out a skinny wooden easel. "It was my daughter's. She's married now and got a husband and a kid to take care of and she doesn't need it. Let you have it for six dollars." He let me have it for five.

It was still snowing when I finally got home. I set up the easel in the living room—my bedroom and now also my studio—and spread out the paint and the other equipment on a little piano bench I had found cast away on the street. I began to paint the snow falling outside my window. I used the zinc white mixed with a hint of black. I flecked the brushstrokes to give the impression of falling snow. I loved the feel of the brush as it swirled paint about, loved how the oil paint glistened in the light as it filled the canvas with color. I loved the sharp pine forest smell of the turpentine as I poured it in the little metal cup clipped to my palette: it was clear I was meant to be an artist.

Everything was falling into place, and I was fast becoming a part of the world I had read about in novels like W. Somerset Maugham's *The Moon and Sixpence* about Paul Gauguin, who had left his wife and children to paint, and *Lust for Life*, about Van Gogh, my hero, who suffered rejection and loneliness and poverty to give his life to art. What a great, noble thing, to give your life to art.

I painted the minute I got home after school, so glad no one was there to break into my concentration, to remind me that I was at home, living with my mother, and not where I dreamed one day of being in my studio in Paris. One day, in Paris, Marilyn would pass by and find me with my model-mistress-muse at my usual café, at my usual table, always reserved for me, and be very surprised to see me and be even more surprised to be invited to my studio, where she would learn from my inspired paintings hanging from and leaning along the walls what a great artist she could have been with and know, like a needle stabbing in her heart, that she had missed her great chance. "Come again, Marilyn," I'd say, "and bring your friend Eugene along if you like."

Tight Pink Sweaters

The Bronx, Pelham Parkway North, circa 1949

A LOOK BACKWARD

My high thoughts of art and fame were frequently accompanied by the burning of lust and the fantasy of sex. Not the sexual act, which was still unclear to my mind, but the idea of what a naked woman looked liked and, most important, what a woman's bra concealed to make men and boys like me mad with desire. Sweater girls were the rage, and I dreamed of seeing what was beneath the sweater and the armor of the bra that gave women so much power. Breasts held great sway in the American male psyche. Archetypes of this kind of mammary power were the screen divinities Sophia Loren, Jayne Mansfield, and Jane Russell, for whom Howard Hughes had devised a bra to give her breasts a maximum lift and fullness in the film *The Outlaw*, which was banned by the Catholic Legion of Decency.

The large-breasted were born lucky and their lives had many advantages; the unlucky ones who came to the world flat as a board stayed handicapped. Less pretty girls with large, full breasts were more desirable than beautiful, flat-chested girls. A girl's "great personality" hardly made up the difference; no one searched for a woman's great personality on a summer beach. Biology is fate, someone said, not realizing, perhaps, that fate meant being born to fill or not fill out a sweater. Along with the rest of the straight boys and young men of that time, I was breast-obsessed, sex-obsessed, obsessed.

When I was thirteen and raging with desire and longing to know the mystery of women, I would concoct some reason to go into my mother's room once she had retreated to bed and to the escape of her novels. "I forgot to say good night, Mom," or I used some other lame excuse, hoping she would not understand that what I had wanted, had hoped for, wished for, yearned for, was to see her undressing to her underwear and bra—or, better yet, to see her naked breasts. I tried to be careful and to time my entrance to that moment, and once I was gloriously successful and found her taking off her bra, setting free her pear-shaped white breasts with small beige nipples.

"Don't come in again without knocking," she said, a bit startled and a bit angry.

I was frightened by her anger, and shamed that she may have understood why I had come into the room. She knew that I knew better than not to knock. But my fear and shame were worth it, because now I knew that a woman's breasts were as beautiful as I had imagined, more beautiful than the photos of bare-breasted women of Bali that I had come upon in *National Geographic* magazine. And now I could also, with this new knowledge, suppose what hid behind the bras of older teenage girls in their tight pink sweaters. Teenage girls, for whom I was invisible and who could never dream that this skinny boy dreamed of them, and squirted quarts of hot passionate semen into his hand at night, in the afternoon, at any time of day when he was alone.

Louie's Luncheonette

The Bronx, Christopher Columbus High School, 1951

Marsha was not beautiful but had huge breasts—the largest of any girl in our high school—and she wore tight sweaters. The boys were crazy for her; some groaned and bit their hand, Italian-style, as she walked by. I was awed by her full lips, by her straight shoulders and her confident walk, head up high, unattainable. I was sure I was not the only boy in school who jerked off at night imagining her.

Marsha was famous but she did not hang out at the cafeteria table with the cool ones; she sat alone, unapproachable, with an open book or with one of her three less attractive slaves, who by association shared her glory. Since she let no boy walk her home or carry her books, and since it was rumored that she went out with college men, she clearly was an "aloof bitch," a "cockteaser," a "cunt." She was, for me, a goddess.

I was walking home from school one April day and heard someone behind me say, "You're the artist."

I turned. It was hard to look at her and not focus on her breasts. "How do you know that?"

"Everyone knows that and thinks you're a fairy."

"Well, I'm not," I said.

"Not an artist or not a fairy?"

I was stymied. I had never known that girls talked so boldly or that anyone would think I was a homo.

"I like girls," I said.

"Well, I never saw you look at me."

"I dream of you," I said.

"Oh, sure."

"I do," I stuttered. "Really."

"Good-bye," she said, walking off slowly. I wondered if she had meant for me to catch up or follow her, but I was baffled and stayed in place.

A week later one of her slaves passed me a note in the cafeteria. It was written in faint blue ink and with almost invisibly thin lines. What kind of pen could do that?

I will be at Louie's tomorrow at 4 p.m. Marsha.

At first I thought it was a prank. And after I sat around waiting long enough, one of the slaves would come over and say, "Waiting for someone?" I would be a fool to go and be humiliated. But supposing she showed up and I didn't? How could I miss this chance?

I got to Louie's early to get a booth. It was empty anyway, the whole stretch of the soda fountain counter with no one there but ketchup bottles and sugar bowls and gleaming napkin dispensers.

Louie, the luncheonette owner himself, came over. "Lime Rickey?" he asked.

"Thanks. Later, maybe," I said, feeling important that he had remembered my favorite drink from the time I was delivering for the butcher the previous summer.

Marsha slid into the booth exactly at four by the fat clock over the door. She was wearing a powder-blue sweater with a soft-looking pink kerchief; she smelled of something wonderful not in nature; she pulled back her shoulders. Louie's eyes popped in a cartoony way.

"I got your message," I said.

"What message?"

"The note you sent."

"Why would I send you a note?"

"It wasn't you?" I asked, sure now I had been tricked.

She waited a long time before she said: "Of course it was me, who else?"

"Oh!"

"Don't you know how to play?"

"No," I finally said.

"Well, I guess I'll go now," she said, taking from her blue purse a giant pair of sunglasses. She put them on in slow motion.

"Going already?"

"Who do I look like in these sunglasses?"

"Like a movie star."

"Sure, but which one?"

"Betty Grable, I think."

"More like Ava Gardner, I think," she said, rising from the table. "Good-bye."

Louie brought over a Lime Rickey. "That's her story. Talks to a guy a few minutes and walks out."

"She's an old friend," I said. "She just came by to say hello."

"She has a lot of old friends."

I hated her. I didn't go to the cafeteria the next day or the following week. I did not want to see Marsha and her slaves having their laugh over me. I got my lunch at an Italian deli close to the school, where I bought "loosies" for a penny a cigarette. The whole pack of twenty cost eighteen cents, but I liked buying one at a time. It made me feel rich. For two weeks I ate Sicilian salami with mustard sandwiches and drank a bottle of Coke. I sat on a stoop and smoked cigarettes for my dessert and wanted not to think about what had happened and not to think that I was an idiot and not to think of Marsha's breasts under her powder-blue sweater. I also took another route home after class. It was longer, but I did not want to see her, to ever see her again.

She found me in the mail. The postcard read: "I like you. Don't avoid me anymore."

I tore it up. But I was happy. Now I no longer had to think of her as a person but as a game I need not play. I returned to the school cafeteria and sat in my usual spot by the window and read. Marsha smiled and waved. I smiled and waved.

The bell rang, the last of the day and the last of the week. I would soon be home and back to my easel and to my beautiful world of paint and canvas and comforting dreams. In a moment, I was out the school's heavy doors and among a throng of students rushing to freedom.

"Don't be that way," she said on the school steps. She was holding her books under her breasts, thrusting them forward like an offering.

I stepped away.

"I was just teasing you."

I nodded.

She was wearing a powder-pink sweater with a blue scarf and a tight black skirt, and I tried not to look at her for too long.

I started down the steps.

"Can't a girl tease you?"

"Good-bye," I said, deliberately echoing her last words to me at Louie's Luncheonette. I had saved it up and was dreaming, during my salami-with-mustard lunches, of a scene where I could use it.

"You stole my line," she said. "And now you owe me."

I walked. She walked beside me, leaving her three slaves behind.

"You don't have to talk to me if you don't want to, but I want to—"

"Apologize?" I said.

"I want to make it up to you. I'm not a mean girl."

"Make it up to me? How?"

"Whatever you like."

I felt myself blushing. "Oh!"

"No, not that."

"What, then?"

"What would you like?"

"Will you model for me?" I heard myself ask.

"You mean naked."

The idea of seeing her naked made me dizzy and blurred the line of trees along the Bronx Parkway.

"Of course not."

"I know I have a bad rep, but I'm not that kind of girl. I write poetry."

"OK. Let's forget the modeling," I said, amazed by my boldness in ever having asked.

We had walked to the street where we had last split off before I had gotten her note, before our rendezvous at the luncheonette, before I hated her.

There was no good-bye this time. She walked away quickly and I did not look after her. I went straight home and reviewed my few canvas-board paintings. One was a study of a bowl of fruit beside a vase of roses that I had copied from an art book; another, the yellow ceramic lamp, two brown chairs, and the fold-up cot in my room, whose window looked on to nothing exciting. The idea for this one came from Van Gogh's painting of his room with a wood-frame bed and straw-bottom chair, everything yellow, gold, orange, with a wall of light blue. Like Van Gogh's, my picture was all swirls, with the paint plastered on thick—"impasto" was the word I had learned; "impasto," like paste, like pasta.

I saw that my still lives were a dead end: even Cézanne had not stopped at apples. My art needed an infusion of figures, of people, of vibrant human life. What would be the point of living with a model in my Paris studio if I could not draw or paint her and bring her warmth and my love for her onto the canvas—as Modigliani had with his mistress, Jeanne?

I sat on my cot and tried to summon noble thoughts that would elevate my art. Long ago, it seemed, when we studied the Greek myths in my grade school Special Progress class, my teacher told us about Plato and his idea of ideal forms and how for everything on earth there was its immortal archetype: a kitchen chair had its perfect echo out there in the world of perfect forms. I wondered about Plato until the afternoon darkened and then I thought about Marsha and fled under the sheets and, with my eyes closed, caressed myself to a silent, creamy explosion.

A Powder-Blue Sweater

The Bronx, the Bronx Botanical Gardens, circa 1952

Someone called me from the street and I went to the already open window. Marsha was standing there. She glowed in the sunlight.

"I was walking my dog and I thought I'd say hello."

I almost hadn't seen the dog; he was so small and white and ugly, with an upturned nose and busy teeth. *Perfect,* I thought, *she has a dog, like her slaves, that gives her no competition.*

"That's nice of you," I said blandly, so commonplace for an artist who would one day live in Paris and exchange brilliant words with fellow artists and poets.

"Do you want to walk with me?"

"Will your dog bite?"

"Only if I tell him to."

"Maybe another time, I'm painting now."

"Sure." She walked away almost to the corner and turned. I ducked my head in.

After a few minutes I heard her call out again. I waited before returning to the window. I made a preoccupied frown so she would know how deeply I had been into my work before her interruption.

"Can I come up and see your paintings?"

We lived on the ground floor, several feet from the sidewalk. Only a low hedge separated us; I could smell her jasmine perfume and feel the softness of her sweater—powder blue again. The blue held more power over me than her pink.

"Not today." I was ashamed of how the apartment looked: the broken-down furniture and the grime from the street coating the walls. Also, I was not sure enough of the quality of my paintings to have her judge and perhaps mock them later with her slaves.

"Don't play hard to get," she said. Her dog quivered and tugged her away with the leash.

"I'll take a walk with you," I said, pretending not to have heard her.

We walked without speaking into the Botanical Gardens and went off the path up into a hill wild with trees and bushes. The dog sniffed the trees and planted a long stream against a baby elm.

"You can kiss me if you like," she said, securing the dog's leash around a thicket.

We kissed. I got dizzy in her perfume and dizzier when she raised my hand to her breast.

"Haven't you ever kissed a girl before?" she asked.

"Of course," I said.

"So why is your face so red?"

On the way back home, and just before we reached my building, the dog, without a warning, growl, or bark, bit deep into my ankle.

The Artist at Work

The Bronx, Pelham Parkway North, 1951

When I was ten, I first heard of the astonishing idea of sexual intercourse, where a man puts his thing into a woman's thing and moves it about until she makes a baby.

"You made that up," I said to my friend Arthur, who, at eleven, already had a faint mustache, which he darkened with his mother's eyebrow pencil, and knew all sorts of strange facts.

"Not only that," Arthur said. "Sometimes a woman freezes up down there and your prick gets clamped inside her and you both have to go to the hospital stuck together on a stretcher."

When I was twelve, I felt the first stirrings of pubic hair. I was too embarrassed to ask my mother what that itchy fuzz was all about, but Arthur knew. "The hair comes first and then you start to get hardons." Then he explained about the hard-ons, how they came over you when you saw a girl naked or even imagined one naked.

One cold, late November morning, a week before my thirteenth birthday, I woke and found white gooey globs on my pajama bottoms and on the sheet. I knew something unusual had happened during the night when I felt a warm flow and surge in my body, but I had not wakened. I thought I was sick, and I was frightened. I washed my pajamas in the sink and sponged the top sheet as clean as I could and hoped my mother would not see the whitish ring that was left behind.

"Hey, Fred, that's great," Arthur said, crushing my hand. "You had a wet dream. I get them all the time unless I jerk off twice a day."

It was only a year later that I learned what he had meant by this and understood its joy and the terrible longing for girls day and night, the fantasy of them that drove me under the sheets whose stains I had to sponge down before my mother woke and discovered my *infamia*. Sometimes I wondered if my mother, in the next room, had heard my moans as the white stuff spurted and slid into my hand. What would she think of me if she knew? I was already living in shame without her knowing.

When I was fifteen, it was Marsha I fantasized about under the sheets, and sometimes she was more real and exciting in my dreams than when we met and kissed and fondled and left each other with bruised lips and indefinite longings.

It was also Arthur who had guided me step by step through the rituals of teenage romance:

1. First, the kiss. No tongue.
2. The kiss and a feel of the breasts with all her clothes on.
3. French kiss, but no slathering of the tongue.
4. French kiss with hand on breast under the bra.
5. Bra off; breast kissing and licking nipples.
6. Rubbing against her thigh with pants on. (Coming in pants acceptable.)
7. Give her a bracelet with your and her names engraved on a little gold heart and let the world know you are GOING STEADY.
8. Put penis between her breasts; slide back and forth until you come.
9. Petting below the waist and beneath the underpants.
10. Guide her hand to your penis and let her stroke you until you come.

11. Slide finger into the vagina. Swirl finger about. Last stop before marriage and the real thing.

After three weeks, I was at rule four when Marsha agreed to pose
for me and one day appeared at my door.

"My mother knows I'm here," she said.

"Why?"

"In case you want to try some funny stuff."

"What are you talking about? What funny stuff?"

"You know very well."

"Have I ever gone further than you let me?"

"No."

"So why are you worried?"

"My mother says I should never be in an apartment alone with
a man."

"That's a good rule, generally."

She looked about for the first time and said what I'd always
dreaded she would say: "How can you live here?"

"It's just temporary. We're going to move."

"Really? That's good. Where to?"

"I'm going to live in Paris as soon as I finish high school next
year."

"With your mother?"

"No, she's going to live in Tuscany, where we have some property."

I heard a dog barking out the open window. "Is that Rudolf?" I
asked.

"I leashed him inside the hedge. He doesn't like you."

"Too bad, I would have painted him sitting on your lap, like in
old paintings of aristocrats."

"Maybe he'll get to like you, one day."

"OK, let's start now before it gets dark," I said. It was only four o'clock in May and did not get dark until at least seven, but I was worried that my mother would return early from work and ruin the intimate atmosphere—what artist's mother walks into his studio while he's painting his model?

I set up a canvas board on my easel and had a few charcoal sticks at the ready for outlining her before I began to paint. I placed her in a chair by the window where we first had chatted and turned her to the light.

"Do you like what I'm wearing?"

"Yes, very much."

"Why?"

"Because."

Marsha was wearing a powder-green sweater and a green scarf. Her black skirt was tight and her legs bare and ripe.

"Is that all?"

"Because you look beautiful."

"I want you to make a portrait of me that will last forever. One that will hang in a museum someday."

"I will try."

"Also, my mother wants to see it."

I made an oval for her head, as I had learned in the *How to Draw from the Model* book that Seymour had finally sold me. Then I drew a larger oval for the chest and abdomen, and two long ovals for the arms.

Marsha yawned. "How long do I have to stay this way?"

"It's not even been three minutes," I said. "Don't break my concentration."

I did my best with the face, but I knew I was in trouble when the eyes seemed too large and the nose too flat. The chest was another problem: How was I ever going to imply the juicy fullness beneath her sweater? I rubbed out the drawing and started again, and now, with Van Gogh–like abandon, I slashed in the paint with my butter knife.

"This is enough," Marsha said. "I've got to go walk Rudolf. Do you want to come?"

"I have to work on the painting."

"Can I have a look?"

"Of course not, I've just started."

She sighed, immaturely, I thought. I walked her to the door. "Don't you want to kiss me?" she said with a make-believe pout.

"All the time."

"Do we have to kiss standing up?" she asked, lightly caressing the back of my neck and sending a current through me.

My cot was too narrow and would not have held us both, so we went to my mother's room and into her bed. My first time in a bed with a woman, so different from lying down on the grass in the park with the dog ready to snap. I felt an unimagined boldness—I was an artist in bed with his model. I kissed and used my tongue. She slowly twirled hers.

I put my hand under her sweater and left it there. She did not take it away. I put my hand under her bra and felt the huge, soft swell of her naked breast. She touched me below and I burst into a warm, steady flow of excitement and embarrassment.

"Can I look now?" she asked.

"When it's done," I said, trying to keep in focus in my role as the artist and not as the boy who had exploded in his mother's bed.

First Review. Picasso Unmasked

The Bronx, Pelham Parkway North, 1951

A few days later, Marsha and I met at Louie's and held hands over the orangey-red Formica-top table littered with the remains of a Lime Rickey, a watery Coke, french fries, and the edges of two hamburger rolls.

"You know," she said, "I've been thinking that I won't model for you again until I see what you've done."

"But this is a process that takes time," I said.

"You just want to get me into bed. Which is OK, because we are going steady."

"We are?"

"Of course! After what I let you do!"

I hoped that no one had heard her, and if they had, what filthy things did they imagine I had done to her? But now that we were going steady, I wondered what more she would let me do.

"Let's go over to my place right now."

"What made you wait so long to ask?"

I paid, took her hand, and walked just short of running across the streets to my house. We rushed to the bed and after few minutes of necking I said, "Take off your sweater."

I was amazed that she did, and without a fuss. We kissed until my lips hurt and my teeth hurt, too.

Then, in a madness of desire, I heard myself say: "Take off your bra."

I thought she would be angry and walk out. But in a tone used to soothe a cranky baby, she said, "Here now," and I drowned myself in her breasts.

"Now can I see the picture?" she asked, putting on her bra and sweater.

"Yes," I said, in a warm haze of satisfaction.

She pointed out that her nose looked like a wedge of yellow cheese; her ears, twin orange slices.

"But it looks nothing like me," she said, summing up the strange concoction on the canvas.

"It's your essence," I explained.

I dared not admit that I had no idea of how to represent faithfully the human face or body—or the form of a dog or a cat or of any animal thing.

"How can I ever show this to my mother? She hates Picasso."

"This was only your first sitting," I said. "I'm sure I can make it more realistic if you want. But then, I might as well take a photograph."

"I want to go home now," she said, her disappointment trailing her all the way to the door and out into the street, where my goodbye wave was not returned.

The Seduction of a Green Cover

Manhattan and the Bronx, circa 1946

ANOTHER BACKWARD GLANCE

When I was ten my grandmother and I went to the city—that's what we called Manhattan—to pick up a cake from De Robertis Pasticceria, between Tenth and Eleventh on First Avenue. My mother had ordered the cake for my aunt Sadie's birthday. There were many Italian pastry shops on Arthur Avenue, a swift twenty-minute bus ride from where we lived, but none, in my family's judgment, was as good as DeRobertis, where they would stop for baba au rhum or a cannoli when they lived on East Twelfth.

We got off at Union Square, as usual, but instead of walking across Fourteenth Street as always, we took a turn and found ourselves on Fourth Avenue, where we had never been. It took us along Book Row, the area between Eighth and Fourteenth Streets, packed with used-book stores with their outdoor stalls. I knew right away that I would go back when I was old enough to travel alone.

I seldom left my neighborhood or traveled to Manhattan, but after I turned thirteen I started taking the subway down to Book Row. The ride from Pelham Parkway to Union Square Fourteenth Street was direct, no changes or transfers, so I was not too afraid of getting lost. On early Saturday afternoons it was easy to find an empty seat and be left quietly to read a book during the hour-long

ride. The subway cost a dime each way, and for another dollar or
even less I could find wonderful books to haul back to the Bronx.
My mother complained, "Where are we going to keep all these
books?" My one bookcase made of boards held up on bricks was
already overpacked and verging on collapse.

"Under my cot, Mom." Where I had stashed the books my
shelves could not hold.

One afternoon, drawn by the title, I bought George Moore's
Confessions of a Young Man from a bookstall for a dime. It had a worn,
leathery green cover and distinguished gold title impressed on the
spine. I read the opening pages out there in the street, and in moments I knew the book was addressed to me. It was about a young
man (like me) who wanted to be an artist (like me) and yearned (like
me) to find his way to become one.

On the subway back to the Bronx, I continued reading, and
as we ascended from the underground to the elevated tracks after
149th Street, passing the littered streets below and the brown rows of
sullen apartment buildings, I felt I had met myself in a past life. Not
only because young Moore had wanted to be an artist, but because
he wanted to live the life of one. His *Confessions* teemed with names
of famous Impressionist painters, of mysterious narrow streets and
smoke-filled cafés, under a Paris sky thick with artistic aspiration.

I promised myself that one day I would follow him to Paris,
where art and beauty counted for everything, and where extraordinary women—as I found in a book of artists photographed in their
studios and on their picnics and in sexy cafés—also came with the
freedom of bohemian life.

My friend Arthur, the expert who had explained to me the mys-
teries of sex, came over to me in the school cafeteria and said, "This
is the book for you." Arthur was the one who had passed around his
copy of Mickey Spillane's *I, the Jury*, dog-eared to the famous scene
of a woman walking into the hero's room and slowly unbuttoning

her blouse—the scene that had inflamed a generation of Bronx youth. Arthur's parents drove around in a Cadillac and parked it in a garage at night and they never seemed to have to go to work. They had recently returned from Paris and had sneaked through customs Henry Miller's banned book *Tropic of Cancer*. Arthur filched it from their bedroom bureau and turned it over to me. "This will make you cream all night," he said. "But you got to give it back before they find it missing." I was thrilled to have this mysterious, forbidden book.

The edges of the pages were folded at the supposedly hot passages. The rest of the book seemed untouched. I read the whole book from first sentence to last, and a day after I finished I started over again. It was a key to the cell I lived in and offered a view of the exciting world outside the prison of ordinary life. The book sang the joy of living unshackled by social norms, conventions, the everyday lies; it was a manifesto for my liberty. Nowhere did I find the supposed sexy filth for which it was banned. There was plenty of sex, but none of it pornographic, and even if it had been, so what? What was all the fuss about? Wasn't sex the stuff of life we lived in and lived for?

Tropic of Cancer tells the story of Henry, the author himself, who, at thirty-five and with just a few dollars to his name, sailed from New York to Paris, knowing no one there, speaking not a phrase of French. In Paris he scrounged money from fellow Americans, went hungry, and yet none of that mattered, because he walked the city like a man crazy in love. A single day wandering in Paris was a day richer, deeper, than his whole previous life in New York working at shitty jobs and starved for a woman's caress that did not require a marriage license. Could I not one day soon do the same as Henry— and young George Moore—and live in Paris a free man?

But first I had to escape from prison. I was bored with my high school classes, with the well-meaning teachers, the students with passion for nothing—except for sex, the only passion we shared. There was nothing in school that opened me to greater poetry or fiction than I had already been reading. I was then in the world of Paul Bowles's *The Sheltering Sky*, with its spiritually lost expatriates wandering through Morocco and its desert outposts.

I thought it was wonderful to be spiritually lost, especially in Bowles's world, so far away from school, from the butcher shop and even Louie's Luncheonette, from my crumbling apartment and my sad mother. But better than Bowles's soulless desert was the glamorous writer's life in Paris that I had discovered in Hemingway's *The Sun Also Rises*. Like its protagonist, Jake Barnes, I, too, would sit with other artists and writer friends—and worldly women—in a café where I could linger for hours drawing and reading at a table *sur la terrasse*, which sounded more heroic than just a table on the sidewalk.

I reread Moore's *Confessions*, searching this time for practical information on how young George was able to pay his way to the city of art and light. I soon discovered the answer. He wrote: "Then my father died, and I suddenly found myself heir to considerable property. . . . I was free to enjoy life as I pleased. Eighteen, with life and France before me."

Expecting no estates to be left to me, I was bitter at my bad luck and chastised myself for being such a dreamy fool. I would have to discover my own way to Paris.

Dancing Daffodils

The Bronx, Christopher Columbus High School, circa 1951

I did not do well in math, and I was rejected for the elite high schools like Stuyvesant and the Bronx High School of Science; so after junior high I went into the general population of Christopher Columbus, which, although not renowned, had some excellent teachers all the same. My favorite was Mr. Francis Anderson.

Mr. Anderson's back was turned to the class; he was dreaming at the blackboard again. The blue suit he wore every day was exhausted and seemed never to have a restful night in the closet or undergo rehabilitation at a dry cleaner's. Tony Gavanti, the class clown and bully, shouted, "Let's chip in and buy Mr. Anderson some new weeds."

Tony was a pimply giant with a slick duck's-ass hairstyle who wore green pegged pants and pointy blue suede roach-killer shoes.

Mr. Anderson wheeled about and said, "Tony, I'm not deaf. But thanks for the thought."

"Don't sweat it." The class tittered. Tony stood and took a bow.

"Where were we, Elizabeth?" Mr. Anderson asked.

Elizabeth Bloom shouted, " 'The Rime of the Ancient Mariner,' Mr. Anderson!"

"Of course, I was just testing you." Chuckles from the class.

Marvin Moyers spoke without raising his hand. "Mr. Anderson, we've been talking about this poem for two weeks. Will it be on the test?"

"As the Boy Scouts say, Marvin, 'Be prepared.'"

Marvin made a sour face and closed his book.

Mr. Anderson, looking about the room, asked, "Why does the ancient mariner have an albatross hanging on his neck?"

Elizabeth and five other girls raised their hands.

"Elizabeth, you know all the answers. Give someone else a chance. How about you, Leslie?"

Leslie took a deep breath: "The mariner wears the albatross because he shot it with his crossbow and his punishment for killing it is to have to have it hang about his neck so that everyone will know that he sinned against nature."

"Very good, Leslie. I see you've been doing your homework." Leslie beamed.

I hated the poem, the lilting seasick rhyming, the corny moral; the whole thing without life, a cardboard boat in a cardboard sea.

We had studied *Romeo and Juliet*, about which Mr. Anderson said, "This is a play about teenagers like yourselves, with problems I'm sure you will understand, because all great literature, no matter when it was written, reaches out to all of us at every age."

"But, soft! What light through yonder window breaks?" Romeo wanted to know. What teenager in all of history had ever spoken like that? I disliked the play because we were told we would love it. I disliked everything official, approved, fixed with the seal of the eternal. If school liked it, it had to be nothing because it was meant to dull us into conformity and not to excite us, disturb us, tell us the truth about life.

"I thought we were going to talk about Wordsworth today," Elizabeth said. Some of the boys called her "brown nose" and "teacher's pet." Tony Gavanti, one day passing her in the hallway, said, "You ass-kissing cunt."

"Yes, Elizabeth, we shall. In fact, among the poems of Wordsworth's we were assigned to read, which one or ones do you like most? Class, I ask all of you the same."

Tony, to everyone's surprise, raised his hand. "Mr. Anderson, can I have the pass? I have to go bad."

"*May* I have the pass?"

"Yes, you may," Tony said.

The roars hit the windows. Tony had done the same routine in math and chemistry and speech.

"Very funny, Tony," Mr. Anderson said. "I hope your great wit helps you land a good job, should you ever graduate."

"Thank you," Tony said. "I hope it shall."

"Class, turn to the Wordsworth poems. Elizabeth, which one have you chosen?"

"'I Wandered Lonely as a Cloud' is my favorite."

"Will you read it aloud, please?"

Elizabeth needed no prompting; she rose and recited. When it was over, the girls applauded—some boys did, too—but two or three expressed other ideas. "Liz," one said, "come with me to the park and I'll show you a plant you've never seen." This was from Murray, who held his crotch all through class.

"Thank you, Elizabeth, very well done. Let's approach this from another tack. What did Wordsworth intend and did he achieve his intention?" Mr. Anderson asked like a man about to fall asleep. He went to his desk and sat, staring at the ceiling. We looked about, wondering what had happened to him. But he soon came to attention and said: "What do you think, Fred?"

Tony wheeled about and gave me the finger. He was my hero, but he disliked me. He had threatened to beat me to death because a girl he liked had asked me, on the school steps, before his eyes, to carry her books home.

I hated this poem, too, but I liked Mr. Anderson because he

always looked sad, because he worked so hard at being nice to everyone, because he was agreeable to even the most stupid and rude students. His kindness made him seem weak, and I hated that some students took advantage of that.

"I like Whitman, Mr. Anderson."

"We all do, Fred."

"He's more direct, more down-to-earth," I said. Then, not to make him feel bad, I added, "But I like Wordsworth, too."

I had made notes in the poem's margins: "Flowers do not 'dance' or 'toss their heads.'" Wordsworth also wrote, "The waves beside them danced . . ." Do waves dance? "And then my heart with pleasure fills, / And dances with the daffodils." So, not only the flowers and the waves danced, but his heart did also.

"Is that all you have to say about this poem?"

"It's full of clichés."

"Such as?"

I wanted so much to blast this silly, banal poem, but I didn't want to challenge a teacher I liked, so I said meekly, "Well, here, for example: 'Continuous as the stars that shine / And twinkle on the milky way.'"

"Clichés may be tired but they are often true and useful," Mr. Anderson said.

"Yes, of course," I said, as if I believed him, but I was afraid to say what I was really thinking: *If this wasn't a famous poem, you would not praise it and you would point out that it is full of useless clichés and contrived feeling.*

Elizabeth could not restrain herself and shouted: "Wordsworth intended to show us the beauty of nature."

"Yes, go on."

"And the daffodils represent the beauty of nature."

"May I ask if Wordsworth achieved his intention? Mary De Falco, do you have an opinion?"

"Yes, I do."

"Well, what is it?"

"He did."

"He did what?"

"He did achieve his intention."

Hands went up again and Irene Mosca said, "There is great beauty in nature if we are open to seeing it. This poem expresses that feeling."

The bell rang, the final one of the day and the week. Freedom. I strapped up my books and made for the door. Mr. Anderson nodded for me to come over to him. I pretended I was absorbed with the rows of photos of cactus and pyramids hung above the blackboard that Mr. Anderson took on his summer vacations in Mexico.

"Do you have a moment, Fred?"

"Sure. Is something wrong?"

"Does something have to be wrong to talk with you?"

"Of course not," I said, half believing it.

"You seem very remote these days. Are you having any problems?"

"No problems."

"Why aren't you as active in class discussions as you once were?"

"I don't have much to say." This was ridiculous because I always had my hand up and my mouth blabbered away about the books I was reading outside of class, trying to make a brilliant point to impress Mr. Anderson.

He dropped some papers into his leather briefcase with the worn handle and ragged bottom and rose from his chair. He looked shorter than when he stood before the class. The collar of his whitish shirt was frayed, and a button was missing from his sleeve. The skin under his eyes was bluish.

"We should have a good talk one day, Fred."

"What about?"

"I'm a little worried about you. You're here but you're not."

We walked out into the corridor; it was seven past three by the hall clock and the students were thinning out. I saw Tony lurking by the exit door.

"I'm thinking of leaving school." I had never told anyone about this before and I was a bit surprised to hear myself say it.

"I'm sorry to hear that. Does your family need your support?"

"Yes, but that's not why." I felt embarrassed to say the rest but he waited until finally I said, "I want to be an artist and live in Paris."

"That's a great idea. Maybe I'll join you." He was laughing, but he was not laughing at me.

"Do you really think it's a good idea?"

"Well, yes and no. No because you should be responsible and finish school. Yes because you have a lifetime ahead of you and you should get the most out of it while you can. After all, it's Paris and not the reform school, where, sadly, many dropouts end up."

"Thank you," I said, and added, "I love your class."

He laughed again. "No you don't."

I started to protest, but he quickly added, "I like Whitman, too."

He lit a Chesterfield, although we were still in the hallway. "Good-bye, Fred. Enjoy the weekend." He waved and walked heavily, his shoulders stooped, to the parking lot.

I walked down the main steps into the afternoon of liberty and sunshine. Tony was there, waiting for me.

I stepped back as he approached. "You got balls," he said, giving me a friendly punch on the arm.

Blindness

The Bronx, Pelham Parkway North, 1951

I took the road beside what was once a horse trail for a riding club up near Pelham Bay Park, which was green and had fancy Tudor- and Spanish-style private houses and seemed like another country, where no one spoke Italian or Yiddish. I passed the Institute for the Blind, with its black iron gates always shut and its mysterious, seemingly uninhabited old buildings in the middle distance. I had never seen anyone on the grounds and wondered if the blind were kept indoors so as not to go astray in the streets and maybe get hit by a car or fall down to China through an open manhole.

I wondered what it was like to be blind, and I thought that death was better. Not ever again to see the sky or a beautiful woman on the street or a movie or a painting or see a girl with her clothes off or see the ocean. I had never seen the ocean, only the tame Long Island Sound whose waters lapped the artificial Orchard Beach where my mother and grandmother and I had sometimes spent some summer hours under a grilling sky, my grandmother fully dressed in black, drawing attention and making me want to turn invisible.

The worst of all: to be blind and never again to see Marsha and her naked breasts with their pink nipple buds.

The Bracelet

The Bronx, Pelham Parkway North, 1951

Thinking of going blind and never again seeing Marsha or her beautiful breasts brought me to call her the minute I got home. She had not been in school for a week and her girlfriends explained: "She's in bed with a bad cold." Each time I had called, her mother said, "She can't come to the phone, Freddy. I'll tell her you called." But this time she came to the phone after I heard her mother shout, "Talk to him, already!" The dog went wild with barking.

"Oh, hello."

"Are you all better? Are you OK now?"

"Of course. Why shouldn't I be?"

"You were sick?"

"Oh, yeah, I forgot."

"Are you well enough to come over?"

"Sure."

"Will you come over?"

"To do what?" And then, in a whisper: "Sex?"

"Yes, sex."

"No."

"Then come over and model for me."

"No."

I laughed as if she were joking, teasing me.

"OK, come over anyway."

"I can't, my boyfriend won't like that."

"Marsha, stop kidding. Come over." I heard the pleading in my voice.

"Fred, you're cute and a nice guy, but without a future."

"Of course I have a future, to be an artist and live in Paris with you."

"That's what I mean, no future."

"Who is this imaginary boyfriend?" I began to suspect she was not joking but still could not believe it was true. Why would she want another boyfriend, and where and when did she find one? I suddenly had a vision that she was seeing Tony Gavanti with his green pegged pants.

"What does it matter?"

"I guess it doesn't," I said. But it did matter, the world's worth. "Is it anyone I know?"

"He's the son of the butcher you deliver for."

"Murray? Is that his name?"

"He likes to be called Morris."

"Marsha, this is crazy. I thought we were going steady?"

"We were, even though you never got me a charm bracelet. But things happen."

I felt myself sinking. "Well, things can unhappen, can't they? I have your bracelet on order at the jeweler's, with our names etched on a gold heart." I had not done this at all, but I knew from my friend Arthur that that was the way it was done.

"It's too late. Anyway, I'm doing you a favor. One day you'll thank me."

I heard her mother yell, "Get off the phone already! Suppose someone's trying to call you?"

I got a little dizzy from all this and felt my chest collapsing and my voice shrinking, turning me into the boy of seven. I took a last chance. "This is a joke, right?"

"Let's say good-bye, Freddy."

"I'll see you at school and walk you home."

"I left school," she said. "We're going to live in Toronto. Morris has a job with his uncle there."

I still didn't completely believe her, but I clung to my last straw and played hard to get.

"OK. Good-bye, Marsha. Keep in touch."

Now I would never see Marsha again or smell her dizzying perfume. Now and forever I would be stuck in the apartment with my mother and all the emptiness of that. I paced about the house in a daze. Finally, I left and wandered about until, as if by magic, I found myself in the Botanical Gardens, where I sat on a rock overlooking the bushes where Marsha and I had first made out. I was sure no one would ever have sex with me again until I was at least twenty-five or was married.

I returned home and started to paint but I felt nothing for it, not even for the smell I loved of the turpentine that I brushed into a little mound of zinc white. I thought about what to do and hit upon the plan of telling her we would get engaged and marry. We would have to wait a bit, because in New York State you had to be sixteen to marry. But if she wanted, we could marry in Kentucky, where fifteen was legal.

Bad News

The Bronx, Christopher Columbus High School, 1951

It was Monday again and I was in school again. In place of the usual noise, the shouts and curses, there was a stillness as green as the walls. Students and teachers glumly, silently milled about the hallway. Mrs. Knovac, the Spanish teacher, had a handkerchief to her eyes, and Miss Wexler, the biology teacher's assistant, was crying; some students, too, especially Elizabeth, who paced the hall with tears flowing down her face. Elizabeth spotted me and rushed over.

"Oh, Fred! Oh, Fred! Mr. Anderson died."

"No he didn't."

"Heart attack over the weekend."

"Stop it. It's not funny."

"He was only thirty-two."

"Thirty-two is old," I said.

"You're a jerk."

The principal's voice came over the PA system announcing that school was closing early; in fact, we could all go home now in honor of Mr. Anderson.

"Didn't you love him, Fred?"

"Of course."

"Not the way I do," she said, as if she was angry with me. She turned and bolted away when she saw Tony approaching.

"Too bad about Mr. Anderson, huh?"

"Terrible," I said, as the truth of his death began to sink in, along with the selfish feeling that he was the one teacher I believed cared about me. From now on, I imagined, I would be adrift, floating from one boring class to another for eternity.

"Take care of yourself," Tony said. "Maybe I'll see you around."

"OK, see you."

He took a few steps and stopped, turned about.

"I'm glad it wasn't you who knocked her up."

"Who?"

"Marsha, you prick, who else?"

The Paradise Movie House

The Bronx, Grand Concourse, 1951

The film *An American in Paris* opened in November 1951. I took the bus to Fordham Road and quick-walked to the Grand Concourse's Loew's Paradise Theatre to see it. I *needed* to see it. Was I not one day going to be an American in Paris? I sat in the rear of the theater in case I disliked the film—a musical with dancing was not for me—and wanted to make a quick exit. It was one p.m., and the house was half-empty, so my getaway would have been easy anyway. I stayed for the second screening. I would have stayed for the third, but it was Saturday, and I had promised my mother I would be home early for dinner so that she would not be alone.

The American in Paris, Jerry Mulligan, was an expat artist who lived in a room on the top floor above a café, whose jolly *patron* and his rounder, jollier wife loved the American and, it seems, let him live and eat on credit. Jerry painted in the open little streets of Paris, his colors golden and rich. He fell in love with a young, beautiful, mysterious shopgirl. Complications eventually do arise, but so what? By the film's end, Jerry and his love run to embrace each other with a joy that would surely last forever.

More than anything I had read about artists in Paris, this movie convinced me that I had to get there before my youth was over. I was sure that, like Jerry, I would find a studio above a café, where I could live on credit—because clearly the French loved American artists and they cared more for art than for money. In Paris I would make great paintings and I would fall in love. It was George Moore again who had led the way or gave me the affirmation I needed to make my decision. "School," he said, "killed the life and love of art." I would not let it kill me.

Coffeepots and Apples

The Bronx, Pelham Parkway North, 1951

I was ready to quit high school at the then legal age of fifteen and a half, but first I needed my mother's permission. She worried that without a high school degree I could never qualify to work in the post office or get any other secure civil service job. She was fearful, too, that I would soon slide into a life of crime—from high school dropout to the juvenile delinquent's school of the streets and from there to the worse school of prison.

"Mom," I said, "don't worry. Paris will leave me no time for crime."

She signed the release papers and set me free.

I found a job in the mailroom of the Sperry and Hutchinson Company, housed in two floors of an office building on Fifth Avenue, a short walk from Union Square. I sorted the mail with six other young men and two retired gentlemen, one a drunk, and I delivered from desk to desk, floor to floor, the correspondence that flowed in three times a day and once on Saturday. I earned fifty-two dollars weekly, and I calculated that by saving seventy-five dollars a month I would be able to afford the cheapest passage on the Holland America Line and have enough to live several weeks in Paris and until my paintings sold, even if they were perhaps not yet ripe for critical acclaim. I was sure that even penniless, like Jerry Mulligan, I would make my way.

At night, after work and after dinner and after my mother had gone to bed, I painted. I had moved from immortalizing the bedroom furniture to making renowned the kitchen with its white-and-red enamel-top table, the old white refrigerator, the old stove with an espresso pot on it, and the three chairs with red vinyl seats. Although everything in the kitchen was static, I painted in the mode of Van Gogh, with vibrating swirls and an impasto so thick that my little tubes of oil threatened to run dry.

I drank while I painted, cup after cup of strong black tea that sent me into exciting shakes—the artist's ecstasy I was certain Van Gogh himself had known. I copied a line from Van Gogh's letters and pasted it on the wall by my cot: "I want to paint men and women with that something of the eternal which the halo used to symbolize, and which we seek to confer by the actual radiance and vibration of our colorings."

I was eager to expand my range beyond the still life and, like Van Gogh, paint living people the way that he had painted portraits of Joseph Roulin, his postman, and Adeline Ravoux, his innkeeper's daughter, and other folk in his daily life.

My experience painting Marsha had taught me that I needed to learn how to draw the human body, the requisite for any serious artist. Even Picasso and Matisse had drawn from the model before they went on their own ways and changed the world. Drawing the nude was the foundation on which the artist's range and power was built, and without that power I would always be limited to painting refrigerators and coffeepots standing beside bowls of flowers and apples.

I had tried to follow the instructions in my book, *How to Draw from the Model*, but I couldn't get beyond the idea of making an oval for the head and then an oval for the torso, ovals for the thighs and the legs and two ovals for the arms. Somewhere in the middle of the torso there were cups for breasts. The book's nude models, obscured

Portrait of me as the aspiring aesthete at age fifteen and a half, meditating on the bridge over the Bronx River. What the Liffey was to James Joyce, the Bronx River was to me.

in shadows, were of no help, either, and I thought, if I was ever to make progress, I would have to take a life-drawing class.

I signed up for a Saturday beginner's life-drawing class at the Art Students League. They accepted me sight unseen for ten classes. I sent the monthly fee of twelve dollars in cash and waited for the receipt, which duly arrived with a class schedule indicating I was to be there every Saturday at nine a.m.

I was sure that in a few weeks or even less I would master drawing from the model and then graduate to painting whatever I wished and in any way I wished. With that power I would reveal the beauty of everyday life, of men tired from a day's work, asleep on the subway, their newspapers still in hand; of a mother and child laughing in a park; of my mother slicing bread on the kitchen table. Van Gogh's beautiful letters, filled with a longing for beauty and truth in life and in painting, made me feel that his was also my longing and that art was a conversation with something higher than even beauty—maybe, as it was for Vincent, with God.

Ideal Forms

Manhattan, Art Students League, 1952

One Saturday morning in September, I took the subway down to Fifty-Seventh Street off Seventh Avenue in Manhattan. In addition to my large sketchpad and batch of charcoal sticks, I carried with me a recent copy of the *New Yorker*. It represented Elegance and Sophistication; just asking for it at the newsstand made me feel special. I had stuffed it into my jacket pocket so that it would be seen when I got to the Art Students League, sure it would declare where I belonged in the world.

Each station farther downtown brought me closer to my new life. The train, elevated until 149th Street, passed tenements through whose naked windows I saw unmade beds, broken chairs, all the visible dreariness of lower-middle-class life, even some steps lower than mine. But soon I would mingle with fellow artists and dreamers of beauty whose devotion to art elevated them above even the prospect of a life of poverty. There was no poverty where there was beauty, and all who created beauty, rich or poor, were equal.

But once I got to the Art Students League building, my grand idea collapsed. I saw right away that I was not dressed properly for an artist. Everyone was wearing jeans, even the women. I was in my tight-fitting, two-year-old blue First Communion suit and blue suede shoes, white shirt, and plaid tie, and I was afraid that, regardless of the *New Yorker* in my pocket, the Bronx hick would reveal himself the moment he entered the classroom.

I waited until the last possible minute, until I shamed myself into some courage, walked in, and took a stool among twenty students chatting at their easels. I got some puzzled but not unfriendly looks: *Has this kid wandered into the wrong place?* The room went still for a moment, waiting, waiting. Then a young woman rushed in and sat on a chair on a raised platform. My heart fluttered. She took off her robe . . . and was naked! Her skin was creamy white, her hair gleamed black and fell halfway down her back, her breasts full with pink nipples—like Marsha's. I was sure I had turned cherry red and was sure that everyone in the room had noticed, including the model.

In 1952, no one was nude on-screen, on-stage, or in the legitimate magazines. Sometimes, but not very often, I found photos of topless women from faraway, exotic places like Bali in library copies of the respectable *National Geographic*. Marsha had made sure she kept her panties on while I fingered her. Until the moment the model shucked off her robe, I had never seen a fully, completely, totally naked woman in real life.

Everyone started to sketch very quickly; then the model changed her pose, her arms raised over her head, her breasts heavy and alone. I started to draw, not knowing where to begin. Before I could even outline the torso with ovals as I had learned from *How to Draw from the Model*, she took another pose. These were the quick warm-ups, but they were too quick for me. I teetered between embarrassment and shame.

I had expected some preparatory instruction on how to draw the body, but there was none of that. Everyone but me seemed knowing and confident as they silently sketched. While I was still floundering, the monitor called for a break and the model put on her robe and disappeared. Some of the students passed by and glanced at my sketchbook, but I was too ashamed to let anyone see what I had done, and I quickly shut the pad with its scrawling lines, the alleged drawings.

I followed some of the students up to the second floor, where everyone was smoking and chatting and laughing. No one spoke or glanced at me. I stood alone, lit a cigarette, and pretended to be concentrating on the nature of good and evil, the meaning of life and death, and Plato's ideas of immortal, perfect forms. But my thoughts ran to how foolish, how stupid I was to come to that room without any previous training and with only a fantasy and desire to be an artist.

Then someone said, "I'm Molly. Come over and join us." She was the model of a few minutes ago; she and other models in their robes were sitting and smoking in an alcove. "Isn't he cute?" Molly said. "I spotted him in my class."

They laughed in a most friendly way and invited me to sit with them. I was choked with shyness, and I smiled like I'd been caught looking at the dirty postcards that my friends had filched from their parents' bedroom closets. I squeezed between Molly and a tall redhead whose fiery pubic hair burned in an open space in her robe. I quickly looked away.

"Why are you here?" one asked.

"Do you have a steady?" another whispered teasingly. It seemed they had never seen someone as young as I in the life-drawing classes. The redhead said, "Did you come just to see girls get naked?"

"Leave him alone," Molly said, putting her arm around my shoulder. "He's sweet."

"I want to learn to draw," I said, in a voice as assured and grownup as I could muster, but whose undertones shouted: "Please, leave me alone—I'm just a kid."

Before I could sink further, the monitor announced that the break was over and we all returned; Molly smiled at me as she went down the stairs. I was back at the easel and flustered, but thrilled by Molly's attention. I wanted to make a great drawing to show her, to please her, to win her. The poses were longer, but that did not help me much. I was still scrawling unsteady lines. There was a faint rustling and a surge of excited electricity in the room. I looked up and saw a middle-aged man walking from student to student and sometimes stopping to comment on their work, sometimes giving only a nod. He was Ernest Fiene, the teacher, and he finally came over and examined my drawing. He stayed silent for a moment, then, pointing to the feet, said very loudly: "What are those she's wearing?"

"She's not wearing anything," I answered, baffled by his question.

"Oh! I thought she was wearing galoshes."

There was some giggling in the room. He moved on to the next student.

When class was over, a tall fellow in jeans and a sport jacket with elbow patches came by and said, "Don't worry, feet are very hard to do. Hands, too." That was kind, but did not make up for my humiliation. I would never be an artist unless I just splattered paint on the canvas with pretended anguish.

All that night in my cot, I thought of Molly and her warm voice. I dreamed we were in Paris, in a sexy hotel room with heavy drapes letting in just a little line of light from the window. She was wearing nothing but my beret. She kissed me everywhere.

A week later, Fiene passed me up on his review. In my fourth week he examined my drawing. I was humiliated that nothing had looked the way I wanted, that there was no relationship between my eye and hand. Molly's full breasts hung like deflated party balloons, the feet belonged to a bear. Fiene, in a loud sotto voce, said: "Maybe you should try the still-life class." No one laughed.

During the break, Molly took me aside and said, "He's a jerk. Everyone knows it." Over the next weeks, the models grew used to me. By late October my novelty had worn off and they talked openly about their boyfriends and having sex with them. I was embarrassed, but, more than that, I was wounded when one whispered to Molly, "That Tony jerk of yours doesn't deserve you."

Molly gave her a sharp glance, as if to stop her from saying more in my presence. But it was too late. Molly had a boyfriend and I was crushed.

I returned to class a few more times, and then, despite the pleasure of sitting with Molly and the models during the breaks and imagining myself an artist among women who love artists, I stopped going. My drawings were no better than when I started—worse, maybe, because now they were not only inept but a tragedy of disproportions. An arm might be the same length as a leg; hands were swelled to the size of footballs. I sulked around, carrying with me the weight of failure.

On my last day, I told Molly I was leaving. She tousled my hair and said, "I'll miss you, Fred."

I was yearning to give her a real, deep kiss, one that would tell her how much I dreamed of her and wanted to live with her forever. I was fighting back the tears. "Miss you, too, Molly," I said.

I left the building without looking back, walking quickly, afraid that someone from my class would see me crying. I melted into the crowd on the subway to the faraway land of the Bronx. Now I was just another high school dropout, and one without the excuse, the cachet, of being an art student with a fascinating future. I was an ordinary mailroom boy in an office with fluorescent lighting and rows of desks and clacking typewriters. All the same, over the following weeks I tried to cling to the idea of Paris because, even only if by osmosis, there, in the art-soaked streets where Van Gogh had walked, I would become the artist I was destined to be.

In place of classes at the Art Students League, I added Saturdays to my work schedule and joined the extra income to my savings for Paris. I still browsed the secondhand bookstores and stalls along

Fourth Avenue on my lunch hour, but I no longer bought books if I could help it, save for the occasional bargain, like a hardcover of *In Dubious Battle*, Steinbeck's novel about the strike in the California orchards, for a dime. I found an ad for the most inexpensive passage on a Holland America Line freighter, and I calculated that, even with helping my mother pay rent and other expenses, I would have saved enough money in a year to book passage and to start my Parisian life. It never occurred to me to learn to speak French.

My Mother's Books

Manhattan, Union Square Park, 1952

At lunchtime, I would sit in a corner of the company's cafeteria and read; in good weather, I would read on a bench in Union Square Park. I read on the subway. If there was no seat, I read standing up. I read: *The Fountainhead, Journey to the End of the Night, A Portrait of the Artist as a Young Man, Under the Volcano*, any book that I had heard or read was important, profound, edifying.

After work, I went directly home to my mother. Without my grandmother there as a buffer, I saw my mother in a new focus. She wore too much dark red lipstick and had too much red rouge on her cheeks. A front tooth was missing, so I understood why she covered her mouth when she smiled. She was so vulnerable, so lonely that I wanted to love her, live forever with her, and work to make her happy—but at the same time I wanted to run, to escape to Paris or anywhere on this earth away from the Bronx and away from her.

After some words about our day over a dinner of pasta and salad, she would go to bed to be with her novels. She liked Rafael Sabatini's *Captain Blood*, *The Black Swan*, and *The Sea Hawk*, and other such romances of high seas and swashbucklers, whose jackets typically featured a woman with bare shoulders bound to a mast and a handsome naval officer, cutlass in hand, fighting off a gang of leering pirates. I snobbishly let her know how mediocre and escapist her books were. "Why are you reading that trash, Mom? There are so many better books."

"I like what I like," she said, half-apologetic, half-defiant.

I had insulted her, and I felt guilty but also resentful, wishing that we could talk about important things and big ideas—Art and Life.

"I'm sorry, Mom. I love you." I didn't know how long it was since I had last declared that.

"My son," she said, "*ti voglio bene assai*." She kissed me. "I know you will leave me, like your father."[3]

---

[3]SONS AND LOVERS
Madelyn Scelfo Tuten (1906–1984)

Eventually, of course, I did leave Madelyn to live on my own. I phoned her a few times a week, and most of the time I was gloomy when I got off. Nothing had changed between us: we were still glued together. She had tried to sound cheerful, as if her life were going well, but her already small world was shutting down. Her sister had died; her brother-in-law, my uncle Umberto, had died; her niece, Jean, had moved to Westchester and her son, my cousin Harold, had died; and her nephew, Big Fred, my sweet cousin, had married and moved to Schenectady, and seldom came again to see my mother. She had no friends. She never had any.

She was in and out of work as usual. She never asked me for money, but once I was working in the Welfare Department in 1964, I started sending her money orders of ten or twenty dollars. She would call to thank me, always adding, "I'd rather see you than have the money. I love you very much. Very much."

I hated traveling to the Bronx—it felt like dying, a little of my coherence, my autonomy draining away with each subway stop that brought me closer to Pelham Parkway. To avoid going back there, I arranged to meet her from time to time for lunch under the Macy's clock on West Thirty-Fourth Street. She knew little of Manhattan and was afraid of getting lost anywhere out of range of what little remained of the garment center. In good weather, we went to a nearby Schrafft's restaurant with its white-gloved women, middle-aged and older patrons, and deferential, seemingly all Irish waitresses. If it was raining or snowing, we'd lunch in the Macy's café itself, where in its brisk atmosphere and the company of mostly younger, sharply dressed women she was ill at ease. She chewed with her front teeth; many others were missing or on the way out, and she took ages to swallow. I pitied her and hated myself for it.

She smiles. "It's grand to see you. I love you."

"You, too, Mom."

"I miss you."

"I hope you're OK, Mom."

"Yes, I am, but I miss you."

We eat. She never finishes her meal and orders coffee midway. She sips it until it gets cold and then orders another.

"This is cold," she tells the waitress, as if the coffee had been brought to her that way.

"Are you OK, Mom?"

"There are mice in the apartment. They live in the kitchen."

"Can't the super come?"

"He says he will, but he never does. And I gave him ten dollars for Christmas."

After lunch, I walk her to the subway station where she had entered and exited since she left ninth grade to work in the garment factories to help support her mother and father. We kiss; I tried to avoid her lips but miss and she smears me with lipstick. She spits into her handkerchief and wipes it off.

"Come back home. You can stay with me until you get married."

By the time she made her way down the stairs and had turned to wave, I already felt guilty for leaving her alone in her little Bronx apartment and angry that she makes me feel guilty for having left her. And I was crushingly sad for the sweet, lost, lonely person she was.

As Madelyn grew older, she became increasingly discombobulated, disoriented, and unkempt. She had stringy, unwashed hair and a face plastered with makeup. She was overripe with perfume. Forgetful, too. She wondered why the waiter had brought her chicken potpie when she thought she had ordered the flounder. "Imagine that," she said. "I would never order chicken." But in fact she *had*.

She was upbeat on the phone, like a woman still in love with the man who had jilted her and was pretending to be awash with suitors and rich with an active social life. But I knew that she seldom left her apartment. She phoned the butcher and the grocery store for delivery; she paid a boy in the building to bring her wash to the Laundromat. She never took a walk or went to a movie: I had bought her a new TV, but she said she disliked watching it alone. "It makes me feel like a shut-in," she said.

"What do you do all day, Mom?"

"I like to sit by the window and listen to the radio and eat cherry vanilla ice cream with a few teaspoons of brandy in it."

"Do you still read in bed at night?"

"I don't like these new books."

Years later, she phoned me in a panic. She was being evicted for failure to pay months of rent. I was shocked, since I had sent her money orders for the rent each month.

"I paid it," she insisted.

But she had not. She had either lost or forgotten to cash a few of the money orders. I later learned that she had also given money to neighborhood kids who came by for a handout, and she had bestowed lavish tips to the delivery people. After I tried contacting other agencies for help, including Catholic Charities, a friend put me in contact with the Jewish Family Services in the Bronx. It did not matter to them that we were not Jewish.

"We're here to help," the counselor said on the phone. I went to visit my mother with the service's team of a nurse, a social worker, and a psychiatrist.

The problem was clear the moment we walked in the apartment. It smelled of rot and filthy rags. Paper and plastic bags of garbage were piled up in the hall; some had holes where the mice had nibbled through. Two mice fled under the stove. Roaches had made the kitchen their palace and did not bother to scamper away.

SOCIAL WORKER: How old are you, Mrs. Tuten?

MOTHER [girlishly]: I'm thirty-five.

PSYCHIATRIST [pointing to me]: Do you know who this person is?

MOTHER: My son, who never comes to visit me.

ME: I'm very sorry, Mom.

MOTHER: But you will come now.

ME: Of course, Mom.

More questions, very gently asked. And then we left. We talked on the sidewalk, under the window where Marsha used to chat with me before our amorous strolls to the bushes on the hill that overlooked the fabled Bronx River.

Psychiatrist: "Don't be angry with your mother. She has dementia."

I was not angry. I was heartbroken for this poor, lost woman who also happened to be my mother. Heartbroken for her sad, shrunken life. Heartbroken that I was the only thing she had to keep her afloat and that I was helpless to keep her above water.

The Jewish Family Services arranged for my mother to have Meals on Wheels, so she could have nourishing food delivered to her. They also sent a nurse to come in a few times a week to care for her, as well as a psychiatric social worker to evaluate her once a month. The psychiatrist advised me to make "other preparations."

"Like what?" I said.

"What do you think?" he said.

In my search for the lost money orders, I found among the papers in her kitchen drawer the name of the cemetery and the family plots that were still vacant. In the Yellow Pages I located a funeral parlor in the Bronx, visited it a week later, and made the arrangements for my mother's coffin.

The funeral home had tried to sell me something very elaborate, with velvet cushions and brass handles and very expensive, durable wood. I opted for the most simple pine box, wondering while I did it if I was not being mean. But then I thought, *Don't be a fool—be realistic. No box will protect her from rotting away.* Yet the feeling that I had wronged her has never left me.

My mother remained another year or so at her apartment. We spoke on the phone, although sometimes it was difficult to find out how she was. She often talked about things that had happened fifty years earlier.

"I was beautiful," she said, "and many men were after me, but they had no charm at all."

One day, the social worker called to tell me that Madelyn had been transferred to a nursing home. They weren't sure if she would be able to ever return to her apartment. Nevertheless, I continued paying the rent in the event she could live at home again. I gave the social workers all the particulars of the funeral parlor.

I had gone to teach in Paris and lived in a large, sun-filled apartment in Neuilly overlooking the Bois de Boulogne. My mother and my old life in the Bronx seemed very far away. But of course that was an illusion because the Bronx lived in me, as did my mother.

One late afternoon the social worker from the Family Service called to say Madelyn had died and was to be buried in two days.

"I suppose I should fly back for the burial."

"If that makes you feel better."

I didn't know what I felt. I thought about how Camus's character Meursault had reacted to the news of his mother's death. But that was only an intellectual ploy to numb my grief, a kind of alchemy to transform my mother's death into a literary event.

I knew no one in the world who had known her. Then I remembered that my former wife, Simona, had been very fond of her. I took a chance and asked if she could go to the funeral.

Some days later Simona phoned me back. "I went," she said. "There was no one there, not even a priest."

I remembered how I felt seeing my grandmother's coffin lowered into the earth and I again felt that despair, picturing my mother's casket slowly being let down into the grave. Now Madelyn was in the earth beside her mother and her father in Woodlawn Cemetery, where a plot was waiting for me. I thought: *I'll eventually join all of them unless I find a better solution, like immortality.* Until then, it comforted me to think I would spend eternity in the same woodsy cemetery where Herman Melville was buried.

Rimbaud in the Kitchen

Elizabeth Charon, her husband, and their two sons lived in a large two-bedroom on the upper floor of the building across our small courtyard. It was James, the younger son, who, when we were boys, without any prompting or cause, threw a stone at me, hitting close to my left eye and leaving there a small white scar, like a knife cut. Thinking it made me seem tough, I boasted to girls in school that I had been in a knife fight over a poker game, the kind I had seen in Westerns and gangster films. The brothers took after neither their father nor mother. They never read a book voluntarily, and they mocked me for doing so. "What'ya reading now, four-eyes?"

I had had a crush on Elizabeth since I was eight, before I even had my first conscious sexual feelings, and now at sixteen, when we became friends some months after I dropped out of high school, I dreamed of her with all of my burning teenage lust. I would see her walking purposefully with a book under her arm, on her way, I imagined, to some glamorous place or on some important mission. But then, on another day, she changed pace and moved like a cat taking its time to a bowl of milk. I masturbated thinking of her. Then I felt guilty whenever I passed her in the street, sure she knew the things I did to myself under the sheets at night dreaming of her.

Elizabeth was universally disapproved of in our building. "Where is she always going alone at night?" I heard our upstairs neighbor ask.

"It's not my business," my mother answered, adding, "With such a handsome husband, why go anywhere?"

"She even goes to Paris without her husband and leaves the boys alone with him. What kind of woman does that?" the neighbor snapped.

One spring Saturday, I saw Elizabeth sitting on a bench in the Bronx Park. She was reading, turning the pages slowly and then quickly, as if she and the book were the whole world and no world else mattered. I wanted very much to know what book so absorbed her while also thinking how beautiful she was. She caught me in my stare; she smiled and called out: "You're my son's friend, aren't you?"

"Yes, I am," I said, not mentioning that we disliked each other, that he called me a fruity bookworm.

"Do you like books? Other than the ones you have to read at school."

"Of course," I said, and nervously began to name a few books I loved. "I like especially *A Portrait of the Artist as a Young Man* and *The Razor's Edge.*"

"I have others you may like," she said. "Come by for coffee, or a glass of wine. Just ring my doorbell and see if I'm free."

A glass of wine with an older, sexy woman who read books: What in the world was more European—more grown-up—than that? Did she know that I was only on the way to sixteen—and that I drank wine only at family meals on Sunday at my uncle Umberto's house?

A week later I crossed the courtyard into her building and rang and was let in. My heart did several quirky skips before I reached the fifth-floor landing, where she was waiting at the open door.

She kissed me on both cheeks. She smelled of lilacs. She was barefoot, in jeans. I thought I could see her nipples pressed against her T-shirt. The living room was three times the size of mine, and bright sunlight filled the clean windows. Unlike my place, all the furniture was intact: no chair or table with a broken leg bound with electrical tape, no lamps with torn shades. Paintings of rooftops with orchards of TV antennas were hung in the spaces between the floor-to-ceiling bookcases.

"They're very beautiful. So realistic!"

"My husband's work," she said. "Why doesn't he just take a photograph?" she added, leading me into the kitchen.

She had made a pot of espresso in an old-fashioned *napoletana*, and while we were waiting for it to brew, I looked too long at her nipples. She caught me and smiled. I turned away to study my empty coffee cup.

"Do you like girls?"

"I love girls."

"That's too bad. My brother, the opera lover, would like you."

"I'm sure I'd like him since he's your brother," I said, pleased with what I thought was a sophisticated answer.

"Have you ever read Rimbaud?" Elizabeth asked. "You burn like him."

She disappeared for a minute and returned with Rimbaud's *A Season in Hell*. "For you," she said. It was the slender New Directions edition that, with five or six other books, I took with me wherever I moved later in life.

She read me a passage in French. It sounded beautiful.

"It's great," I said.

"So you speak French?"

"I plan to learn it because I'm going to live in Paris and be a painter."

"An artist! Wonderful. You will love it there, Fred, and you'll never want to come back."

"My mother says you've been to Paris."

"Yes, but never for long enough," Elizabeth answered, with a make-believe sigh.

The doorbell rang, and her sons crashed into the kitchen, sending me dirty looks. They were in muddy baseball uniforms, and the younger had a streak of blood down his nose. They had just returned from a game; the other team had tried to cheat, so they got into a fight. "Guess who won," James said. They grinned and swung their bats and poked them toward me.

"Stop it," Elizabeth said, in a deep voice that scared them and even me. They withdrew without a word. She grew silent, brooding. Then she brightened up. "Visit me again. Come when we can really talk. And let me see your paintings one day."

That would be the day, I thought, imagining myself toting my paintings of chairs, a cot, and black streets up to her apartment and having her glance at them and, without a word, showing me to the door.

But I did visit her again, and often, pacing myself so as not to seem avid for her attention, her beauty, her sophistication. One day, she lent me the novel I had seen her reading on the park bench, Djuna Barnes's *Nightwood*.[4]

"Let me know what you think," she said. I had wanted to like it because she did, but I couldn't follow the story. I did not even understand if there was a story, but there were passages of intense, shadowy beauty that made me wonder what new world I was in. I also tried to make sense of Joyce's *Ulysses*, another book she gave me, holding it out like a treasure.

"This is the one, Freddy. This is the alpha and omega of literature. This is all novels rolled into one."

The book left me baffled, although I knew there was something extraordinary going on in Joyce's ocean of words, and I felt special just trying to fathom them. What was wrong with me that I failed to have a clue to what anything in it meant or was supposed to mean?

"How's it going with the Joyce?" she asked from time to time.

"Just great," I said, with feigned enthusiasm.

She was the guiding mother I had wished for. She was also the woman of pure sensuality over whom I was spending loads of sperm under my sheets at night—afternoons, too.

I liked to think that she saw me as the son she had wanted, instead of the two louts living under her cultured roof, but, whatever the reason, I knew she liked me and liked my wanting to be an artist and to live in Paris.

"But one is never alone in Paris," she said when I asked if I would be lonely there, not knowing a soul. "An artist like you will make friends in a week. And I have some people there for you to meet. But brush up on your French."

I was ashamed to tell her that I had not yet made an attempt to learn the language. Somehow I believed that by some magic I would start speaking French once I was in Paris.

We sat in her kitchen—her favorite place—and over coffee talked about novels and poetry. I liked Whitman and his singing in ordinary language, his love for the human body and its beauty. I treasured his embrace of the vast expanse of life, his finding miracles in it everywhere. He spoke to my heart, I told her.

"He's easy to like," Elizabeth said. "Like Ravel, when you're young. But Whitman won't last when you grow older."

"Then I'll never grow older," I said.

I knew that I would and she would, too. Would she one day outgrow her need for me? And where would I be then, without her?

---

⁴PARIS AND *NIGHTWOOD* YEARS LATER

Perhaps it was Elizabeth who drew me to any woman I saw reading, and to be curious to know what she was reading, snobbishly gauging her beauty to her taste.

Once, fifteen years later, when I finally made it to Paris, I saw an elegant woman in a café fixed on a book. She was at the same café table and with a book over the following five days. Finally our eyes met, and she smiled. I took the courage from that smile to approach her and ask in my most polite way, and in my crippled French, what she was reading.

"*Nightwood*," she said, showing me the cover. "And you?"

I held back my surprise and my wanting to tell her how I had been introduced to the book when I was a boy years ago in the Bronx, a boy with a crush on a woman who resembled her, answering instead: "*The Third Policeman*, by an Irish writer. I'm not sure it's translated."

"I have read it in English," she said, adding, "I have wondered what you were reading all these days, and wondered if you were a simpleton."

She did not appear the next day or the days after, which I ascribed to my intruding on her privacy. I had become friendly with Marcel, the headwaiter, who said, "She comes here every spring and early fall for seven days and sits with a book, speaks to no one, and waits for no one. She is not French, and she is not English or American. She leaves extravagant tips above the *service compris*, so we don't care how long she sits, even when we are busy. She drinks Kir Royale. Anyway, she is beautiful."

I imagined her world, and years later I wrote a novel, *The Green Hour*, inspired by her and also infused by the memory of Elizabeth.

Trash Cans and Kafka

The Bronx, Parkchester, 1952

One day Elizabeth said, "You're too isolated, Freddy. You should meet a real artist." I thought she meant her husband, who hardly ever spoke to me and sent me icy looks, but that was not it: she wanted to take me to meet her friend, an artist who lived a little more than a half-hour bus ride away. She had spoken to him about me, and he was interested enough to invite us over.

He lived in a small apartment in the huge, maze-like middle-income Parkchester housing complex. From the approach, I could not imagine that any kind of artist or anyone with a soul could live there in those buildings. I did not see a single tree or patch of green to lift the spirit.

John Resko greeted us with a broad, welcoming smile, and that made me like him right off. We went into his small living room, where there hung two large paintings of garbage pails, gray with faint red lines trailing along their sides, standing in a flat, gray, anonymous field. They had a gentle sadness to them, garbage pails without friends or a street to belong to. I thought them beautiful and their sadness spoke to me, as I had always linked beauty with sadness, my mother being my earliest model.

"Who painted them?" I asked. "They're wonderful!"

"I did," John answered, like a shy boy.

Five or six African sculptures and masks rested on a table set against the wall. I had only seen their likes in books, and here they were in real life. Elizabeth caught me staring and said, "John's an expert on African art."

He laughed. "I'm more of a looter. African sculpture isn't meant for museums or homes," he said, "so I feel a little guilty having them here. After all, how would we feel if people had gone to a church and took the paintings off the walls and sold them in a marketplace far away?"

"We have done that for centuries," Elizabeth said.

"What do you think, Fred?" John asked.

"All art is beautiful," I said, not knowing what I meant, but wanting to seem like I did.

"No argument there," he said, in a way that made me feel welcome.

John went into the kitchen, giving me a moment to take in the room. Black scatter rugs on the wooden floor; four sling chairs, two red, two black; a phonograph player on a blond-wood credenza with a stack of LPs standing neatly in racks; and a bookcase my height, packed tight with hardcovers. No disorder, nothing broken or makeshift, everything clean. The walls looked freshly painted.

I had thought that artists lived in a kind of deliberate anti-bourgeois mess, and here I found myself in a home neater than any I had ever before stepped in, even Elizabeth's. I was not sure that John was a real artist.

John returned with a tray of demitasse cups and a tall espresso pot, steam curling from the funnel, as it did in comic books.

"My wife would like to meet you, but she may be late from work," John said.

"You'll like her, Freddy, she's beautiful," Elizabeth said.

I was miffed at being pegged as just a superficial boy who liked only good looks, so I said, "I'm sure she's intelligent, too."

John smiled. "Yes, and kind."

I felt profoundly grown-up sitting on a canvas chair and drinking espresso in a room of books and paintings.

"Elizabeth tells me you've dropped out of high school," John continued, "and that you're an artist."

"Well, I want to be."

"He's going to go to Paris to paint," Elizabeth said.

"That's great. You'll love it there."

"Were you there long?" I was excited. John had actually lived in Paris, so clearly his life in Parkchester was just a temporary circumstance and did not disqualify him as an artist.

"In my imagination."

I quickly recovered from my disappointment when he added: "Have you read Kafka?"

"Not yet, but I heard he's great. I like Hemingway and Mark Twain and Melville, too." I was happy that he was interested in me and, in the way that the self-absorbed young never wonder about the lives of the older, I never thought to ask anything about him.

In a low voice, and in what sounded like an official tone, he said: "Ever been in trouble?"

I thought he meant trouble with girls: Had I got one pregnant?

He did not wait for my answer to add, "With the law?"

I was surprised by the question, offended by it.

"Not at all, ever."

"In my time," he said, "we thought high school dropouts went to work in the factory or were sent to jail." He laughed a warm, deep laugh. "I must be thinking of leaving grammar school."

I nodded as if I knew what he was talking about. Who ever drops out of grade school?

"Anyway, Freddy, it's Kafka out there."

"It's Kafka everywhere," Elizabeth said.

John broke out into a laugh. "Oh, boy, how true."

I was left out of the joke. The only thing I knew about Kafka was that he was a man who wrote depressing books.

John pulled out a book from the shelf, Kafka's *The Trial* in hardcover. "Let me know if you like this," he said.

"I'll give it back when I finish," I promised.

"It's a present. Or pass it along if you like, Fred. That's what books are for."

The doorbell rang, and John smiled like a happy kid. Anita, his wife, walked in. She had long black hair and olive skin and she flashed me a warm smile. I had a crush on her already.

"John told me we'd have a guest," she said, "but I didn't know it was Tony Curtis." I was embarrassed but flattered, since Tony was the current rage among the neighborhood teenage girls. Not only was he "gorgeous" and a "dreamboat," he was one of ours, a Bronx boy.

Anita turned to Elizabeth. "But maybe he's more like Brando. What do you think?"

"More like Rimbaud, I think."

Feeling bold, I chimed in: "Maybe you can fix me up with your sister?"

"Come over for dinner," Anita said. "Let's find out what's in your head first, then maybe I can dig up a girl your own age." She kissed me on both cheeks, sending me to the clouds.

Anita and Elizabeth disappeared into the kitchen, leaving me with John, face-to-face on our sling chairs. "Women," he said with a sigh. "What would our world be without them, Freddy? Or Dostoyevsky? But I'm sure you know that."

I nodded and made a note to read Dostoyevsky.

Elizabeth and Anita soon returned, but Elizabeth was anxious to leave and rushed into making our farewells. Anita was tearful; John somber. The three hugged and kissed and then went into another round of the same. John gave me a strong handshake and a pat on the shoulder.

"Come over again and let me see your paintings whenever you like."

I wanted to say more than thank you: I wanted to say how grateful I was for showing me a little of his life, the life I had dreamed of, one of books, music, art, and a beautiful woman—the artist's life. But instead I said, "Thank you, I would like that." I was happier with the idea that John wanted to see me again than with the prospect of showing him all of my ten clumsy paintings.

Elizabeth was silent on the bus ride back home. I wondered if I had made a fool of myself and had disappointed her. Finally, four stops from our station, she took my hand and said, "I wanted you to meet John and Anita before I left for Paris."

"Great. Bring me back some Henry Miller books, please."

"That may be a long time away, Fred. I'm going for good. But I wanted to leave you in good hands. I know they both like you. I knew they would."

I was stunned. "What do you mean, 'going for good'? You're never coming back?"

"Of course, for visits, and the boys are always welcome to visit me on holidays, maybe even a week or two over their summer vacation."

We stepped off the bus and made for home. I was in grief, and I dragged along. But Elizabeth was in her speed mode.

"I've got much left to do before I leave. I haven't even started packing yet."

"Don't leave," I said, seeing my father, suitcase in hand, disappearing toward the subway station.

We stopped in the courtyard. She turned to me. "Freddy, I'm in love. He's Parisian."

"Is he an artist?"

"A Joyce scholar, and a man I'm in love with and want to be with while there is time left to us both."

"I see," I said, seeing nothing but that I would be left all alone with my dreams and ambitions, and with no one to feel that they, and I, were valuable.

"Maybe one day you really will," she said.

"I'm sure."

"Do you know who finally convinced me to leave? John."

"Why would he do that?"

"Not convinced me, but he told me what I wanted to hear. That he would leave Anita and live in the street rather than stay in an unhappy life. That freedom was everything in the world. He should know, Freddy."

"Why?"

"Let him tell you, Fred."

I thought I caught a glimpse of her large, sour-faced husband peering down at us from the window. Then the light went out.

"I will miss you," I said, in my most brave way, masking, I hoped, the little boy I was. Soon, like my father who had left and Mr. Anderson who had died, Elizabeth would also be gone.

I came home to find my mother staring at the blank face of the TV.

"Mom, don't you know how to turn it on?" I asked jokingly.

She was silent for a few moments. Then she let it all out. She had lost her job, months ago. She tried to make do with her unemployment checks, but they quickly ended and were never enough to live on anyway.

"I even used up all your share of the money for expenses, but it was not enough to cover the full rent."

"How much do we owe?"

"Three months, and I got an eviction notice. Are you angry?"

"No." I was not angry; I was sick. Now I understood why she

was always there when I got home from work and why she had left after me in the morning, saying her workday had been shortened.

I now had to raid my savings to pay the current rent and the arrears in full, as well as take care of our living expenses until she found work. If she did not get a job soon, I would exhaust my meager savings and Paris would be out.

I could not sleep even after I turned off the light. All that work I had done to save for Paris had been for nothing. Maybe I was never meant to go there, to be an artist there. Maybe I was meant to spend my life living with my mother, taking care of her until one of us died. John's words about freedom spun in my mind: Why was he, as Elizabeth had said, the one to know best its meaning?

Something I had read some weeks earlier welled up in my mind. I turned on the light and pulled out from under my cot a stack of the past ten issues of the *New Yorker* and read the table of contents of each. It was in a magazine from two months earlier that I found John Resko.

The Bronx, Pelham Parkway North, 1952

I had not matched the name with the man I had met, but the *New Yorker* profile was about John Resko. He had been raised in the Lower East Side and been a merchant seaman, and at nineteen had a wife and child to support. During the height of the Great Depression, he could not find a ship or work of any kind. In his desperation, on February 5, 1931, John and an older man, a seasoned criminal who had cajoled him into joining him, set out to rob a grocery store in the Bronx. The owner came at him with a broom. The older man slipped John a pistol and said, "Shoot him!" John shot and killed him, and was caught right out in the street. He was tried and sentenced to die in the electric chair.

John had no criminal record, and many people from his neighborhood in the Lower East Side testified that he was a good boy who, for a moment, had gone wrong. The foreman of the jury said that Resko had been a tool "in the hands of a hardened criminal." Appeals were made to the then governor, Franklin Roosevelt, who, only twenty minutes before John was to be walked to the electric chair, reprieved him. John was given a life sentence and packed off to Clinton prison in Dannemora, then called, for its harsh conditions and remote location, Little Siberia.

There John began to make drawings of prison guards and convicts, and he eventually made oil paintings: scenes of men warming

themselves over cans of fire in the prison yards, of men sitting deject-
edly in their prison cells. Eventually he gained the attention of Carl
Carmer, a noted author of the time who was interested in prison
rehabilitation. Carmer was struck not only by John's art but also by
his intelligence and sweetness. He began the long work of getting
him released from prison, enlisting a range of people, even Groucho
Marx, to petition for John's parole. After nineteen years, John was set
free. He had painted a door on the wall of his cell, opened it, and
stepped into his freedom.

African Masks and a Lesson

Manhattan, Carlebach Gallery, 1952

It was a Saturday morning. The phone rang. My mother called out from her bedroom, "It's for you." No one had ever phoned for me before except Hyman, my boss from work at the mailroom, to say there was an emergency, that the Saturday man had not shown up, and to ask me to come in and sort the mail. Extra pay.

"Hi! Freddy, it's John. Elizabeth's friend."

"Oh! Sure." I was nervous.

"I'm going to the city this afternoon and thought you might like to come along."

"Of course," I said. "I'd go anywhere with you."

He laughed. "I bet not. But this is to an art gallery. I thought you'd like it."

We took the clattering Third Avenue El down to Fifty-Seventh Street. John was friendly, smiling but mostly silent all the way; I was, too, having no idea what to say to a man I hardly knew. I was relieved when we arrived in midtown, at Third Avenue, with its low- and high-end shops and dark bars. We walked to Carlebach Gallery, a nowhere-looking place under the shadow of the El. We had come all the way down to deliver John's text for a forthcoming African sculpture exhibition at the gallery.[5]

This was the first time I had ever entered a private art gallery; I always felt that such chic places were only for well-dressed, well-heeled, serious-looking adults. So I was uncomfortable walking in, even under John's wing.

"Carlebach is a sweet guy," John said. "You don't have to be shy with him."

I wondered how John had sensed my anxiety, my fear of being found a kid under my rebellious artist's pose.

"Julius, this is the young artist I told you about," John said, introducing me to the gallery owner, a kind-looking man. Most older people looked kind to me then because I had thought that life had made them wise.

He shook my hand. "I hope we will see your work one day." I was pleased, feeling puffed-up and just a step away from the door to a better world. But in my heart, I also knew that that door was shut to me because I was not a real artist but a pretend one. All the same, I mustered up my courage to say, in my most adult voice, a line I have never heard except in movies or on the radio: "Nothing would please me more." That sounded so phony that I was sure John was embarrassed for me, maybe ashamed he had brought me there.

Carlebach soon got to the business of the payment for John's text. "Would a check be OK, John, or would you prefer cash?"

John looked about and landed on an African mask and said, "Actually, I'd prefer this."

Carlebach flinched but, with a polite smile, said, "As you like, John. You always know the best ones." He wrapped the mask in many sheets of newspaper, tied it, and handed it to John in a brown shopping bag. It was very quiet when we made our good-byes.

John and I stopped at a nearby luncheonette for ham-and-egg sandwiches on rye toast and coffee. I had never had a sandwich like that, but I ordered what John ordered. John was silent, his hands folded. The sandwiches came fast and I started eating right away, but John was in a trance.

"That's one of the most beautiful masks I have ever seen. It's worth much more than what he owed me for my work."

"That's great, John," I said, thinking he was pleased about the bargain.

"Do you think so?" he said with a smile that suggested sarcasm. He finished one half of his sandwich and, with his head lowered, asked the waitress, "May I take the other half home, please?"

"Sure, why not," she said, whisking the plate away.

"Sometimes I forget I'm not in prison," John whispered. He drank his coffee in a dreamy way. "One day I would like to live in Manhattan and not have Anita working." I sensed that what he said was not what he had been dreaming about over coffee.

"That would be great," I said, imagining how wonderful it would be to visit him in the exciting city and not in the boring Parkchester in the depressing Bronx.

We left and strolled about until we paused at a shop. John asked if I thought Anita would like the red dress that was in the window. "I have no idea," I said, feeling the less for having none. Then we started walking toward the subway, but before we got there John turned us back to the gallery, where Carlebach was sitting at his desk, staring at a Benin mask like a man in love. He seemed surprised to see us.

John handed over the bag with the mask, saying nothing. Carlebach beamed. "You're a gentleman, as I have always thought," he said. He went to the rear and presently returned with an envelope, which John took without opening. They shook hands. We were again on the elevated, Bronx-bound.

"I feel better now," John said above the train's screeches. "Who wants to go around feeling bad over an African mask?" Then a moment later he added, "Or over anything, if you can help it."

As we were approaching our stop, John said, "I'd invite you to dinner at home, but now I have enough to take Anita out and maybe catch a movie, too."

He took a twenty from the envelope and said, "Buy some good brushes."

I did not want to take the money, but I wanted to take it. It was a fortune. I did not buy the brushes. I gave my mother ten dollars and bought books with the rest on an excursion to Book Row. I found a book of poems and drawings by Kenneth Patchen for a quarter. John had told me about him: how Patchen hand-painted his own books. I read: "The stars go to sleep so peacefully." Patchen was sentimental, but I didn't care. His sentimentality had pain and love and feeling. So much feeling. To feel, to feel: What matters more than that?

---

[5]CARLEBACH GALLERY

Carlebach Gallery specialized in African sculpture and Mesoamerican art. Julius Carlebach sold works to the famous American collector Peggy Guggenheim and had connections to the European surrealists, who were then living in New York, having fled from Hitler. Carlebach himself had escaped the Nazis in 1937 and started his gallery in New York in 1939. I only recently learned, much to my shock, that Carlebach died at the age of fifty-five from a heart attack. I had met him when I was fifteen and he was forty-two, which, to me then, seemed ancient.

Carlebach was one of the few galleries then showing contemporary American art. There was such a little market for it then. Roy Lichtenstein's first solo show was mounted there in 1951. These were paintings in a cubistic mode of Native American scenes and Old West motifs; it was some years before Lichtenstein became famous as a pop artist. When Roy and I became friends in 1964, we noted that we had missed meeting each other at Carlebach Gallery by a mere few months.

Tattoos

The Bronx, Parkchester, 1953

I visited John as often as I could. Once or twice, he and Anita invited me to dinner: one thin hamburger on a plate, some boiled carrots, a glass of red wine, a slice of Italian bread. "John has to be careful what he eats," Anita said. "The food in prison ruined his stomach."

"Maybe it's been the food since I got out of prison." John laughed. I joined in.

Sometimes John and I spent an hour or two alone when Anita was still at work. There were so many questions I wanted to ask him.

I was hungry with wanting to learn what adults knew about life, and the questions that I wished my father had been there to answer I now put to John.

"Are you afraid of death?" I asked. John was in his black sling chair, me in the red. There was a big pot of espresso on the coffee table, which was also loaded with art books, only some of them from the library.

"No, but I want to live." He was smoking an unfiltered Camel cigarette and, imitating John, so was I. I had switched from Marlboro, which John found too anemic.

"What happens after, John, are you afraid of that?"

"There is nothing after."

A year earlier, I stopped going to church, stopped taking Holy Communion. As an experiment I took Communion without going to confession beforehand, just to see if, as I had been told, Jesus would strike me dead and thus prove to me his existence. I trembled at the altar, letting the sacramental wafer melt in my mouth, and waited for the bolt of punishment. By the time I got home, alive, I was sure that religion was hocus-pocus. But maybe there was still God anyway.

"Nothing at all?"

"Why are you worrying about it?"

"Because it's so painful to think that all this is for nothing. What's the point of living anyway?"

He laughed. "When you figure it out, tell me."

On the wall behind him there were large paintings of trash cans, different from the ones I had seen on first meeting him. The elongated red lines were a deeper red, like thin rivulets of blood. I wished I could paint the beauty of trash cans. By now I was painting very little and had started writing poetry instead. I suspected the poems were worse than my paintings, but they were not as costly to produce, a consoling virtue. Writing poetry let me still feel myself to be an artist and not a total failure sorting and lugging mail in a windowless office.

I wanted to be like John as much as possible. When I told John I wanted to get a tattoo like his, a small blue star between his thumb and forefinger on his left hand, which he covered with his right when sitting and talking, he threatened that if I ever got one he would never speak to me again.

"Apart from sailors, only hoodlums and gang members sport tattoos," he said. "By the way, this reminds me: Have you started thinking about going back to high school?"

"No, I'm not thinking about it at all, John."

"I have a high school equivalency diploma," he said, "and it's embarrassing to hang out with a dropout like you." He was joking, but I was stung. "Go to Paris after you graduate," he said. Paris seemed far away, and my dream of it and of being an artist was fading; but, mostly to please him, that fall, after a year away from classes, I returned to the death of a thousand cuts of formal education.

Molly

Like an escapee from prison who cannot hold out in the wild, I, the big dreamer, the would-be adventurer in life, fled back to the safe slammer of high school. John had said that among the cons in Dannemora there ran a debate as to which was preferable, a hard prison with a short sentence or an easy prison with a long sentence. School was easy and long and, just as I had left it, boring, uninspiring, with hours of sitting and learning little.

What I had been reading outside of class—Hemingway's *The Sun Also Rises*, James's *The American*, Melville's *The Confidence-Man*—was more interesting than the books like *A Tale of Two Cities* and *The Scarlet Letter* that we were made to read for class. The very fact that they had been assigned made them unreadable.

The teachers were just teachers, not writers or poets or artists, but the best were intelligent, well-meaning, and decent. Many had left behind or had failed at fulfilling their own dreams and were making their way through life honorably. All the same, I resented sitting at a desk like a baby in a high chair being spoon-fed processed, sanctioned culture.

About my attitude, John said, "You don't have to like the system or the institution. But pay its dues to get what you want in the long run. Feel above it if you like, drop out again, but the institution will be there long after you are gone."

I was stuck in high school, but I was sure I still had a few years left to be Rimbaud, to have a creative and adventurous life, to travel, to live free and with some elegance and meaning. When would that happen, though? I sent my poems all the way to Manhattan, to the magical, avant-garde publisher New Directions. One poem began: "Kyphosis of the mind / Is no crime." No question, the editors there would be impressed by the unusual use of the medical term "kyphosis" in the literary context I had placed it. I received a little handwritten rejection note. It meant they took me seriously! It felt like I was on the track to the wider artistic world, one that was sure to include love.

I often dreamed about Molly, the model at the Art Students League, and had never stopped thinking of her beautiful body and her tenderness with me. "I will miss you," she had said. Maybe she was thinking of me, too, missing me now as I had missed her. I often imagined I would see her again—maybe invite her out for dinner in a little Italian restaurant in Greenwich Village, one with checkered tablecloths and a candle stuck in an empty bottle of Chianti. I had yet to go to such a place.

One day John said, "Go see her. Start small and ask her out for coffee."

"She's twenty-one. She'll laugh at me."

"I bet she won't, Freddy. You have to take chances sometimes."

I did not tell John that I did not want just to ask Molly out for dinner or coffee; I wanted to ask her to come to Paris and live with me. I would devote myself as never before to painting and become a great artist—and maybe even a valuable poet. Molly and I would sit in our café and read and draw on the paper tablecloth and later meet fellow artists and poets for dinner. Afterward she and I would walk arm in arm at night along the glistening Seine to our little apartment under the eaves, the moon thick in our window. Molly and I would live every hour, every day with passion and joy.

One Saturday, I took John's advice and subwayed down to the Art Students League. I sat in the little alcove waiting for the class to break, in the hope that Molly would come up for a cigarette, as she always had. Several times I was on the verge of running away before I could make a fool of myself. What if she didn't even remember me?

After a while the students wandered in, chatting, giving me glances; the models followed, surrounded by clouds of cigarette smoke. Molly was not among them, but the redhead Sally was, and she walked right over to me, giving me a big, warm smile and a kiss on the cheek.

"We all wondered what happened to you."

"I decided to go away and paint on my own," I said, as if I had sailed to a faraway exotic land, as one of my heroes, Gauguin, had done.

"Do you want to sit with us awhile?"

"I have to rush," I said. "I just wanted to say hello to you and Molly."

"She woulda loved seeing you, but she's left."

I tried to mask my disappointment, but not well enough, because she said, "I'm sorry."

"Well, I'll come by again. Please let her know I was here."

"Of course, if she ever comes back."

"To work, you mean?"

"No, to America. She went to live in Brazil with her boyfriend."

"Oh!"

"I see," she said. "Well, she had a little crush on you, too, in case you want to know." I was sure she heard the disappointment in my voice.

I dragged myself back into the sad street, into the sad sunlight, and went to the sad corner of sad Seventh Avenue and sat in the sad luncheonette with a cup of sad, watery, burnt American coffee and imagined Molly standing by a palm hut on a green sea, smiling happily, her hair even longer. She was waving to me.

Tables and Whales

The Bronx, Parkchester, 1953

One evening I came to John and Anita's for dinner and found in the dining room a new, gleaming, ash-blond wooden table.

"When did you get that?" I asked.

"I made it," John said with a kid's pride. People build tables and all sorts of things, although I never yet had met any who had. John's table was sturdy, smooth, elegant. There was nothing crudely home-made looking about it. John said he learned how to make it from library books. He bought the wood, paid a local carpentry shop to use their equipment, and, presto, there was the table.

"There is nothing you can't learn," he said. "There is nothing your mind can't do."

I was almost sold on the idea, but building a table wasn't strong enough proof I needed to keep me painting. I was losing the will, the belief in myself to devote my life to painting and perhaps, at the very best, only to end up a decent artist whose skill never matched his vision. Years later, I realized what a fool I was to surrender because of an idea of perfection—how many middling artists and poets and writers are minnows who swim as whales? They appear impervious to self-doubt, their egos seemingly ironclad. They use what little they have to will themselves to success, or at least to fool others into believing in their worth.

Post Office or College

The Bronx, Parkchester, 1953

I finally got off my very rickety high horse long enough to get my high school diploma. But now that that was done, John said, "You should go to college."

Even though I had balked and railed against formal education, strangely the idea appealed to me. I understood that in college, unlike high school, I could read anything I wanted and, I had been told, no one was made to go to classes. College had an added appeal: no one in my family had ever finished high school, let alone gone to college. I would be the first. What else spoke for the American dream?

But to what college and with what money? My grades were so poor that a scholarship was out of the question. The only place that might take me was a rich kid's fun-house school where grades were overlooked. Of course, I did not have the money for such places. I had never heard of college loans.

John said, "Freddy, I'd give you the money if I could."

I knew that. I knew he was hardly making the rent, and he would be down the drain without Anita's salary. As for family money, my mother depended on what I could give her, and that prompted me to find work with a steady income and job security. "The post office," my mother suggested. "It's permanent work with a pension and paid vacations." She had had long talks with our postman, an Italian who had found security in America delivering mail three times a day and once on Saturday. His son had various pseudonyms, among them Evan Hunter, because he had gone to Evander Childs High School and Hunter College; he was better known as Ed McBain, one of the country's leading crime writers.

"The postman's son's very famous," my mother said. "Get a steady job like his father and have a family and give your children a chance for success."

The Letter

Manhattan, The City College of New York, 1954

In 1954 the City College of New York was tuition-free but only for those with grade averages well above the 90s. If you did not have the necessary grades, you could take a test open to anyone with a high school degree, but the word was that you had a mouse's chance of scoring high enough to be accepted.

John said, "Take the exam, Freddy. There's nothing to lose."

One cold fall morning with hundreds of others in the Great Hall of the college's Shepard Building, an old, cathedral-like Gothic stone pile—Kafka's impenetrable castle come to life—which even from a distance gave me chills, I took the exam. I skimmed through the math part because I had failed at algebra—a mystery to me—and I had to beg the principal to be allowed to take it again in summer night school. The higher reaches of abstract thought were beyond my grasp, in spite of John's claim that one could learn anything.

The entrance exam lasted three hours. When we all left, I heard, "That was a breeze. Are they kidding?"

I thought I had done well but not brilliantly enough to slide in. On the subway home I wanted to die and be over with my empty future before I had worked all my life to get there. But in the spring I received a letter saying I was accepted to one of the City University colleges, of which there were five in ascending reputation and importance, with the City College of New York, then called the

Proletarian Harvard, at the pinnacle. I was to come for my assignment to one of the colleges.

I returned to the Great Hall. Behind its stage stretched the mural by Edwin H. Blissfield called *The Graduate*, a celestial, golden light of success glowing on a graduate in full academic gown and mortarboard about to be handed his diploma. One day I, too, would stand there bathed in that golden light, diploma in one hand, a paintbrush in the other, my mother one of the assembled thousands looking on with tears of pride.

The man at the reception desk looked me up on a huge printout sheet, rose, and extended his hand. "Congratulations, you've made City College." My pride inflated me like a Thanksgiving Day balloon. I could hardly squeeze through my apartment door, and I floated above my cot for three nights.

John and Anita were thrilled for me.

"See?" John said. "It never hurts to take a risk. Come over next week. I have a present for you."

"I can't wait, John. What is it?" I was hoping it would be one of his grim prison drawings that I thought held as much truth as Goya's paintings of madhouses.

"Hold your horses. Come over and find out for yourself."

Anita came to the phone. "Congratulations, handsome. Maybe now I can find you a date."

"Anita," I said, "what does John have for me? I can't stand the suspense."

"It's a Japanese print," she whispered into the phone. "A Hiroshige print he's been saving for your birthday. But don't let him know I told you."

Overcoats and Penmanship

Manhattan, The City College of New York, 1954

Within weeks I was already disappointed with college. It felt like an extension of the high school nullity, like I was once again in the student's baby high chair. I returned to my old rebellious, childish tricks. I walked out in the middle of the class to go to the bathroom for a smoke and took my time daydreaming. When I finally returned I sat tilting the chair back on two legs. This was my mixture of insult to authority and my insolent attention getting. The professor seemed oblivious to my antics. In some ways he seemed oblivious to the class.

The professor, Norman Schlenoff, had asked us each to write an in-class essay about ourselves, especially what we had read and cared to read. As a writer-poet who was in correspondence with the esteemed New Directions publishers and who was asked to submit to them more of his work, I was packed with resentment and wished to let the professor know who exactly he was dealing with. I wrote boastfully about my artistic aspirations and my desire to live in Paris. About reading, I mentioned Rimbaud, Hemingway, and Joyce, and I added Henry Miller for shock effect. A week later I got back the essay with a grade of B– and a note that Dr. Schlenoff would like to see me in his office.

The office was a cubicle barely large enough for one, with a dim overhead fluorescent light, and a small desk with a gray, rubbery top.

This was not what I had seen in movies set in an Ivy League or a fancy Oxford University office, and there was no sherry. For a free education you got the genteel reform school spartan look: the toilets had no doors—no one seemed to know why, unless it was to prevent us from masturbating in public; a pane in Schlenoff's class window was missing and one was cracked, and the room was kept freezing, so we wore our overcoats indoors; the radiator pipes clanged and banged like swords on a shield. At the time, all of that was expected, part of the small price for paying nothing to be at the Proletarian Harvard.

Dr. Norman Schlenoff did not appear to notice his icy classroom or the dreary little office where we sat almost knee to knee. He had a swan's beak and an indefinable foreign-accent honk. In class he smiled with his every sentence and smiled at everything we said. He always seemed on the edge of telling a joke to a cloud floating high above the window. Everything was ironic: he was in a secret, ironic relationship to the class, to the chalky blackboard, and even to the banging radiator pipes.

He pulled my essay from a little stack of blue books and said something I did not understand, then said it again. I finally got it. "I don't know French," I said.

He seemed disappointed. But then, very gently: "Perhaps you would like Rimbaud more if you had read him."

"I have read him," I said, hurt, as if being accused of lying.

"You have read him in translation, I suppose." I nodded. We turned to the matter of my little blue book essay.

"You're interesting, Mr. Tuten, but your prose is less so." And then he pointed out why: the least of my flaws were grammar, syntax, spelling, punctuation, and organization. He didn't mention penmanship.

"Why do you use the possessive as if you were translating literally from Spanish? You say 'the house of my uncle' instead of 'my uncle's house,' for example."

Somehow I believed that the Latinate possessive had weight, dignity. I had gotten that idea from my uncle Umberto, who would say, "Have you just come from the house of your mother?" I had always thought that my visit was made all the more glamorous by his elocution.

All my big sense of myself, all the grand thoughts that had made me feel special—where were they now? How had I ever gotten into this college? On orientation day, in the Great Hall, we were all congratulated for being accepted: "You are all exceptional," the academic dean had said. "Now, look to your left and look to your right. You may never see these people again." The standard for admission was high; so, too, was the standard for our remaining there. If you let your grade average slip too far, you were sent back to the street. And from there, where? The gutter?

We went over the essay, and with each comment and correction I fell lower and lower until I crashed back to the earth, a mere boy. On the saving side, Schlenoff seemed impressed that I had read as much as I had, and not just the standard literature; he was touched, he said, by my wish to be an artist and to live in Paris.

"Have you ever been there?" I asked with undisguised admiration.

"Oh, I have spent some time there. You would like it," he said. "Actually, you should be there now."

Only when I left his office and sped downstairs to the cafeteria did I consider the double meaning of his sentence. By the time I entered the warm, safe haven of the cafeteria, I felt twice deflated: I was both a worthless student and the fool of grandiose dreams.

I told my friends about the conference with Schlenoff. They laughed. "He must love you, with a B-minus." That helped a bit but didn't keep me from feeling down.

"He's a strange bird," another said. "He doesn't even have a doctorate in English but some weird degree from a French university."

The idea of his having a weird degree—that he himself was a weird item in a conventional academic world—made me like him, even though I was afraid of his Olympian distance, the way he seemed to be mocking everything on earth, especially my naïveté.[6]

---

[6]ADVICE
Norman Schlenhoff (1915–1983)

While Norman Schlenoff did not have an American doctorate, he actually had a degree from the Sorbonne, a *Docteur d'État*, a diploma with *Mention Très Honourable*, the French equivalent of summa cum laude. His thesis, written in French, was on beauty. He defended his thesis orally before a committee of five specialists in the field. I understood finally why his colleagues always approached him with a kind of friendly deference. He later wrote and published books on the French neo-classicist Ingres and on Romanticism.

In 1964, when I began to teach at City College, I went to my first department meeting and Schlenoff came to sit beside me. The topic for the meeting was whether to change the number of a Composition Class from 1.1 to 1.2. Considering the subject, the meeting was strangely heated. Schlenoff turned to me and said sotto voce, "If you stay here long enough, you'll never write a word."

Some four years later, I ran into Dr. Schlenoff at the Metropolitan Museum of Art. I watched him stand before a painting, studying it for a long time. It might have been a Poussin. I went over to say hello and he greeted me warmly and even remembered my name. He had long left teaching and was a private art dealer, specializing, I think, in pre-nineteenth-century and earlier European art.

I boasted that I was writing a lot about art for *Arts* magazine and volunteered that I was especially fond of the Pop painters like Lichtenstein. "I am surprised," I said. "I have never seen you in the galleries, especially at Castelli, where all the new painters are showing."

He gave me a kind look, but one that also suggested that I was something of a fool. "There are galleries where one must never be seen," he said. "Only the most vulgar people go there and only the most vulgar nouveau-riche collectors buy that work."

"Oh," I said, feeling that I had again disappointed him in the way I had when he learned I did not speak French.

I lost touch with him after that encounter and learned only recently that he died in 1983 at the age of sixty-seven. He had been married to an art historian and had children. There is no other record of him that I could find.

Mexican Murals and Exile

Manhattan, City College Basement Cafeteria, 1954

The City College cafeteria stretched along the dark basement of Shepard Hall, like the mess halls in black-and-white prison movies. Brown, linoleum-topped, bolted-down tables (in case of a heated political argument?) were lined up on either side; the four tables in the center aisle were known as Red Square, for the various shades of leftist students who, as if it were still the 1930s, argued there on the finer points of Marxist theory.

I had joined the bohemian table, where I had made friends with English majors and aspiring poets and fiction writers. I was awed by Eli, a senior whose parents—and he, in his free time after school—ran a hole-in-the-wall soda fountain/candy shop in the west Bronx. He wrote with Céline as his model and, to my envy, left school, bused down to Mexico City, and stayed there writing novels and letters to us describing his loneliness. Bruno was a poet in the Dylan Thomas mode and, over coffee, declaimed his sonnets with quivering, dramatic pauses. Natasha, the table's intellectual and quick-witted deflator of the pretentious—contrary to what I would have expected—adored him. I adored her. But she seemed so sophisticated, so assured in her literary opinions, including about the novels she had read in French and Russian, that I was happy to stay in her shadow and be tolerated.

I had spent as much time in the cafeteria as in my classes, cutting several to drink coffee and talk. The argument of the moment: Who is the greater writer, Proust or Joyce? I had not yet read Proust, but—following my aesthetic principle that the more difficult, the more abstruse, the better—I argued for Joyce's greatness. The bohemian table was leftist enough to decry Kapitalism but we were above, we thought, the crude Marxist idea, preached at the tables of Red Square, of art as a tool for revolution. Our heads dwelled in the pure, noble spires of art and ideas, while our feet—as Danny, the defector of Red Square, had said—"dragged in the capitalist muck."

Danny was a soft-spoken Mexican. We loved him because he never had dogmatic schemes for changing the world and took our artistic pontifications in stride. He was an engineering student but did not sit with the slide rulers and instead had fixed himself with us at the bohemian table. He was respected for reading to us in Spanish poems by Pablo Neruda but mostly because he was studying something difficult, something practical that one day would get him a job and a place in the world.

Danny often spoke affectionately of his father, a renowned Mexican artist, and spoke about Mexican painting, about which I knew nothing. One day he brought me a book, *Mexican Painting in Our Time*, written by Bernard Meyers, a professor at City College. I was immediately smitten by the boldness of the art and by the undercurrent, if not the current, of its political consciousness. I had not known that such art had existed. Danny said that in Mexico, after its great revolution, artists like Orozco, Siqueiros, and Rivera had devoted themselves to mural painting because they thought that was the best way to show the Mexican people their own history, from the invasion of the conquistadores to their capitalist exploitation in fields and factories.

This was not easel painting for a gallery or for the homes of rich collectors but art that was meant to be seen on the walls of post offices and school courtyards: art for the masses. Art that would have more meaning to people's lives than, say, paintings of nude women or bowls of fruit with a wine bottle, or an abstractionist canvas that referred to nothing but itself, the ultimate goal of art for art's sake.

The Mexican muralists had the same mission as the religious painters of the past: to instruct, to inspire. The muralists depicted how the Church and the rich, the military and the state, crushed the poor and the powerless. Rivera's murals, in particular, presented the Mexican people with their history and a glimpse of their earthly socialist salvation in the not-too-distant future. The murals were meant not to unite all classes but to encourage class warfare in the struggle for social and economic democracy.

The artist, James Joyce believed, should be "like the God of creation . . . invisible, refined out of existence, indifferent, paring his fingernails." I was coming to think there was something dead about this conception of the artist that had made no connection between art and the lifeblood of people who worked and suffered. I saw the artist in combat with all society, with all forms of conformity that would attempt to fit his originality into a conventional mold.

I loved Joyce's hero, Stephen Dedalus, who believed only in art for art's sake. But I also loved Diego Rivera, who had lived in Paris and was a cubist painter before returning to Mexico to subordinate his art in the service of the revolution. Strangely, I found no dichotomy between the individualistic and the subservient vision, believing that both could be combined. Sometimes I wondered about myself and my contradictions and I decided that I was a true aesthetic schizophrenic.

I was transforming myself from an aesthete to someone who saw no conflict with the idea of art as some form of social mission. The place that had promoted that art was Mexico, its mecca. I wanted to go to Mexico.

I was in love with the cafeteria. The college was just a place that housed it. I would leave my mother's apartment early and get there by eight, have breakfast, cheap and good—sausages and scrambled eggs, home fries, rolls with butter, and a mug of coffee for a dollar eighty-seven—and maybe show up for a class or two. I would spend the rest of the day at the table, or go to the library and roam the stacks and then return to the table. I would stay there until late afternoon, and when there was no one I knew left to talk to and the cafeteria was starting to fill up with the evening-class students, I would leave the campus reluctantly for the seemingly never-ending subway ride home. I'd read, and sometimes I was so absorbed that I would miss my stop by several stations. It seemed days before I could return to my real home, the cafeteria.

I read *The Fountainhead* for the third time. It convinced me that I was one of the rare Elect, born not to take the conventional route trod by others, the Ordinary Ones, the professors who feared originality, the students who studied, tried hard, got to some uninspired place, and died there. I was like Ayn Rand's superman genius, Howard Roark, and, like him, I was above churches, law courts, universities—certainly above the petty classroom—so I never needed to study, never needed to write my required papers, never needed, even, to come to class. I knew there were consequences, but I dismissed them and lived on an island of self-certainty and grandiose dreams. I was an artist; what artist writes papers and takes exams? I wrote poems and stories on a black Royal portable typewriter, using a piano bench for a desk. I still had some months left to match or to fly above Rimbaud's greatness before he quit poetry at nineteen.

One day, toward the final weeks of the semester, I found in the mail a notice of my academic expulsion. I was to see Professor Barber, the dean of academic affairs. My grades averaged a D. My highest grade was a B– in composition with Professor Schlenoff.

The dean was full of quirky energy and high-pitched goodwill. "Clearly you're bright, Mr. Tootin," he said, "or you wouldn't be here at City. You scored high on the entrance exam."

I finally felt the weight of the expulsion, of my having to leave the college, the cafeteria. I was ashamed. He studied me for a long moment while I held back my tears.

He saw them welling up and gently said: "Let's give you another try. Suspension for only a semester. Come back next fall on probation: B average or better. I'm sure you can do even better than that."

I thanked him. He must have felt the true gratitude behind it, and he added, "I'll mail you an official reinstatement for next September. If you have any problems, come by my office when you return."

"I will never forget your kindness," I said.

I was too humiliated to tell John or my mother about my suspension. I pretended to be going to school but I was really taking the subway to my job in the Sperry and Hutchinson Company mailroom, where I was again employed full-time. Now, maybe finally, I could save up enough money to go not to Paris but to Mexico.

Prison Walls and a Memoir

The Bronx, Parkchester, 1955

Doubleday had commissioned John Resko to write a book about his prison life; he spent his mornings and afternoons banging on his typewriter and didn't answer the phone until after five. I visited him and Anita for dinner once a week. He asked about school. I lied, told stories about history and literature classes that I invented. He did not press me but at times, like the murderer Raskolnikov, I yearned to confess. John may have suspected the truth, especially when I had invented two wholly different class schedules, but his mind was filled with his day's writing and it spilled into his conversation.

John phoned to ask me to come to his place one evening. He rarely called; it was always I who made contact, who always needed him. I thought it was a good time to tell him about the expulsion, to finally stop the lies and the guilt that came with telling them.

He opened the door warmly, as always. But I could see he had forced the smile.

It was only when John was writing his book that I ever saw him gloomy, dark. All those memories, the harshness, the brutality of twenty years of prison life that makes suicide a welcome option to a lifetime of withering, without hope, in a cell, lights off at nine, with roaches and rats and bedbugs for roommates, welled up in him as he wrote.

We sat silently for some minutes. Then, with his eyes closed, he said, "Sometimes it's good just to be still and brood. Maybe indulge yourself with a dose of self-pity. Have you ever done that?"

"Too much," I said.

"That's OK. Just don't let yourself sink in it for too long or it becomes the whole life."

"What's the matter, John?" I asked, nervous about reversing roles and making a fool of myself in the matters of the grown-up world.

He nodded to the wall, where, in place of the trash can, were black-and-white drawings of a man sitting in a dark cell; a man being beaten by guards with clubs; the splattered body of a man seen from high up on a prison tier; convicts in a yard warming themselves over a barrel of fire, stone walls reaching to the sky.

"I couldn't make those drawings in the joint or I would have been sent to the hole or worse. So I did them recently as an *aide-mémoire* for my book. Not that I needed much aid."

"But you drew a lot in prison. Isn't that how you got out?"

"Sure, but I always wanted one day to graduate from drawing to painting in oils on canvas. But prison rules did not permit oils, so that was that."

"What were they afraid of?"

"A secret weapon concealed in the tubes? Or maybe a poison so that the con can commute his own sentence before doing his time? Who knows, Freddy. Prison is its own world, and it makes rules to protect itself."

"Did you get them to change the rules or make an exception for you?"

"That's a good one, Fred."

"I guess I'm naïve."

"Let's say that maybe you'd last fourteen minutes in prison. Make that ten." He laughed like he loved me.

"You're right," I said.

"Do you know who Lucky Luciano is?"

"Don't make fun of me."

"I thought you might have mistaken him for a character in a Chandler novel. Anyway, his friends called him Charlie. He asked me to call him that. He was still so powerful, even in prison, that the guards called him Mr. Luciano. Both of us grew up in the Lower East Side, so we were like *paisanos*, and we chewed the rag over the old places we remembered, like a barbershop that sold French postcards and weed. Anyway, he liked me and my drawings—I think I may have made a few of him.

"One day he said, 'Kid, you should be doing oils, like you want.' I told him that the prison regulations forbade it and I thought that was that. But a few weeks later two guards rolled in a trolley with three huge boxes to my cell. Boxes packed with brushes and large tubes of oil paint and rolls and rolls of canvas. Turpentine, even.

"The hack says, 'Present from Mr. Luciano.' Luciano could have anything he wanted sent to him. He was a star. Even the worst hacks were grudgingly respectful.

"I went to thank Charlie. He said, 'Johnny, everyone should work with good tools.'"

"That's a great story, John. Will it be in your book?"

"Maybe, but I have to be careful not to irritate my parole board. They could send me back if they wanted."

That idea frightened me. That he'd go back to hell. That I would be alone again.

Months later he called to say the book was finished and had been accepted by his editor. John said proudly, "The copy editor remarked that there was almost no work to be done: perfect spelling and punctuation." The book was called *Reprieve*, and it soon would take John on a road to a new life.[7]

ᴊOHN'S LIFE IN L.A.
John Resko (1911–1991)

Reprieve was published in 1956 to critical success, but was not enough of a commercial hit to make John rich, or to allow him to move to Manhattan, or to sweep Anita away from her job behind the sales counter. But his personal story was unusual enough to get him invited, in 1957, to the popular quiz show *The $64,000 Question*. The city streets were silent when the show went on: If you had a TV, you were home watching. The contestants were given questions of escalating difficulty; you could stop at any stage and take home your earnings, and if you answered them all, week by week, you'd reach the highest rung, the sixty-four-thousand-dollar question.

I went to a neighbor's house to see the show. John was charming and calm, and the famous host, Hal March, seemed to like him. John got as far as the eight-thousand-dollar mark, and his question was on African sculpture. They brought him a mask to identify. He said it was so-and-so from so-and-so. Hal March consulted his card and said, "I'm sorry, that's wrong." But John gently insisted that he was right. There was an awkward moment, and March said they had to consult with experts in the field, and that John was to return the following week.

He did. March said he regretted it, wished it were not so, but John had made a mistake. The audience let out a moan of sympathy. As a consolation prize, he was given a Cadillac. John made a gracious bow, thanked everyone, and was accompanied off the stage. John said, "Freddy, I still think I was right and they were wrong." It was a little hard for me to believe that, and I think my expression showed it. John laughed. "What do you think, Freddy, isn't a man entitled to his mistaken beliefs?"

John sold the Cadillac. "What do I need a car for in the city?" he said. "Anyway, I don't have a driver's license and I don't think I'm ever going to get one." He didn't realize then that he was going to leave New York. In the fall of 1957, he and Anita packed up and left for Los Angeles, where he was hired to consult on a prospective Hollywood biopic based on his book. He was also invited to write on spec for the successful TV series *Alfred Hitchcock Presents*.

At first he and Anita were not happy in LA. He wrote me: "It's not smog out here—it's a rank, fuliginous overcast of opium fumes that makes everything seem pretty and eternal and palm lissome and pastel sweet. I'm afraid Anita has succumbed to the pipe dream and is unable to experience the under layer of stifling, watery shit which is the true foundation of Hollywood—I loathe it and am impatient to return to the world of real people—people who sweat and belch and squeeze pimples and grope each other honestly."

But John slowly warmed up to the place. He appreciated the climate. Years in the piercing winter cold and damp and the burning summer heat of Dannemora had injured his health, and he thrived in the reliable sunshine and comforting warmth of Los Angeles. He learned to drive and got his license, but most of the time, on her days off from work, Anita had to drive him from place to place, which was not many places, since John stayed home most of the time developing scripts and ideas for TV projects and consulting on the script for the movie being made from *Reprieve*. He bought a get-around-the-town used car, which in the movie world made him a loser. As a writer, he was the lowest person on the totem pole.

"One look at the car had the guard at the studio gate make a few phone calls before letting me through. I didn't even get a salute and a good morning smile," John said, laughing. I didn't laugh.

The film, *Convicts 4*, came out in 1962. It starred Ben Gazzara and bore little resemblance to John's book. It was heavy-handed, disjunctive, with little cameos of stars like Sammy Davis Jr. to give celebrity glamour to the dark story of prison life. Sammy Davis Jr. played a convict like he was mugging onstage with the Rat Pack in Las Vegas. Ben Gazzara played John Resko like a second-rate Method actor. All in all, the film was a flop.

John called me from LA: "Have you seen it? What do you think?"

"It's terrific," I said.

John laughed. "Come out here and be a movie producer, Fred. They can sell you the idea the world is flat and that they're going to make a movie proving it. It's not a great film; don't worry about it."

"No kidding, it's really good. I enjoyed it."

"There's a saying in prison: When you get caught, keep to your story. Did you learn that from me?" His laugh warmed me. I had missed that warmth.

Then he added something I had always felt but had never heard voiced from him. "Love you, Freddy."

In 1968, I was in Los Angeles to write a piece for *Arts Magazine* about the Art and Technology show at the Los Angeles County Museum of Art. I visited John and Anita in their apartment, the twin of his modest Parkchester flat, except that the African sculptures were missing. He was as cheerful as ever, greeting me with the same warm smile he had the day I first met him. Anita kissed me: "How's my little Tony Curtis?"

Anita was working as a salesperson in a department store again, and John was having some undefined trouble with his eyes, so he couldn't drive to shop for dinner. We walked to a small Italian restaurant nearby, and all was good cheer. The owner, Mario, with his pencil mustache, came to greet us; the two waiters were professionally polite. John studied the menu like a man panning for gold.

The waiters were funereal and served the courses all at once. The dinner: soggy pasta and canned tomato sauce; the veal, like creamed rubber; the spinach, greenish mush; the after-dinner espresso, bitter and burned. John said he loved it from start to finish. Anita smiled weakly.

"Hard to find great little places like this in LA," John said. "Even in New York anymore."

"It's really great," I said, trying to muster up enthusiasm.

Anita said, "Nothing like this place," and winked at me, her fellow conspirator. "By the way, are you still with that girl who made you so crazy? The girl who looked like Elizabeth Taylor?"

"They all make him crazy," John said.

"I'm married now," I said. "I've forgotten everyone but my wife and you."

"I told you that he was married," John said, and he and Anita went back and forth on whether he really had. Now they seemed like a sweet old couple, with the juicy sexual life drained out of them. I thought: *Will this happen to me, too? Will I grow old and tame, become half of a cute elderly couple that bickers over where the remote was last seen?*

Slowly, after the second espresso, more bitter than the first, it leaked out that John's eyesight was disintegrating and that he had sold his car—Anita now had to take a bus to work—but not only because of his failing vision. John had written one or two episodes for the Hitchcock show, and that was about the sum of his television career.

"TV writing is drying up," John said, "if it's not already a Sahara, with no oasis in sight."

"What about your screenwriting projects?" I asked.

Anita said, "No one is taking John's calls anymore. His friends," she said. "His great friends!"

"Things change," John said sweetly. "New writers, new studio heads, new fashions in everything."

"John always takes the Olympian view," Anita said.

"Freddy, you never talk about yourself. What's the big mystery?" John asked.

I was reluctant to talk about myself, feeling that my life was on the ascent and theirs was on the slide. Not that I was living in abundance and ease, but I was writing, married, living in a cozy apartment facing Tompkins Square Park, teaching at City College, and on the way to getting a PhD in literature. I was happy for the first time in my life; my happiness, I imagined, was a gulf between us. I hated myself for feeling that. A shitty little ingrate and a snob, I called myself. But the feeling of that separation between us still remained no matter how many times I repeated that.

The restaurant's eight tables were now empty, and, without asking, Mario brought us the check. I took out my wallet and said, "It's my turn." Anita was silent, but John said, "You are our guest, always," and, to Mario's obvious discomfort, John said, "Put it on my tab, please."

Anita left three singles for the waiters.

We exited the restaurant with less cheer than when we had arrived. John said, "I owe them a painting in exchange for dinners." Anita stayed silent.

We waited for the cab I had ordered from the restaurant. We hugged, we kissed, we said, "I love you." John gave me his warmest smile. My cab came, and soon I was on the way to my friend's house in Beverly Hills with its Lichtenstein and Warhol paintings. There, in bed, I was wrapped in sadness. Sadness for John and Anita and sadness that I had no power to help them. And frightened of John's failure and wanting to run from it and from him. Run from my fear of my own failure, of a future hand-to-mouth existence, of me alone, back in the Bronx, in an apartment with broken furniture and torn lampshades. I recalled what John had said to me long ago about my self-pity, whining about a girl who did not reciprocate my love: "What will you do when you have real problems, Fred?"

I called John from time to time, and wrote to him with greater and greater infrequency. He was always cheerful; there were always projects looming—a film script, or maybe an art gallery, for real art and not the fashion of the moment.

I phoned him from Paris in 1978. "John, how are your eyes doing?" I asked, remembering the trouble he had been having years ago.

"I'm blind."

My heart sank and kept sinking. "John" was all I could say.

"It's all right, Fred, I'm so glad to hear from you."

Then, in 1981, my youthful dream came true: I was finally living in Paris—not in a tiny flat above a café, but in a large empty apartment in Neuilly-sur-Seine, a quiet, elegant section of Paris. It was the apartment of the great writer Raymond Queneau, my editor at Gallimard, who had become my friend and whose family let me live there after his death.

On impulse, I phoned John in LA. Anita answered in a cautious voice, but she brightened up when I said my name. She told me right off what I was afraid to ask: "John's dead, Freddy. He had been paralyzed from the neck down," she said. "He lasted that way for a few years. He wasn't able to speak, but he smiled at me a lot."

I went silent, feeling that sickening darkness when someone you love has left you or has died, and you begin to realize that you will never see them again, ever. Feeling crushed for Anita, too, alone, old, in LA. With what kind of money? Feeling sad for myself, too. A link to my former life was broken, and more links would break until I was the last link to myself, and one day that link, too, would be broken.

"He was a sweet man," she said.

"I loved him very much, and I love you, too, Anita," I said, thinking as I said it what a selfish, stupid jerk I had been, so self-involved all these years not to have taken a minute to call to see how they both were. In my heart, I knew I had been afraid to learn he was sinking into poverty, blindness, isolation, mirroring my own self-doubts. I had not wanted to see him as a man in trouble: a father is meant always to be a hero who never ages and stays virile, potent, and never in need.

"Where is he buried?" I asked, as if my visiting his grave one day would make up for all the calls I had never made and the letters I had never written.

"You remember, he always said he would give his body to science. Well, he did."

He had always said he would donate his body to some medical school: "A cadaver for students to learn about the anatomy firsthand," he said, "otherwise the corpse just goes to waste." But his death had seemed so far away then, and I had never believed that he would die or that anyone I loved would ever die. I still found it inconceivable that my grandmother wasn't waiting for me to come back from school with a bowl of *café latte* and some day-old semolina bread waiting for me on a plate.

I saw John on a metal table, his body carved up, his face skinned to show the muscles to the medical students. All that life and thought gone, reduced to meat to be dissected by people who had no idea where he had come from, what long struggle he had had to leave a prison cage and to see the trees and the moon.

"Do you need anything, Anita?" I asked.

"Like what, Freddy?"

It was hard for me to say it, fearing she would think I was pitying her. "Money. Do you need any?"

"Oh! No," she said. "I'm OK. Thanks, anyway. I have a part-time job in a luncheonette. I'm the morning cashier."

I remembered how beautiful she had been and how I had lusted after her. I remembered how affectionate and sexy she had been without putting it on. I remembered how much John had wanted to free her from working menial jobs—from working *any* jobs—and let her take acting classes. We said our good-byes. I could not bear to put the phone down.

A few weeks later Anita sent me a package with several of John's prison drawings, studies of guards and fellow convicts huddled in the prison courtyard with no sky. I kept them in a closet until I had enough money to frame them. But then, when I did, I could not find the drawings in the closet or in the whole of the apartment. Had I disappeared them in my guilt?

Years later, I published a novel about Van Gogh's final three days before he committed suicide. I wanted to put into the book, *Van Gogh's Bad Café* (1997), all the love I felt about Vincent and his work, and maybe something about John's sweetness, his innocence, slipped into my portrayal of Van Gogh's character. When the novel was finished I dedicated it to John, using the last line of his memoir, when he steps out of the prison gate to freedom, for my novel's epigraph: "The trees were so close I could smell them and the road began singing to me." Even though he was dead and would not know it, Anita would. I sent it to her at the last address I had. It was returned, "Addressee Unknown."

Leonard and Belinda

Manhattan, The City College of New York, 1955

In the fall I returned to City College, my rescue ship. Fear of being thrown again into the open sea goaded me: I climbed down from my Olympian perch and I studied relentlessly. I got As on my exams; I got As on my papers. I sat respectfully in my seat and waited for class to be over before I went for a smoke.

I took a fiction-writing workshop with Irwin Stark, a novelist, who conducted his class dramatically: He bellowed, he gesticulated, he threw little pieces of chalk at the students to emphasize a point. He told jokes. He did not wear a jacket and tie. He favored the gods of Realism and Verisimilitude—the sputtering sound a cigarette makes when it hits a wet gutter, the stink of rotting garbage in a knocked-over pail in the summer heat. I distrusted his flamboyant presentation—he strived to be loved—and his pedestrian, realist aesthetic was everything I disdained, despised. I wanted lead to be spun into gold, not gold into gutters and cigarette butts: I wanted ashcans to be pyramids to heaven. I studied with him a week or two before switching, within the time limit the school permitted, to Leonard Ehrlich's fiction-writing class. His class was not popular.

Ehrlich, the author of one novel, *God's Angry Man*, about the abolitionist John Brown, was a trim, bespectacled man, soft-spoken, dapper in a conservative way. He wore dark gray flannel pants, a herringbone jacket, and a silent tie; his shoes had a golden burnish.

He looked at you with his head turned to one side as if studying you with one suspicious eye while the other was doing who knew what. He was friendly but reserved. Unlike Professor Schlenoff, Ehrlich was not a Francophile; he did not carry with him the rare air of fin de siècle Europe, or of its literature and art. Irony did not seep through his speech or his demeanor.

Ehrlich measured the students' stories, and all writing, by its music, freshness, conviction, insight, clarity, wisdom, and—a word he frequently used—"dignity." His most severe criticism of any author was that his or her work lacked dignity, meaning it was lazy, trite, ordinary, that the prose was cowardly. My stories got a B– at first; when I abandoned the junior Hemingway pose, they rose to a B+.

Perhaps to please him, I tried to purge myself of Hemingway's declarative sentences and his nuts-and-bolts view of life as simply something to endure with courage and grace. I also tried to write on a higher, more intellectual plane and with greater complexity of language.

One of these lofty attempts was "The History of the Radical Movement," a claustrophobic tale about a solipsistic youth in a rowboat who wonders whether he should drown himself or join with the radical Catholic Worker movement. In the margin Ehrlich wrote in a tiny, tight hand, "This indicates much potential talent, but the story as written is pretentious and overwritten and rather obvious in its treatment. This suggests, however, that the writer will in time do better and perhaps excitingly better work!" I was stung by his assessment but, on looking over the story, which I have kept with me these sixty years, I notice that the charge of pretentiousness was warranted, considering how I chose, for example, the word "fulvous" instead of "brownish," thinking that the former might indicate my acquaintance with the dictionary.

I also included on the title page of the story, which was all of ten pages long, two epigraphs, both from Albert Camus, the intellectual god of the moment, to further indicate my gravitas and the high level of my seriousness. Camus: "The unity of the world, which was not achieved with God, will henceforth be attempted in defiance of God," and the other: "But no mind is impartial when confronted with life and death."

Ehrlich's words "much potential talent" carried me along for years while I wondered when the "potential" might explode into the "actualized." Of course, I need not have wondered for so many years if I had only sat and done the work. But there were too many terrors there for me to expel before I would come to that.

One of the reasons I loved coming to Ehrlich's class was Belinda, who never turned in a story. She sat straight, silent and beautiful. She seemed older than us, but that may have been because of her composure and erect posture, and because she came to class dressed like a mature woman and not in the uniform of just another bohemian student. She wore skirts and soft blue sweaters and high heels. Her black hair was beyond long and astonishing in its sexual power. I approached her after class.

"Would you like to have a coffee with me?"

She turned, smiled politely, and, in a heart-stopping Spanish accent, said, "Maybes other times." One afternoon I saw her and Ehrlich enter a taxi and speed down Amsterdam Avenue.

I went to the college library and read Ehrlich's novel, wanting to find out what made him so smart as to brush Hemingway aside. I was impressed by his lyricism, the powerful sweep and charge of his sentences:

"He walked with a long springing step and an inward air, his right shoulder thrust forward as though to meet life full on. He had a power of quickness and no fear; knew how to fade in a swamp or ride like a wind through hills; and he would stand and shoot against twenty."

I understood that Ehrlich was a fine writer and that his was an exceptional book, but as with other novels one respects but does not love, reading it felt like an act of literary duty. However beautifully written it was, this novel about John Brown and his murderous, moral righteousness did not draw me in. I was nineteen: I wanted Hemingway's cool and sexy characters in cafés and bullrings, and I wanted prose as understated as the characters. I wanted Paul Bowles's alienated wanderer under a vast, empty desert sky; I wanted Céline's brave, solitary man journeying to the end of the night.

When he was twenty-seven, Ehrlich was sprung into the literary world with his debut and only novel, *God's Angry Man*. On October 30, 1932, the *New York Times* said: "It is a work of art, powerful and exciting." The reviewer concluded: "To approach this novel critically after a day spent in abject surrender to its power and beauty is a difficult and ungrateful task. It is the kind of work which one should approach again after a space of time before defining. It does not yield itself to ready discussion. It is too disturbing. But that it is an outstanding novel by a new writer who has now achieved significance is certainly no more than a cold statement of fact."

He was soon famous and moved among the literary lights of the day; Carson McCullers was among them. He had a future and everyone was waiting for his next novel. He was writing it. He summered at Yaddo, the artists' colony in Saratoga Springs, to find the peace to do his work. He went to San Francisco to find peace, where there was not enough of it. He returned to Yaddo.

In New York he rented a succession of large, roomy apartments in the Upper West Side of Manhattan. He kept moving from one apartment to another. When he heard the flush of a toilet or the banging of a steam pipe or the rattling of a window or the sound of a child's voice or a cat's purr through the walls, or a footstep through the ceiling, he fled. He needed absolute silence, or else his writing day—his day—was ruined. He went into classical psychoanalysis five days a week. It was some years before the shrink finally spoke and said, "You might try dancing to loosen up." Everyone was still waiting for his next book. Years passed, and then no one was waiting.[8]

---

[8]EHRLICH AND MY GUILT
Leonard Ehrlich (1905–1984)

In a letter from Truman Capote to the distinguished literary critic and poet John Malcolm Brinnin, Capote says, "Yaddo, yadddooooo . . . through the ages; don't you ever get just a wee bit tired of going there? You're going to end up like Leonard Ehrlich . . ." (Truman Capote, *Too Brief a Treat: The Letters of Truman Capote* [New York: Vintage, 2005], pages 179–80).

I never sent Ehrlich my first novel after it was published in 1971. I look over my reasons and fail to find anything in our relationship our friendship that would justify my neglect. Leonard had always been more than kind to me. But I think I feared he would find that my novel, a great deal of it made up of a mosaic of quotations and literary parodies, lacked what he found paramount in literature: dignity. I feared that he would see in my pastiche a facile attempt to avoid the serious work of crafting sentences each with their own music and energy and conviction. Perhaps I also had a not-too-unconscious desire to break from exactly the kind of studied writing that Ehrlich—and my hero, Hemingway—had highly prized. Kill the father so that you can be free.

We drifted far apart. Or perhaps it was I who had drifted, fearing that his aura of failure was catching, and now that I had become a published author of one novel, there would be no second and I would drown as he had.

In my writing about him, and I hope lovingly so, I seek to address and perhaps, in some way, redeem my guilt for having abandoned him: he who was my friend and who had needed friends.

Cocktail Party by the Hudson

Manhattan, Riverside Drive, 1955

Leonard had never been married, had never lived with a woman or a man or a dog or a cat or a goldfish. He loved women. He had no children. He did not drink or take drugs. He made and stayed friends with some of his students, me among them. He gave cocktail parties at his apartment and invited a mixture of a few, very select, students—one of them, beautiful Belinda—and other writers, friends from his era. He rarely invited his colleagues. In any case, most of his colleagues were married and lived and traveled in bland coupledom; to invite them meant there would be polite, maybe even interesting conversation, but without erotic hope in the room.

Leonard invited me to one of his parties, telling me to come at six. I arrived at his building on Riverside Drive and Eighty-Fourth Street at five thirty and, to kill time, walked almost to the Hudson. It was broad and frightening to me, like the wide avenues of the Upper West Side. I stared at the river and beyond to the Palisades of New Jersey, where I had been twice as a boy, to attend grim family funerals where I was obliged to kiss the corpses of distant cousins stiff in their caskets. Farther west was America, where I had never been except in books, and what for me was the land of great Dread: the insane, murderous South of Faulkner and Twain, the strike-breaking West of John Steinbeck.

I didn't know how long to linger on the view, not wanting to get to Ehrlich's too early or too late. Finally, I walked in the building at ten after six. There was a uniformed doorman and an elevator with a man also in a uniform conducting it. The ride ground away slowly, and I didn't know if I was expected to talk to the man at the elevator wheel. It was so strange to be in this paneled box pretending he was not there.

We stopped: top floor. Leonard came to the door full of smiles and cheer. I had never been to an apartment that large: the living room alone was twice the size of my Bronx apartment. The floor was carpeted, not wall-to-wall, but with rich-looking reddish-brown rugs; the ceilings went to the clouds. There were no shirts or pants hanging on a chair, no broken lamps. You could see clear through the sparkling windows.

Leonard was casual: jacket and flannel trousers, but no tie. Guests had already arrived, which made me feel like a chump. He introduced me: "Fred's a gifted writer," he said for my tag. There were smiles and nods all around, and I was glad no one asked me what I wrote. I was afraid I had nothing to say, and that anything I did say would be adolescent, unworldly, reeking of the Bronx. So I retreated to the window and again studied the Hudson and the mysterious America in the distance.

Belinda came in twenty minutes later, wilting all the women in the room. She was in pedal pushers, a pale blue sweater, and black flat shoes, Capezios. Her black hair gleamed. I kissed her on the cheek the way Anita had taught me. She smiled and wafted away. Belinda lived in the distant Land of Refinement, where, cross-legged, she read poetry on the carpeted floor, Ravel's "Pavane for a Dead Princess" floating in the background. Belinda was always polite to me when we were with Leonard; otherwise I was invisible. I often masturbated imagining her, spending acres of sperm before daybreak. Sometimes I wondered if I was using it all up and if I would have any left for sex when it counted, like in a marriage. But Belinda was worth it.

Leonard introduced me to a burly man, Albert Halper, who looked like what I had imagined was a boxer or a longshoreman. Years earlier he had published a novel called *Union Square*; because I liked the title, I had bought it for a dime on Fourth Avenue. He was surprised I had read it; I was surprised to meet my third living novelist, and one I had actually read.

He gave me a powerful, beefy handshake. "Lenny tells me you're writing a novel."

"I would like to."[9]

"Well, throw everything in it, even the kitchen sink," he said. Halper crushed my hand, said good-bye, and went off for a drink. I was left standing alone and uncomfortable, just as I had been ten minutes earlier. Frank Sinatra was crooning on the phonograph and Leonard was dancing with Belinda. I did not dance—had never danced, was too shy, too self-conscious. But not Ehrlich: he was breaking from an orderly fox-trot into arm-flinging, free-wheeling wildness. I was embarrassed for him, but envious, too, that he could be so unabashedly uninhibited. I hid in a corner. I kept drinking. Finally, it was seven thirty, and a few people started to leave, off to dinner or to the theater or to have sex, to go wherever they belonged. I barely stayed sober enough to thank Leonard for a "wonderful evening," just as they said in the movies. I felt smaller than when I had walked into the party. A boob, a hick, a failure, a zero.

In just an hour and a half I had downed a dozen canapés before I stopped counting and had knocked back eight Scotches neat. I was reeling, and I threw up just as I stepped off the Pelham Parkway station platform. People walked around me holding their noses. I found some scattered pages of the *Daily News* in the trash can and spread them over my vomit, the souvenir of my glamorous life. All I could think about on the walk home was my shame for the disgusting mess I had left behind for someone else to clean up. I washed up and, with a quick good night to my mother, I went directly to my cot. Belinda spun in my drunken head.

---

⁹MY FIRST NOVEL

Years later, in 1971, I published a collage novel, *The Adventures of Mao on the Long March*, and I often wonder whether it was Halper's words that had encouraged me to be bold and to weave everything into the narrative: cameos, parodies, quotations from literature, including Walter Pater, Friedrich Engels, and Jack London. Halper also said, "Kid, it's your first novel. No one's looking over your shoulder. You can do anything you want. In fact, you can always do anything you want." He laughed. "But that doesn't guarantee you'll get it published."

What neither Halper nor I could foresee was that the most difficult book to publish was my first, which was rejected by every publishing house in America, and often with rude comments. The most gentle was: "Why are you sending me this, it's not a novel." The book was published in 1971, after floating about since 1969. The history of its publication is in the preface to the New Directions Classics reprint of the novel, including the story of how the artist Roy Lichtenstein was instrumental in having it published.

Soft Porn and Unfinished Novels

Manhattan, Times Square, 1955

Some weeks later I subwayed down to Times Square, to one of the all-night movie houses that showed films that came as close to porn as the laws of the time allowed. There were no sexual acts or nudity in these films of pre-liberated 1955. There was usually a story line with a moral or instructive tag to justify the tantalizing erotic action to the censors. I was watching, in a packed audience of men with coats on their laps, a movie with a first-person voice-over.

She was a model, she said, whose early experiences looking for work in New York had almost led her into a degrading, sordid, low-life world. Hers, she said, was a cautionary tale for all the naïve, starry-eyed girls out there just off the Greyhound bus from Kansas and looking for fame and riches.

Her flashback: She is walking through Times Square and stops to check a newspaper with her pencil-circled ads for models. She looks up. She is at the right address. Cut to a small room with three cigar-smoking men reading the racing sheets. She walks in and, with no further ceremony, one of the men says, "Let's see what you got."

She produces a résumé from her large shoulder bag. The man says, "Come on, kid, you know what I mean."

Close-up: She looks confused.

"Don't waste our time. You wanna be a model? So strip."

She reluctantly slips off her skirt, leaving her in stockings, a garter belt, and high heels. The camera rests on her forever.

"OK, OK, now let's see the rest."

She is taken aback. Bewildered.

"Come on, we haven't got all day!"

Button by button, she slowly undoes her blouse. She has on a black bra. She stands nervously and defiantly.

Then: "The bra, too."

She puts her arms behind her and unsnaps the bra.

At the moment we were about to see her breasts, a black rectangle blocked the view. There were groans from the audience. I sent up a few myself.

Close-up of the three men at the desk, their eyes popping.

"Now turn around."

She takes a lifetime before she comes full circle and a man orders her to part her thighs. She spreads wide to unabashed moans in the audience. Cut.

Then followed scenes of several other young women repeating the same stripping routine. More groans and moans from the darkness.

In the final scene the same stripping routine started with another shy, hesitant, beautiful woman. The woman was Belinda.

There were other short films, but I left, wanting to keep Belinda fresh in my mind until I got home, where, more crazy for her than ever, I spent the night in reverie and lust.

I said nothing to Leonard about Belinda and my movie house adventures, not knowing whether my report of Belinda's film life would upset him. I also didn't want him to think less of me for my having gone into a seedy theater servicing the fantasies of lonely, sex-hungry men and boys like me. Perhaps by coincidence, Belinda did not show up for the end of the spring semester, and there was a void in the classroom. A week before school ended, Lenny said, "I miss her, Fred."

"We all do."

He gave me a suspicious, not-too-friendly look. "Were you in love with her, too?"

"No," I said. "I just liked her very much."

"Well, she's gone now."

We taxied to a kosher dairy cafeteria favored by the Upper Broadway intelligentsia. There, over coffee and free rolls, he told me this story.

Belinda lived with a drug addict. Sometimes he beat her, made her lie on the bed naked, and whipped her ass with his belt. She did not like the beating, but she liked that he was crazy-jealous for her, and she thought his belting her proved it. She did all kinds of work for him: as a model sometimes and as an actress in smut films; sometimes she turned a trick for a john her boyfriend had carefully chosen. Sometimes she asked Leonard for money.

"I give her money from time to time. Gifts to a friend, not payment for sex."

She had told her boyfriend that Leonard was her mentor, her platonic friend. "Bullshit," he said, and smacked her around. One night, some months earlier, Belinda had been in Leonard's apartment past midnight, when there was a smashing at the door and the boyfriend screaming, "I know you are in there. Come out, you bitch."

And then he added. "You, too, you fairy, come out and fight like a man."

"Belinda and I stayed very quiet and hoped he would think no one was home. He finally stopped banging and left. It was very frightening. I wonder how he ever got past the doorman."

I was embarrassed by his confidence, wondering why he would tell this story to me, his student and thirty years his junior. How little did I understand how lonely he was; I thought that old people had already had their time for life, for passion, and that they should be grateful and mellow into a kind of sexless, passionless wisdom and serenity.

"I'm sorry she's gone, Leonard." I was, but more for myself. None of the girls I knew at City had her style, her silent you-can-never-have-me look; none drove me to such melancholy. I thought of returning to that movie house in the hope of seeing her again standing in her high heels and stockings, and with the mad hope that, for once, when she took off her bra, the censors would have forgotten the black bar.

Leonard and I left the cafeteria and shook hands. I was about to leave for the subway when he said, "Can you come over to my place now? I'd like to show you something."

His apartment was quiet, empty, even with its furniture, without a hint that anyone lived there, not even a plant. I sat at the bare living room table while he vanished into another room, returning, finally, with two file boxes, holding them as if what was inside would explode if shaken. He opened one. It contained the typewritten manuscript of his second novel. In the other box was another manuscript, his third novel.

"They are both finished. Except the final chapters," he said.

He teared up and I turned away. I wanted to vanish but I also wanted to hug him.

"I can't finish them. My analyst said I have problems with completion." He paused and gave me an anxious glance. "Not with everything, of course. No one else has seen them before. I wanted to finish them first. I didn't want to be someone forever writing a novel in progress."

"Some writers take a lot of time," I said. "Like Ralph Ellison, still working on his second novel."

"Yes, forever. Does anyone take Ellison seriously anymore?"

"I never thought of that, Leonard."

"I'm sure *he* does. All the time."

He took a manuscript from the box and held it as if the pages would disintegrate.

"I thought I would read you the overture. May I?"

"I'd be honored," I said, frightened, however, that I might dislike it, and then what would I say?

His voice started off dry, reserved, but it grew with confidence and vigor over the course of the four pages. The "overture" followed a man walking, enveloped by traffic noise: the screech of bus brakes, the whine of sirens, the whir and hum and clang of the city streets—what Whitman called the "blab of the pave." The man was indifferent to the lights, crossing against the red, stopping at the green. He was in his thirties but he looked tired and much older. He was alone. From the first page you knew he would always be alone.

"It's a novel about a composer," Leonard said. "He's composing in his mind and oblivious to everything but the sounds of the streets."

The prose had all the sureness and cadence of his first novel: the writing as rich but not as overripe. You knew this was an artist, not just another willed writer.

"It's beautiful," I said. He gave me his one-eye, shy, suspicious look.

"Yes," I added, "it's wonderful, Leonard."

He smiled a pained, sweet smile, and his eyes went moist again.

"Am I still a writer, Fred?"

"Of course you are."

"Even if I'm not writing?"

"You are always a writer," I said, not sure of what I meant but sure that I was right.

He walked me to the door. He made as if to hug me, then stopped. We shook hands. "Take care of yourself, Fred."

He stood by his door until I entered the elevator. On the way down, I thought: *Go back and ask if he wants to go to dinner. Or, better, offer to take him to dinner.* But something held me back, a fear that he would think I pitied him, but also a fear that I would not know how to cheer him up.

He had set unrealistically high standards for himself, unforgiving of anything less than perfection. I was too young to understand that I could have suggested he dictate the final chapters to me, or to anyone, and be done. I was reluctant, as his student, to tell him that, or to recite a line I remembered Gauguin had said about starting to draw: "When you hold a pencil, hold it loose." I should have learned that myself earlier, before I spent years trying to write the perfect paragraph, the perfect story, the perfect novel, and staying, like Leonard, frozen in the process.[10]

At the spring semester's end, Leonard took a leave from the college and went to live in San Francisco. And that summer I went to Mexico.

---

[10]REPORTS OF MY DEMISE

It took me seventeen years to publish my second novel, *Tallien: A Brief Romance* (1988). I often thought that Leonard Ehrlich had put a curse on me, or that he had infected me with a version of his perfectionism. Of course, this thinking was a rationalization. The fact was that I was afraid, because the reception for *The Adventures of Mao on the Long March* was more than favorable and had set up expectations in me and in what was then the very small publishing world.

One day, Susan Sontag and I were walking to her home after lunch, and she said that some people were giving up on Ralph Ellison, whose second novel was years in the making and still had not come to fruition. But then she turned quickly to me and said, "But no one's thinking that about you, Fred." This was only four years after *Mao* was published. When I went to live in Paris, I heard reports that the reason I had left America was that I would never finish a second book and that, in fact, I had fled the country to hide my shame.

Manhattan, The Sperry and Hutchinson Mailroom, circa
1956

I had continued working after classes and on weekends in the mail-room of the Sperry and Hutchinson Company on Fourteenth and Fifth. They were famous for their S&H Green Stamps, which were given to people with purchases to paste into little booklets and mail to the company in exchange for toasters and golf clubs and other household and semi-luxury items.

Mail came from all over America; stamp-filled booklets and let-ters to the company arrived by the thousands every week, filling huge canvas post office sacks that needed sorting and had to be brought to the appropriate desks. Eight of us sorted and slid the mail into designated wall boxes, put rubber bands about the finished lots, and laid them out by floors. I had crushes on at least five of the secretaries on the upper floor, and I tried to finish quickly so that I could cart the mail there while I was still fresh and chipper. The secretaries giggled and smiled when I passed by their desks, and one, Sylvia, with whom I was particularity smitten and whose cleavage occupied my fantasies, said, "Fred, you're too young for me." She was twenty-one and went to night school at Brooklyn College.

"I'm old enough to marry you," I said. I had learned that there was no flirtation more sincere and effective than the expressed in-tention that a date might lead to the altar.

"I have a boyfriend," Sylvia said. The inevitable boyfriend, true or not, was a woman's solid and usually effective shield from further advances. I still longed for her but I retreated. I wish I had thought of answering what years later I heard my friend the Spanish novelist Julián Ríos say to a woman who rejected his invitation to Madrid on the grounds she was married: "I'm not a jealous man."

Hyman, the mailroom supervisor and my boss, was a high school dropout, about sixty, a former merchant seaman who, after he left the sea, had worked his way up to a high position in the post office bureaucracy in New York. When he retired he could have gone to Florida and died in the sun, but he loved working, loved schmoozing and kibitzing with everyone high and low, so he gladly worked long hours in the company's vital mailroom. He was the first there, at six thirty or earlier, and the last to leave, which he did slowly and only when the last secretary had left her desk and gone home.

He chatted, he joked, he flirted. He was the company's clown and, with his Groucho Marx stoop and loping walk, he was allowed everywhere, even permitted to step into—without appointment—the private offices of the reserved, seldom-seen elders, the executives E. J. and F. W. Beinecke. Everyone wondered how he had such license to roam about at will and chat up the bosses and terrorize the secretaries.

"Every company has a company spy," he said to me one day when he came looking for me in the bathroom and caught me, book in hand, taking a too-long toilet break. "Maybe I'm one, and I'll report you to the personnel manager"—a skinny middle-aged woman who, he frequently and loudly announced, "had tits like golf balls."

"Are you the company spy, Hyman?" I asked, not out of concern but out of curiosity that such a strange thing existed.

"I'm no stooge, kid. I hate rats. But I just want you to watch out."

When he was young, Hyman had read a book a week from a

duffel bag of books he hauled onto the merchant ships, leaving the books aboard for others when he finished his tour. He liked Westerns and detective novels, but above all he liked Jack London and Henry Miller. Hyman had sailed the world twenty times over and thought those writers, like himself, had lived, knew life, and were no "sissies." Hyman was crude and sentimental, loud and fearless. He'd say to secretaries who were snippy with him: "Kiss *mein tukhus*, I'm Jewish." He liked to recite to me a merchant seaman's ditty: "I'll wipe your brass / I'll kiss your ass / May I have another trip, sir?"

E. J. Beinecke, a partner of the family that owned the S&H Company, was a lover of literature and a renowned collector of Robert Louis Stevenson first editions and literary papers.[11] One day Hyman sent me uptown to a wood-paneled bookstore with mellow lighting and soft carpets to pick up a book for E.J. My world had stopped at Book Row, with its musty, dusty piles of books and sagging shelves. Here the clerks wore suits and ties, spoke in whispers, and handled the books as if they were gold bricks. I brought the wrapped and boxed package back to the office and to Hyman, who made a point of delivering it himself to Beinecke as if he had personally taken on the mission of retrieving and safeguarding it.

"Always keep your boss glad he hired you," Hyman said, taking the elevator to the upper executive offices.

The bookshop and the mysterious book stayed in my mind, as if I had been to a holy place and had transported a holy relic. I had now seen that there was a world of books, of art, much larger and grander than I had ever imagined, and that there was a world high above the Bronx but that it was not impossibly out of reach.

On his own initiative, Hyman went to E. J. Beinecke and got him to pay for my plane fare, cover tuition for my trip to study at the University of Mexico's summer program, and give me one hundred dollars toward my expenses. Hyman told E.J. that I was an ace student—not true—and that I wanted to be a writer—true—and that I was a hard worker—somewhat true.

"Go thank him," Hyman said. "Wear a jacket and a tie. And don't forget to kiss my ass every day."

A week passed before I was ushered into E. J. Beinecke's thickly carpeted office with its burnished wood paneling and lamps that radiated an amber glow of well-being. The rosy-cheeked, white-haired man behind the mahogany battleship of a desk was E. J. himself, on whose two secretaries' front desks I had daily piled mail without ever once glimpsing the grand man's face.

He looked me over a few moments before saying, "Good morning, young man."

"Good morning, sir."

"I hope you have a successful time well spent in Mexico."

"Thank you, sir."

He did not extend his hand, but he gave me a friendly nod and smile and then I was once again out into the arena of one hundred typing desks and fluorescent lights.

Hyman, wishing he could still travel as he had when young, loved the idea of my going to Mexico. He booked me on a Mexican airline that made a stopover in Havana. I could stay a week in Cuba if I wanted and resume the flight to Mexico City on the same fare. He also booked a room for me at a hotel a few steps from the ocean and hassled the travel agent to give me a discount lower than even the summer's reduced rate. "I bring you a lot of company business," he said to the travel agent on the phone. "Don't make me take it elsewhere."

Hyman even set me up with a driver in Havana to show me the town for eight dollars a day plus gas. "He used to drive me around for years, before I got married," Hyman said. "He'll take you places you'd never see on your own. His name is Herman, close enough to mine, so you'll never forget."

[11]THE BEINECKE LIBRARY AND ME

E. J. Beineke was one of the founders of the Beinecke Library at Yale, where, many years later, I did research for my doctoral thesis on James Fenimore Cooper's novel *The Bravo*, set in eighteenth-century Venice.

My 1956 ID card for summer school at the University of Mexico. Studies apart, there were many adventures.

Art Deco Eden

Mexico City DF, Calle Michelet, 1956

In the summer of 1956, I was nineteen and my whole world up to then had fit inside the boroughs of New York City, from Pelham Parkway to the Bronx Zoo or the Bronx Park or Arthur Avenue. I had taken the subway to City College of New York at 138th Street and Convent Avenue, and sometimes even to the downtown reaches of Manhattan, to the Museum of Modern Art on Fifty-Third Street, to Greenwich Village and coffeehouses like Le Figaro on Bleecker and Rienzi on Macdougal Street, or to my beloved bookshops and stalls along Book Row on Fourth Avenue. I must not forget that I also roamed the movie houses around Forty-Second Street, where, to hide my shame, I went only under the shadow of night, and so saw nothing of normal life in the course of the day.

But now I was in Mexico City, studying pre-Columbian art and mural painting at the University of Mexico's summer program. A schoolmate from City College and I shared a furnished apartment in a beautiful art deco building on Calle Michelet, in a serene, tree-lined bourgeois neighborhood. Hyman had found this Eden for me through his countless networks of favors given and received, and because of him I came to live in a solid and well-kempt quarter for the monthly rent of one hundred and eight dollars. I understood Hyman, for all his crudity, wanted me to taste the life of a gentleman of some ease.

Diana

It was about two on a sunny afternoon and I had just returned home from my classes at the university and was in the vestibule opening my mailbox, when a limo drew up. A blond woman with huge black movie-star sunglasses, a tight black dress, and high heels slowly stepped out of the limo and walked in, a bit wobbly, giving me a wide smile and a smashing "Hello!"

"I'm Diana," she said. "I'm from Minnesota, and you're from New York. I can tell by your shoes." She laughed. Her breath stank of alcohol and minty mouthwash.

"I'm studying at the university," I said, not mentioning that it was just for the summer.

"You must be a medical student."

How old does she think I am? I wondered. I said, "I'm considering that, actually."

"That's great. The world needs smart doctors."

"Thanks," I said, and felt stumped, with no idea how to advance the conversation. But she made it easy for me. "I live here," she said. "But I supposed you guessed that much, or why would I be looking into my mailbox?"

She did not open the mailbox but fumbled with the key in the lock and finally gave up.

"Good-bye," she said. "Good to meet you, and maybe we'll run into each other again someday."

I was excited by her womanly dress and womanly everything, and I was amazed that she had even allowed me a moment of her life. But her good cheer and openness gave me a burst of confidence, and I found in myself a new, sophisticated, urbane, worldly, and totally smooth self and said, "My roommate and I are having some people over for drinks tomorrow. Please come by; I know they would love to meet you. Say around six?"

"Sure," she said, giving me a kiss on the cheek before disappearing into the elevator.

My roommate was certain I had invented this blond goddess. Why had *he* never seen her? I finally convinced him with the argument that she might have a friend—for him. I had already made my claim but knew in my heart that my sophisto pose could not last long, and that this woman—unlike those folk singing lefty girls I knew in the Bronx and at City College—would find me both immature and inexperienced. She was older than I, but I could not judge by how much; in any case, she was of the grand and elegant world of beautiful women who wear perfume and dresses in the afternoon and ride in limos, and I was a boy from the borough famous for its zoo.

My roommate and I went to the local *supermercado* and stocked up on Scotch and vodka and bourbon and tequila and sparkling sodas, marveling at how inexpensive it all was—ninety cents for a quart bottle of Johnnie Walker Black Label! We spent the rest of the afternoon cleaning up our rooms and making some order of the living room. The kitchen sink was soon naked of dishes, and the glasses looked obscenely clean. We scrubbed the bathroom floor and tub and washed the sink until it shone right from the factory. We had no friends to invite for our little cocktail party, so we invented the implausible story that they had all canceled at the last minute because

of a pneumonia epidemic that had spread across the university and
that, so far, as North Americans, we were resistant to this strain of
Mexican germs and had been spared.

At seven she was not there, nor at eight, nine, ten, or eleven. By
midnight we turned in. I promised to pay my roommate for his share
of the liquor.

The doorbell rang at two in the dark morning. I came out in a
T-shirt and boxers. Diana stood at the door wearing a great smile
and holding a bottle of champagne.

"Where is everyone?" she asked, walking right in. Spared the
pneumonia fiction, I said, "Gone home early. We have classes in the
morning."

"I like educated men," she said. "It cuts out the small talk."

"I'll be right back," I said, wanting to go to my room and put on
my trousers.

"You're OK as you are," she said, adding, "This place has no
charm. How can you live without charm?"

"It came furnished," I said, embarrassed mostly by the two large
prints of pink flamingos over the credenza.

"I'll bring you down some things, dress the place up a bit."

I stood there in my briefs not knowing what to do next. But she
saved me from further embarrassment, saying, "Let's get some glasses
and pop the champagne."

We sat at the table drinking from tall water glasses emblazoned
with red palm trees, the only kind we had. And when we finished
the champagne in short order—she slugged it down like water—she
asked, "What else you got?" I pointed to the credenza, where our
newly acquired liquor supply stood unopened and guarded over by
the flamingos.

She examined the Scotch bottle label: "*Hecho en Mexico.* Do you
know what that means?"

"It means made in Mexico."

"No, it means made in a sewer and tastes like sewer water. But it improves with ice. Do you have any?"

"Oh—yes," I said.

"Better yet, do you have any vodka—even the Mexican kind?"

I brought out from the fridge a bottle whose label with its bulbous turrets and snowy scene proclaimed the Russia of the tsars and Dostoyevsky but whose 80 percent alcohol was distilled in Jalisco. I forgot the ice.

"Don't worry about the ice, it's cold enough," she said, filling our glasses to the rims.

We drank. I sipped; she guzzled. I heard the bedroom door open; it was my roommate in gray flannel pajamas, a robe made from a carpet, and wine-colored slippers. All he needed was a stocking cap to complete the picture of how he—and thus I—was so *square.* I was so pissed off that he had broken into our little twosome that I almost forgot his name.

"Hi," she said. "I'm Diana."

He grinned and sat and drank Scotch minus the ice. He didn't speak. He stared at her with a sleepy grin. He drank more and turned greenish. He tried to kiss her good night but missed her cheek.

"It was fun meeting you," she said, after he had already left the room. She was almost done with her second glass of vodka; I was an inch into my second when I started to slide a long slide under the table. I was out before I hit the ground. I woke up in a strange bed in a strange room with vases of flowers and with Diana propped up beside me.

"Your come tastes very sweet," she said.

"Thank you."

"Innocent, I mean."

A young maid, who said, "*Me llamo Theresa,*" came to the bed with a tray of cream and sugar and coffee for one: me. She smiled.

"*Buenos días,*" she said, and left with an even wider smile. I had no idea where I was, but I knew where I was.

"Do you smoke?"

"Yes, all the time: Camels," I said.

"I mean Mary Jane."

She laughed and cupped my balls. It was then that I realized I was naked under the covers. My clothes were piled neatly on the chair by the door.

She poured my coffee and doused it with cream. "One sugar or two—or three?" She laughed.

This was deeply familiar, and joyful. Francesca, my grandmother, had given me coffee and hot milk and semolina bread when I came home from grade school. My friends went home to chocolate milk and cookies, in the all-American model. To fit in, I lied that I did, too.

Theresa reappeared with an ice bucket with a bottle of French champagne and a bottle of vodka. "It's the real stuff," Diana said, pointing to the label. I drank the coffee and she downed the champagne, chased with more gulps of vodka. She lit up a very fat joint and offered me the first hit. I declined politely, telling her the story of my last smoke, when the world went spinning and my heart pounded to get out of my chest.

"That's a tragedy," she said, "like having an allergy to life. I hope you don't mind if I smoke."

"Not at all," I said, slowly trying to piece together what had happened after I passed out the night before, wondering how I ever got to the elevator and into her bed.

The sun powered through the large, clean window; the sky was cloudless and exciting in its blueness. She smelled of a stale perfume that still had the power to make me lovesick. I turned to kiss her. We kissed and I went for more.

"It's too early," she said. "Anyway, don't you have to go to school?"

I had forgotten the university, and I no longer cared if I ever went again if I could wake each morning with her.

The night table clock said a quarter past one. On a normal day I would have finished classes and headed home by this time. I *was* home but just missed the earlier step.

"It's a very informal university," I said. "It's a just-go-when-I-feel-like-it kind of thing."

She gave me a look that said, "Stop the bullshit." So I added, "Well, I'm pretty serious about it most of the time."

"What do you actually do there, anyway? Chase girls?"

"I study Mexican mural painting and pre-Columbian art," I said defensively.

She laughed. "The commie art. Are you a little commie like everyone else from New York?"

"Well, I'm not a fascist. And you?"

"Don't get so hot under the collar. I'm just playing."

"I apologize," I said, not meaning it.

"Loosen up, Freddy. The world's worse than you think but not as bad as you think."

"What?"

"Figure it out some other time." She kissed me.

Theresa walked in with a sheet of lilac-scented paper on a silver tray. Diana looked it over and I took a peek: it was a list of five first names with phone numbers.

"This is from the last two hours," Theresa said. Then, turning to me, she asked if I wanted an *aspirina* before I left.

"You don't need one, do you?" Diana asked. I was slow but I got the point and waited for Theresa to leave before I got out of bed and dressed. Diana gave me a big, sisterly kiss on the cheek.

"Mind if I don't see you to the door?"

"That's OK. Sure," I said, wondering if she was being impolite by an etiquette standard I did not know. Then I thought: *She is shy about my seeing her nude in the daylight.*

I got as far as the hallway when she called out, "Wait a minute." I halted. She was beautifully naked. She threw her arms around my neck and kissed me again and said, "You're sweet. Stay sweet."

Mexican Skies and Dark Cantinas

Xochimilco and Plaza Garibaldi, 1956

For all my desire and dreaming of Diana, I was not sitting alone in my room waiting for her knock at the door. I was absorbed with my love for Mexico City and for Mexican art, going to all the places in the city that had the murals of the giants, Orozco, Rivera, and Siqueiros. I took a bus as far as Chapingo to see Rivera's fresco of juicy Mother Earth watching over us from up high. I had seen Francisco Goitia's famous *Old Man on a Garbage Heap* in Bernard Myers's book and was fascinated by the painting and the man who had authored it. Goitia himself had become a hermit and a mystic and was known for sometimes burying himself in the earth, his eyes toward the sky and God.

I learned that the man considered the grandfather of Mexican art lived less than an hour's trolley ride away in Xochimilco, but the address I was given was very general. I was told not to worry; everyone knew where he lived; just ask the trolley conductor.

"Goitia is always there," a Mexican fellow student told me. "He is famous for never going anywhere and seeing no one." Goitia had no phone, so I took my chances.

I rode out of the city until finally the trolley was clacking through cornfields. The driver called out my stop; there was nothing but tall cornfields on either side. I asked him about Goitia, and he said "*el loco*" was over there, pointing to someplace in the distance. I saw a little footpath and took it, wondering if I could find my way back and when the next trolley would come to return me to the city. I came to a wooden shack; chickens were running wild. I called out but there was no answer.

"He's sick," an old woman in a nearby shack told me, surprised that I had come to see him. "He's in the hospital."

I waited a long time for the trolley to return. I studied the surrounding cornfield and the cobalt sky, and listened to the chickens cackling away. I was so far from the Bronx, but I had never felt so close to home.

My friend Danny at the bohemian table at City College had written to his father about me and he took me under his wing a week after I had arrived in Mexico City. He introduced me to the artists who had formed the Taller de Gráfica Popular, a collective devoted to lithography with a social bent. The TGP had the same aim as the muralists whose art I'd been busing around Mexico to study, but they worked on a small scale, making prints easily reproducible and affordable to the poorest: art for everyone.

I liked their art and I liked them: they were warm to me and to each other. I was invited to little gatherings at their modest apartments with plants in the windows and prints by fellow artists on the walls, and I learned how to drink tequila the Mexican way, with salt I licked from the hollow near my thumb, followed by a bite of lime. I was proud to be accepted; I was the gringo mascot who loved Mexican art.

I had a crush on Mariana Yampolsky, a thirtyish American artist and photographer who lived in Mexico and eventually became a Mexican citizen. She had an affectionate way with me that made me feel loved. I envied that she had changed her life so completely, living independently as an artist among artists. Her example further convinced me that I had to be free, but what did that mean? I seldom thought of Paris now: *la vie bohème* seemed so anemic and narrow and precious, so much a part of my childish escapist self, a dream of a pure world and a pure art high in the pure clouds. There was no ivory tower in Mexico.

"You should see more of Mexico," Mariana said. "Then you should come live here."

"With you," I said.

"You're very quick, *compañero.*" She touched my cheek. "Not that I mind it."

My friendships were not always so easy. I clashed once with

Bullfight in Mexico City, 1956. I went there to see what Hemingway had seen and returned having seen it.

Dosamantes when he assured me that Mexico would have another great revolution, a socialist one this time.

"The United States will stop it," I said. "They will send in the troops like they did in 1914, except that this time it will be with whole armies."

"The Soviet Union would go to war if the USA did that," Dosamantes said.

I laughed. "Go to war?"

Another time he explained to me that Abstract Expressionism was being taught by American artists in Mexican art schools as part of a CIA plot to undermine the politically driven Mexican art. I laughed at that, too, only to be amazed to learn years later that he had been right.

Even with these little parties and gatherings, and the classes I was attending, there was much room for me to wander the city, even at night, alone, in the darkest streets. I was naïve and fearless about going to new places, especially dangerous ones like the Barba Azul, a bar on the dark Plaza Garibaldi, a place, had I known, I should not have ventured into even with a heavy tank. Barba Azul had a long wooden bar and booths with hard benches, but after a few shots of tequila the benches went soft. Mariachi bands, playing for tips, strolled in and made the place bounce, and everyone sang along— me, too: "*Ayee, Jalisco no te rajes.*" I felt very Mexican.

Everything about the Barba Azul was exciting to me, even the toilet stalls that were kept packed with ice and quartered limes to deodorize the urine, and the tile floors paved with sawdust that were continuously swept and refreshed with more sawdust.

One night three very elegant young Mexican couples in their twenties came in, slumming, like me. They took a booth and soon went into an uproar of drink and fun. I wished I were among them, so filled with life, so sexy. But after a while one of them slapped his girlfriend, accusing her of flirting with one of his friends; the friend

immediately got into the act and called the man a coward for slapping a woman. Tears, cries, shouts. The two men went out into the
dark street, followed by the whole bar and the bartender, who was
holding a bat. More name-calling between the two, then fists, then
one drew a knife and stabbed the other. I stood there entranced by
the drama, thrilled. Passion, honor, death. This was the very real stuff
of life that writers were born to experience!

But then someone took me by the sleeve and said in English,
"Get out of here right away." Everyone else was running away, including the two who had been fighting, although the one who had
been stabbed and was bleeding through his shirt did not run so fast.
He held his hand over his bleeding chest and was carried along by
his slapped girlfriend. I ran, finding a taxi meandering in a dark side
street. I arrived home and didn't even argue with the driver when
he invented a new surcharge to the meter. I didn't care whatever the
price was; I was so grateful to have found him in that empty side
street and so grateful to be home.

You like it raw until it gets too real, I said to myself as I turned off
the light. *You're just a bourgeois jerk,* I added. *Good night, jerk.*

Dosamantes later explained to me that if you are a witness to an
accident or a crime in Mexico, the police have a right to keep you
in the country until all the legal proceedings are over—which might
mean years. This frightened me more than the fight in the plaza, so I
stayed clear of the Barba Azul after that and kept to the tamer streets
and bars without fire, although I missed the wildness. I thought:
Would I ever have experienced this excitement in a café in Paris?

Ice Cubes and Caviar

Sanborn, the Reforma, 1956

For all my adventures, I still thought about Diana. I thought about her in class, during the lectures on Mexican mural painting. Slides of Rivera's workers and peasants marching with scythes and rifles and led by a mustachioed man in a huge sombrero and riding a white horse merged with Diana's face and shoulders and breasts and creamy flat belly. In my battle between ideas and sex, sex always wins. In a choice between anything and sex, sex always wins. Reveries of sex will be my companion on my deathbed.

Diana followed me most of the day and in my sleep. I did not have her phone number and I thought it not polite to ring her doorbell cold, so I squeezed a note into her mailbox—a note I had written many times over, trying to find a tone at once friendly but not from just a friend; casual, but suggestively at the edge of erotic familiarity.

I finally hit upon: *It was wonderful meeting you. May I invite you to dinner, at your convenience?*

No word from her in the following days, and there was no response note in my mailbox or under my door. All the same, my roommate was a bit in awe of me, having seen her, the divinity. He said, "You lucky bastard. How did you get so lucky?"

I was not in love with Diana, but I wanted to be in her sophisticated aura and all the sex that went along with it—imagined, because I had no memory of sex with her the first drunken night I slept in her bed.

A week or two passed since I dropped off my dinner invitation and there was still no word from Diana. I started to think that I did not miss her.

But then, at three or four or five in the morning, there was a ringing, then a pounding at my door. I knew who it was. As much as I wanted to go to the door, I was crushed with sleep. More pounding. "Open the door, you little Bolshevik, I know you're in there!"

I was worried that Diana would keep pounding until the neighbors went wild and started their own shouting, to be followed up later by complaints to the building's manager. I finally opened the door, pretending I had heard her knocking only a moment earlier. I yawned twice and blinked my eyes.

"Come up for a drink," she said, more of a command than an invitation. Her lipstick was smeared. She was swaying.

"I have an early class," I said, which was true. But she slowly came into erotic focus and the classroom melted away.

She was carrying an armful of bags filled to the brim.

"Aren't you going to give me a hand?"

My roommate called out from his room, "Hey! Bring her in."

She did not want to come in. She ordered me to take the bags and follow her in my pajamas and bare feet up to her apartment. All the lights were blazing; they were always on when she left the house, she said, day and night, so she did not have to worry about coming home in the dark. We emptied the bags on the kitchen table: three tins of Iranian caviar, still cold; four bottles of vintage French champagne, lukewarm; and a silver pail of maybe a hundred chocolates in cellophane wrappings. And there were more little precious-looking items I could not identify.

"Santa came early this year," she said when I asked where it all had come from.

She started drinking the champagne with a single ice cube in a water glass—her favorite glass, it seemed, for any beverage, even water. "You know, Freddy, people put an emphasis on the right glass for the right drink. But I think that's all bull to make everything seem fancy."

"Simplify, simplify," I said, telling her, in a puffed-up way, that it was a quote from Thoreau.

She made an innocent face. "Gee, you mean Emerson's boyfriend?"

I was embarrassed for being such a snob and she saw it, saying, "I'm just kidding you. But don't you think I've ever read a book?"

I wanted to say, "I have never seen you read even a magazine," but of course I didn't.

She spooned me the caviar directly from the tin. I had never eaten caviar before, but I didn't tell her that. It was unpleasant, slimy and salty. *Who eats this stuff?* I wondered. And it was supposed to be very expensive! However, I dug in and soon liked it better, and after the third heaping spoonful I couldn't stop.

By the time we were on the second tin, Diana said: "Oh, shit," and turned over the bags still on the table. "I forgot the toasts."

There were none, but we polished off the second tin without them, and the champagne, too, and a half glass of cold Russian vodka for her, followed by a fat joint that gave me a contact high and the feeling that very soon I would be sick.

She was smiling in a woozy way. "I've saved the best part for last," she said, rising and taking me by the hand to bed.

I was half-drunk and excited to see her strip down to her black bra and black panties, black garter belt and black stockings—like a girl in a black-and-white stag movie or the one with Belinda that looped forever in my mind. She staggered into the bed, where I was nervously waiting, naked.

"You have a funny body," she said. "Flat, like an Etruscan's."

"You're so beautiful," I managed to come up with, not knowing the words to say how amazed I was by her body, so golden and with such wonderful curves.

"You don't have to do anything," she said, going down on me. I came fast; she swallowed and licked the little bit of sperm that clung to the edge of her lower lip. "Good night, my little commie," she said, giving me a kiss on my forehead.

She was soon in dreamland and I thought I had better leave before I missed another class. I slid to the edge of the bed, but with her eyes still closed she took me by the hand and in a little girl's voice said, "Don't leave yet. Don't leave me."

I stayed beside her trying to sleep but it was not until broad daylight that I did.

The maid came in and repeated the breakfast of my first stay. She was even friendlier this time and said to Diana, "*Muy guapo,*" and "*Sí joven.*"

It was noon when we were finally out of bed. She invited me to shower with her. I did, the first time with anyone, the first time I saw in her soapy wet body how beautiful it was to be alive in the morning with a woman who excited you.

I didn't know what to do for the rest of the day. She looked about as if she was wondering the same until she said, "Let's go to Sanborns and get some lunch, my treat."

I had never been there, having heard it was a place for tourists and Texans. Of course, I was neither.

"It's the only place to go where you can eat the salad—not that I eat salad," Diana said.

I knew what she meant, having gone through a bout of dysentery the first days I had arrived in Mexico and making it worse by drinking tequila, which I thought would kill the bad bacteria in my intestines.

Diana called for a car and soon we were down the Reforma and in Sanborns and at the counter, where all that was missing for the idyllic Norman Rockwell magazine cover was the strawberry ice cream float for us to share, one straw for each.

She looked over the bilingual menu for what seemed an hour before saying, "I'm not really hungry."

She ordered a Coke without ice. I followed her lead.

"Don't drink stuff with ice in it," she said. "Even here in Sanborns, you never know if the water is healthy."

She sipped her Coke and studied the glass a few times as if to see how much of it was left. She smiled and it made me happy to be there with her in the friendly bustle of the restaurant among American voices.

Then her mood swung and her good cheer vanished; she turned and said, "Why did we come to this dump anyway? *Vamanos.*"

There was a cab line right outside. Diana did not say a word all along the way and stayed fixed in a faraway stare. I wondered if I had done something wrong and, fearful of making it worse, remained silent, too.

Then she turned and very loudly said: "You know, it's not just Sanborns; it's Mexico City and its whole world of low-class ignorant idiots with money."

"There are rich idiots everywhere."

"Yes, but in Paris they dress better."

"What's wrong, Diana? Did I do something to upset you?"

She smiled. "Don't be so nice to me. I can't stand it. But don't change, either, or I'll hate you."

I wondered if she ever wanted to see me again. But then a week passed and we spent four nights in a row together. I was prepared and even had a toothbrush at the ready. I was missing classes but I didn't care. But I did care, worried the university would drop me: "Good-bye, foolish gringo!" Hadn't I learned my lesson from being expelled from City College?

Then Diana vanished and it was two weeks before I saw her again, late in the afternoon, when she showed up at my place, sober and somber in a nervous way. She was wearing a scarf over her head and the huge sunglasses when we first met by the mailbox. We sat in my living room, which was no better furnished than when we first met.

"Didn't Theresa bring you a pair of chairs and a coffee table?"

"Not that I know of," I said.

"Don't you like me anymore?"

"Of course I do."

"Then why haven't I seen you?"

"You've been away, I suppose."

"Why haven't you called?"

"I have: I got some answering service."

"They never gave me the message. Why didn't you just come up?"

"You told me never to."

"I haven't been there anyway. Do you want to come up now?"

"More than anything."

We were soon up in her living room; the windows were shut and the room felt dusty and hot, as if they had been shut for weeks. But then again, I was sure she lived only in her bedroom. She took off her scarf and sunglasses; she was bruised about the left eye. She caught my look.

"Some guys just like slapping you around."

"What guys?"

"Use your imagination," she said.

She disappeared and returned with an unopened bottle of vodka and a single glass and poured herself a tall one.

"I don't think you should drink in the afternoon. It starts a bad habit," she said.

I felt a great tenderness for her, as if I were the adult and she the child. "Diana, do you want to go for a walk in the park, get some fresh air and a little sun?"

"Come over here, you little jerk," she said with a great, happy laugh. We were sitting on the spotless white sofa and began necking like kids in the back of a movie house. I put my hand on her breast and squeezed.

"You don't have much experience with girls, do you?"

"Not in a big way."

She spread her legs and guided my head downward, where it had never been. "Lesson one, my little student," she said.

After the rest of the day had vanished and night had vanished, there was breakfast and sex and another midday followed by a long nap. Diana was gone when I woke. Theresa brought me coffee and, on the tray beside it, a blue envelope with a handwritten note. *Be away for a while,* it said. *Here's something to keep you company when I'm gone.* There were two five-hundred-peso notes inside the envelope, about eighty dollars, a fortune.

I did not see or hear from her for a week, and I mustered up the courage to go up to her apartment and found Theresa, who assured me that *la señora* was on vacation, maybe Acapulco, or just somewhere, *quien sabe?*

Somehow I was relieved. I needed a rest from Diana and even from her exciting lessons, which had sometimes left me feeling exhausted and longing to hibernate.

Adios, Muchachos y Compañeras de Mi Vida

Mexico City DF, Pedregal, 1956

A few days before I was to return to New York, Theresa came to the door as I was packing and said that Diana was in the hospital and wished I would visit her.

The hospital looked more like a luxury hotel where she had her own sunny room filled with bowls of flowers, the notes still attached. She was sickly white and had a tube or two in her arm. Her blond hair was matted. She was worn-out, looked ten years older, but she was cheerful, and asked me to draw the single chair close to her.

"I had a botched abortion and almost bled to death. I think the doctor who did it was drunk, but he was very good-looking." Her voice was full of sunshine and pain.

"I'm so sorry," I said, then realizing how lame that sounded, I added, "I wanted to say good-bye before I left. I'm going to miss you so much, Diana." I could feel my tears starting to come.

"It was fun, you little red."

I took her hand and kissed it. I kissed her face. I started to embrace her but she said, "It hurts me down there, so don't hug me too close."

I kissed her eyes and took her hand again, holding it for a long time, as if not to lose her like a balloon on a string. I started to feel that I loved her but then wasn't sure that it was really love that I felt, but the sorrow of my leaving her.

"It will be OK," she said. "Send me a postcard sometimes."

"I will," I said. "One every day."

Isn't it true, I thought in the taxi back to my apartment, that with every good-bye we die a little? And with someone you love, you die a lot. How much life in us is left at the end, when there have been so many good-byes?

On the Road

From Texas to the Bronx, Fall 1956

The Mexico we had left behind was ripe, red, warm. Its road to America was bordered by lush, dark green hills, and yellow and blue wildflowers spread themselves everywhere along the mountain passes. Children waved to us, smiling, as we drove by, and I saw men and women splashing water on each other, laughing as they bathed naked in a pool fed by a gentle waterfall. I loved even the crisp, blue, cloudless sky that had covered Mexico, the sexy Eden I had left behind.

But now our car sped us over the endless dry, hot flatness of Texas. Strange huge black bugs zinged up to the windows, so we had to keep them closed and ourselves steaming within.

We flashed by pasty people dozing on suburban porches fronting scorched lawns: my fellow Americans in their arid, colorless world. The little I saw from the car window assured me that America was, as Henry Miller had written, an air-conditioned nightmare. I was sick at heart not to be in Mexico, and I was shrunken by the vastness of Texas, a country in itself. Humbled, too, by how little I knew of my own land, having always lived in the Bronx and never having seen a steer or a horse or a sky the size of the world.

Larry, a young American I had met at the university and whose Ford we were in, drove in a maddening stop-and-start way that made me seasick. He was ill, feverish, even some days after we had stopped in Ti Belinda to get him a shot of penicillin; his penis had been burning, and it was in flames when he pissed. He wondered why. He had spent his last month in Mexico going to a brothel twice a week but made no connection between that and his malady. His sickness worked in my favor because we often had to get off the highways and stop in diners for him to piss away his infection, and I had time to write postcards to Diana from Brownsville, Laredo, Austin, New Orleans, and some swampy, forbidding towns in Louisiana; time to send passionate greetings from wherever I could along the way. The cards grew more cheerful the farther north we went, and by the time we got to New Jersey, I was pure optimism.

But no sooner had I returned to City College than I went back to my indolent ways of life as a student. I enjoyed the few excitements that came from sitting again in the cafeteria and talking politics and art—could a fascist be a great artist?—and staying glued to the tables after all my classes were done, and I would linger there into the early evening, staying through the comings and goings of friends headed to their classes or on their way back home. Maybe one of them was a girl I was interested in, or maybe I would go with her and friends out for a drink at the Emerald, one of the last Irish bars left in Harlem. Or maybe I would just dally in the cafeteria as long as there was a hint of company. I never wanted to go home to that tiny apartment with my abandoned, husbandless mother and her grief.

Beautiful Mexico was behind me. I was in New York, a student again, riding the subway to the nowhere Bronx where the local bars provided free TV and bowls of free pretzels and peanuts, and where no one but an occasional weepy drunk sang. Had they, in the 1956 Bronx of Seagram's 7-and-7 and boilermakers, ever sat in a bar drinking tequila or mescal with a fat worm soaking in it, and heard strolling bands of mariachi singers who made your heart pound with joy?

I wrote to Diana several times over the next months but received

no answer; finally, my letters were returned marked "Addressee Unknown." I gave my phone an experience it had never known before:
I placed a long-distance call and had the operator connect me to Diana's private number. The line had been disconnected. I had no idea
how to find her, and I feared that she had now vanished from my
life. And then I waxed philosophical, cosmological: "We all vanish," I
said aloud, and the pronouncement elevated me, as if in making it I
was, for the moment, as tall as Death.[12]

---

[12]DIANA UNTO DEATH
Diana Harris (1930–1960)

In 1960 my former roommate told me that some newspapers had reported that
Diana died of a morphine overdose in her apartment in Houston, Texas. She
had been famous, known as Lady Diana Harrington, the Golden Girl. She was
a star in a call girl ring in New York's café society of the 1950s and was one
of the highest-paid prostitutes of her time, supposedly making as much as five
hundred dollars a night. She had been arrested as a material witness against the
pimp ringleader, Mickey Jelke, heir to an oleomargarine fortune.

In exchange for her evidence, she was set free and told to leave the country.
She went to Mexico. She became increasingly addicted to morphine and went
to live in Texas, where drugs were allegedly supplied by a doctor who was also
her lover. She deteriorated to such an extent that by the time she died, her rates
had gone down to fifty a throw. She was twenty-six when I met her; she died
at thirty.

She lived an intense burst of life, where most of us string along, eking out
a pleasure here and there. Most people I met were not as warm, as generous, as
honest, or as fun as Diana. Stuffed shirts and hypocritical moralists and misogy-
nist politicians, pimps for the wealthy and for giant corporations, don't have
an ounce of her integrity and spirit. She injured no one but herself and gave
others much pleasure.

Before the Bar with Dignity

Manhattan, The City College of New York, Fall 1956

Mexico filled my thoughts, even months after my return to the city. My friends at the college were interested in my stories at first, but they'd had enough after several retellings of my adventures. I told them of the knife fight at the Barba Azul, about the artists I had met and the great public murals, which I compared to those decorating the Sistine Chapel, in Italy, where I had never been. I never mentioned Diana. Who would have believed me? But then my roommate told them about her. This seemed less interesting to the men than to the women, who asked me such questions as: What kind of perfume did she wear? Did she paint her nails? What color? And her toes, too?

Natasha, the red-haired intellectual queen of our table, asked, "Is sex different with her than with regular women?"

This was dangerous territory, mostly because I didn't yet have that much sexual experience to know, but also because I sensed a trick.

"All women are regular women," I said.

"Do you know any regular women in the whole college who wear perfume or paint their nails?"

My roommate's description of Diana as a glamorous being had elevated me by association and made me interesting, even desirable—so much so that the worldly Natasha, who had spent two summer months on a scholarship in Paris, took me aside one late afternoon and said, "Let's have a drink later." And we did, at the Emerald, the seedy Irish bar on Amsterdam Avenue.

The Emerald was always empty; its clientele had long ago moved away or were dead. Mike, the hatchet-faced barman, was sullen and unwelcoming and as mute as the TV high above the bar. All the same, I loved it there: I loved the liverwurst on rye, made to order and just forty cents with a draft beer; I loved the bowls of hard-boiled eggs on the long wooden counter, worn, I glamorized, by fifty years of hard working-class Irish elbows.

Natasha and I drank: she had vodka—"American-made swill," she said—on the rocks and I had a proletarian rye with a beer chaser. We rushed into books—*The Idiot*, our favorite. She had read it in Russian, which her mother, who had fled the Bolsheviks a few years after the 1917 revolution, spoke at home.

"Dostoyevsky is much greater than you can imagine from reading him in the English translation," she said, adding that the American novel was immature—like Americans. "You know nothing of life, you simple-minded, cheerful Americans."

"Am I simple-minded, Natasha?"

"Yes." She gave me a big smile.

This was an exciting, new Natasha, not the studious one who punctually did all her work and got only As and never seemed to date. Or, as she had said once, "I have no time for boys, and all American men are boys." Even her hair was exciting, a vibrant red, like the inside of a pomegranate.

It got uninvitingly dark outside; through the dirt-streaked window, the lamppost on Amsterdam Avenue sprang to life with a dull eggshell-white glow. I hated the idea of leaving the bar, of leaving Natasha, but how long could we stay before I slid under the table? And this time there would be no Diana to transport me to her bed. It was late enough to suggest that we go to dinner, but this—the issue of whether she would expect me to pay for her share aside—was above the level of my daring. The law was that you had to ask a woman for a date—a movie and pizza—at least a week in advance; for pride's sake she would not accept if you called later than that, even if she was free.

I imagined my walk to the subway on 125th Street and the ride all the way to Fordham Road in the Bronx, then the lumbering bus to Pelham Parkway. An hour and a half if I was lucky. I wished I could fall asleep under the table and be done with it. She said, in a thick, throaty way I had never heard before, "Come with me."

We grabbed a gypsy cab right off and drove down to a dark street in the Nineties. The garbage pails were overflowing; the underlit hallway stank of urine. Up, up, to the top floor and into a railroad flat—an apartment with a long corridor and rooms off the hall—until we reached a room with a sagging bed.

I needed a bed. I needed to sleep. But Natasha had other ideas. And we tried to implement them. Natasha was naked, stunning in her white, white skin and full, beautiful, delicately freckled breasts. She had been concealing this ravishing body under goody-goody peasant skirts and billowy blouses, but her unshaven legs, like a colony of crawling red ants, made me queasy. But I was in luck: Natasha passed out and was soon snoring. I read her body for long minutes, focusing on her torso, her heavy breasts. And then I was in dreamland, dreaming of Diana, pale in the hospital, saying her tender good-byes.

I woke at nine and Natasha was still sleeping. But she opened her eyes and said, "Don't tell anybody." I splashed water on my face and rinsed my teeth with a stinging spearmint toothpaste and then I was down on the street walking back toward the college. I stopped on the way at the Emerald for a shot of rye, a beer chaser, and two hard-boiled eggs.

Mike said, "Go for another round, sonny, on me." This was the first time he had ever spoken to me in a full sentence or offered me a drink. I felt in luck: first Natasha, and now recognition by Mike, casting me among the elect.

"Thank you," I said, and, hoping it wouldn't be too familiar and break the thread of our progressing relationship, cautiously added, "Mike."

I downed the rye and started to feel like a grown man. "Good-bye, Mike," I said, but Mike was deep into his *Daily News* and simply nodded. The nod was enough to make me feel special.

I was halfway up the block when on impulse—for the glamour of the thing—I doubled back to the bar and downed another beer and rye. I was woozy, but I felt powerful. I looked at myself in the tired, weak mirror and, paraphrasing Hemingway, said, "There is nothing left but to stand before the bar with dignity." I was thinking of having another drink to accord myself the full measure of dignity befitting a young writer standing at the bar in the morning having woken in bed with a beautiful woman.

I said good-bye to Mike again; this time he pulled the newspaper to his face and said, "You said that already, sonny."

The Intellectual at Large

Manhattan, The City College of New York, Fall 1956

I got to the school just in time to make Professor Hans Kohn's ten o'clock class, The History of Ideas. The little amphitheater was packed, and I had to sit high up in the crowded stairway. Professor Kohn seemed never to have had a childhood: he was born venerable, was nursed in a venerable library, and had worn a venerable pin-striped suit in his crib.

He sat at his desk with a few books piled up by his side and started slowly, quietly, and, with a Germanic accent that spelled intel-lectual wisdom and scholarship, he swelled passionately to his theme.

"The Romantics believed that the city—civilization—cor-rupted, and that people who lived closer to nature have higher moral values and live in communal harmony. This is the fiction Rousseau created and that was bought by the upper classes and the aristocrats in the French court before the Revolution decapitated them.

"But the truth is that the natural man is fraught with taboos and injunctions greater than any codified laws, and he lives in fear of nature and its countless threats. The natural man does not wander about in hills and dales rhapsodizing on daffodils."

The show-offs among us gave a polite laugh—we had all read Wordsworth, it signaled.

"The natural man and the civilized man murder all the time, but with different tools."

He saved time for questions at the end. Few asked. We were entranced by Kohn's wisdom, which came not just from books. We all knew his history: born in Prague, a POW in a Russian camp for four years during World War I, moved to Palestine in 1925, and came to live in America in the early thirties. He started teaching at City College in 1949. His was a class I never wished to miss and whose syllabus I followed to the letter. I was a little drunk and felt bold and maybe wanted to show off to the class, maybe also let him know that I took all this seriously, that *I* was serious, and that he should notice me.

"In Marx," I said, "the idea is that when we shed ourselves of capitalist competition, of the exploitation of labor, we will have rid ourselves of wars and crime and the like, and we will all live in harmony." I had impressed myself.

"Maybe," he said, "and maybe someday fish will sing opera."

Laughter all around. Even from me.

"Freud says, in a footnote to his prophetic book *Civilization and Its Discontents*, that even under communism, men will find a place and a way to use their aggressive nature."

I was humbled and tried to recover: "Professor Kohn, that supposes we are aggressive by nature, born that way. Isn't that just an a priori, unverifiable assumption in the same way the Calvinists believe we are born rotten with original sin?"

He studied me while the class went chillingly silent, waiting for him to go in and kill the big shot, then he answered, "That's a very good point, and I would once have argued the same as you against unproven claims that we are born this way or that. I do not like unreason and hope that nothing I have ever said in class may lead you to think so. But in this case, in life, I think that it is wiser and safer to assume that we are all murderers and that without the restraints put on us we all will murder, torture, and kill our neighbors. Freud quotes Plautus, who says, 'Man is a wolf to man.'"

"Thank you, Professor Kohn," I said, grateful he had not made a fool of me. There was some faint applause in the class, but for whom or what, no one was sure.

Later that week, I was in the subway going from school to the Museum of Modern Art. I opened the novel I had brought to read in the museum's garden, when I saw Professor Kohn sitting opposite me. From shyness, I pretended not to see him but he called out, "Young man! Hello, young man. Aren't you that student in my class?"

Before I answered, he added, "Come sit here if you like," indicating a vacant seat beside him.

It was strange to see Professor Kohn not behind his desk, which had seemed attached to him, and I felt bashful and uncomfortable sitting so close beside him. I wondered—as always—what to say that was not banal or stupid or both. No need to have worried because he took the lead and asked: "If you had to flee your country, what valuable thing would you take with you across the frontier?"

"As much money as I could."

"You would be robbed by the border guards. Do you mind my asking what you wish to be your profession?"

"I want to be a writer."

"You want or you write?"

"Both."

"And whom do you read with conviction?"

"Hemingway."

"Yes, of course."

I didn't know how to take that. Was he making fun of me for my obvious taste?

"Well, I read a lot of other things, too."

"That's very good," he said. "And how many languages do you know?"

"A little Spanish. I'm studying it now."

"Learn a few more so you can translate for a living and write anywhere."

We had long left 125th Street and were approaching Fifty-Ninth, where I was to get off, but I did not want to leave him.

"How many languages do you know, Professor?"

He laughed. "Oh, I have had to do a lot of traveling and been stuck in places, so I picked up a few languages. So, did you think about what you would take across the border?"

"I have no idea, but I would be sure to take my portable type-writer with me."

"What for? You can always find another when you get to safety. I mean, what thing would you take so you can *live*? *¿Entiendes?*"

"I give up, Professor. I guess I would just have to kill myself."

"Many have done the same, so that's not too funny."

"That was dumb of me. I'm sorry, Professor."

"Stamps," he said. "Some are worth a small fortune, and you can slip them into your wallet."

"That's amazing!"

"By the way, *The Magic Mountain*, even in translation, is for you."

I had heard of it often and had tried reading it, but I could not get beyond the snooze-worthy opening thirty pages.[13]

We were suddenly at Fourteenth Street. "Thank you for your time, young man."

"It is me who thanks you, Professor," I said, after fumbling for words.

"You are a good boy," he said. "Don't waste time."

How did he know that I killed time, assassinated days and weeks of it dreaming and sitting in the cafeteria and, like the lonely drunk at the bar, talking to anyone at hand? The professor's parting words frightened me. I *was* a time waster, a daydreamer, a failure at twenty! And without a penny to buy a rare stamp to see me safely across the border.

[13]THE SPELL OF *THE MAGIC MOUNTAIN*

I did not know then that one day Thomas Mann's book would change my life and become the foundation for my novel *Tintin in the New World* (1993), where the fabled young reporter and his sidekick, Captain Haddock, and the dog, Snowy, meet the characters from *The Magic Mountain* on the heights of Machu Picchu.

The novel opened me to the vast encyclopedic, philosophical world, which the protagonists refer to and debate. But, on a more personal level, its theme of unrequited love spoke to me, not as a literary trope but as a theme central to my life and, eventually, to my writing.

Lord Byron and Smoke Rings over Broadway

Manhattan: Museum of Modern Art; Times Square, Fall 1956

I got to MoMA two hours before closing. In those innocent days, before art had become a mass audience spectacle, it had a spiritual quiet and stillness. The garden with its Matisse and Maillol and Picasso sculptures was all mine. This was my oasis of beauty, my refuge from the Bronx, which I wished to escape from permanently. I sat under Rodin's huge sculpture of Balzac and opened Paul Bowles's *The Sheltering Sky.*

Soon I was with Port, dying of typhus in a little dark mud-brick hovel of a far-flung hospital in the Sahara Desert. What had started for him as a touristic adventure was ending in misery and death. But he had been dying spiritually before he and his wife, Kit, first set foot in North Africa in search of something to refresh their fruitless lives. Port was sexually estranged from his wife, but he was also estranged from everyone and everything, and, like the desert surrounding him, his soul was arid. I found it beautiful, noble, to slide into eternity among the dunes and the camels and the little colonial French fort in the oasis where Port had made his final way.

Compared to Bowles' North African world, my earlier dreams of living in Paris seemed so tame and ordinary, so civilized. I imagined myself like Port, wandering through silent villages of sunbaked mud, and falling in love, as he had, with a blind dancer and waiting to die, not old in a boring, bright, noisy hospital but in a hovel with a narrow window open to the night stars and to God, who was not there.

"Fred!"

It was Lenny, a premed student with Dumbo ears whom the girls hated and loved. He hung out with us at the bohemian table when he was not at the lab dissecting a baby shark. He copied sonnets from an anthology of love poems and slipped them into the books of girls he was trying to seduce. He had cultivated a great tragic façade— the poor man's Lord Byron of the Bronx, Natasha called him to his face—and an exquisite set of manners that opened all doors. I had been with him once when we walked over to a table of four young women neither of us knew and he said, "Ladies, excuse me, may I engage you in conversation?"

No one said "Please go away" or "Don't bother us."

"Sit down with us," the most beautiful at the table said, "and your friend, too."

Lenny had more girls than he could handle, and he was always looking for even more. The men, we hated him. He told me one day that he always came to our bohemian table because arty girls put out. "Fred," he advised, "just take the arty ones to a folk concert or to an art movie house for a date, and then you're in."

I was astonished to see him appear in the museum garden.

"What'ya doing here?" he asked.

"What are *you* doing here?" I replied, not too brilliantly.

"Thought I'd stop by to check the talent. You can't imagine how many chicks I've picked up here. They can't get over seeing a guy alone looking at paintings. I had one follow me from the Impressionist gallery down here to the garden wanting to know if I was an artist."

"Which you said you were?"

"Of course not. Why be caught in a lie so soon? I told her I was a poet, the truth. And she asked me if I ever read Rilke's *Letters on Cézanne*. I love Rilke and I love Cézanne but I had not read that book, I said, and she told me all about it on the way downtown to Café Figaro on Macdougal Street, and even mentioned it in bed the next morning."

"That's great," I said, "but I'm reading right now."

"Oh, sure. Don't let me stop you." He drew up a chair beside me and went into a deep, meditative pose. I could no longer concentrate on Port, his fever, and his dying under an indifferent sky.

"What'ya reading?"

I showed him the book. He recorded the title and the author in his pad. "I know there's a whole bunch of books they like, and it's always good to drop them in a conversation."

"I can give you a list one day and you don't even have to read them."

"You think so?"

"Well, maybe just read the jacket copy."

"What about *The Idiot*? Natasha is always swooning over it."

"Actually, it's called *The Moron* in the English translation."

"Very cute," he said. "It's a good thing I can take a joke."

I felt guilty for teasing him, for my envy of his looseness and daring, guilty that I was turning into a small-time literary snob or maybe just a plain snob.

"I'm just kidding."

"That's OK. Hey, you still have a job after school?"

"I'm off today."

"Oh. Because I may have something for you where I work."

He had a job we all envied. He sat behind the Camel cigarettes billboard of a man blowing smoke rings. The smoke puffed out twenty-four hours a day. They were nationally famous, those smoke rings over Times Square; even parents from the outer boroughs would make the trip to show their kids that wonder. Lenny worked one of the eight-hour shifts behind the billboard and was paid to do little more than make sure the steam machine that sent out the huge smoke rings through the hole that was the man's mouth kept working, so he had a huge amount of time to study or nap or do whatever he wanted. For all his goofing and chasing women, Lenny was a straight-A student, necessary for anyone who hoped to get into medical school.

"Are they looking for someone?"

"Sometimes, and I could put in a good word for you."

"Thanks. Please keep me in mind," I said, already grateful and more guilty than before for being such a snot to him.

He flashed me a big smile. "Hey, if you're free, why don't you come down with me now and I'll show you around?" Port would have to hang on awhile longer and wait for my return before he slid into eternity.

I was rarely in the Broadway area, except when I got off the subway and sped directly to the sleazy soft-porn movie houses, hoping not to be seen by anyone who might know me. So this was a new place for me: the towering billboards, the knots of awed tourists and their guides, the flow of people from all over America whom I otherwise, in my Bronx and City College enclaves, would never see. We went up into the Hotel Claridge and took the stairs up to the billboard's behind-the-scene mystery. Lenny was excited to show me a peephole that looked onto the streets below.

"I'm like God being up here," he said.

Lenny was right. I felt Godlike, up above the world, surveying the movement and sway of human traffic. Below me were people without names or voices, bodies without history, without joy or tears. But then I came down a bit, and I realized although I was perched up high, I belonged in the street. I was one of the flow beneath me, and God was regarding me in the same way, indifferent to whether I was ill or in love. I thought of Port, just another dead ember; there were mountains of them, of us, just waiting. I was reveling in the bittersweetness of this profound reverie and deep thinking but was interrupted at its climax.

"Cool, huh?"

"Very," I said. "I see why you like working here."

"I'm going to get a pair of great binoculars and scope out the talent in-depth."

"Thank you. I guess I should let you get to work."

"Gotta study, Fred."

I started to leave, when, drawing a bottle from under a stack of newspapers, he said, "Let's seal it."

"Seal what?"

"Our friendship, dummy."

He half filled two paper cups with Seagram's 7, a blended whiskey I disliked and usually chased with beer. He knocked it down in a flash; I sipped it like sherry. He gave me a sympathetic look: "Whataya, some kind of fairy?"

"I don't usually drink rye in the afternoon."

"Sure," he said. "Anyway, I got to get cracking with the books. The next time I'll fix you a dry martini."

I forced a laugh. I was at the door when he came from behind his desk to stand inches away from me. He wore his tragic poet expression. "You could do me a big favor. Put in a good word for me with that Russian with the big tits. I got a thing for her, but she treats me like small-time potatoes."

All the guilt I had earlier felt for being a snob and a snot to him vanished.

"Maybe when you get me the job," I said, as coolly as I could.

I was halfway downstairs before he shouted: "Tell her we're great friends."

Vodka, Bread, and Pickles

Manhattan, Amsterdam Avenue, Spring 1957

One cold, winterish early April afternoon, Lenny and Natasha and I found ourselves alone at the bohemian table when everyone else had left for home.

Natasha pointedly addressed me: "Let's go for a drink."

Lenny, who for the past half hour had been silent and meek and ostentatiously reading *The Idiot*, chimed in: "May I come along?"

Natasha: "You may say 'can,' as you always do."

Lenny: "Can I come along?"

"Don't you have to go to work?" I asked, hoping he would get the point and bow out.

"I was having such an interesting time that I called in sick an hour ago, and they didn't mind because they have five subs itching to go at any minute."

"So, what did you find so interesting, Mr. Poet?" Natasha asked.

He took his time, made his tragic face more suffering than ever: "I'm crazy for your big tits and I've been wondering what color your nipples are."

I expected her to smack him, but she said, "Ask Fred. I'm sure he remembers."

He gave me a look of surprise and high regard.

"I'd rather learn in person."

We rose to leave and Natasha said, "You may come, but only if you buy us all the drinks."

"I'm loaded," he said, showing us a wallet stuffed with bills.

The mute TV over the Emerald's bar flashed static waves and broken wavy images. It was the first time I had ever seen it on.

Mike yawned as we walked in.

"Closing soon," he said, "unless you're an Irishman." He smiled. I had never heard him speak so much, but then I realized he was flirting with Natasha.

"We are all Irish here," Lenny said.

"The lass, too?"

"I'm Irish as long as you keep the bar open," she said.

"All night, then."

"I see that a beautiful woman can melt the stoniest heart," I wanted to say to Mike, but I thought it best to keep this piece of wisdom to myself, considering that now he and I were on intimate terms.

It was six thirty when Lenny ordered the second round of gin martinis with extra olives. When Mike finally brought them, he said, "I'm clean out of olives, except for the lady."

Lenny said, "OK, just keep 'em coming," laying a five-dollar tip on the now-empty tray. Mike yawned, held the bill up to the light as if pretending to see if it were a counterfeit, and slipped it into his apron pocket without a thank-you.

"Big shot," Natasha said to Lenny. "*Etot mujik nichego krome deneg.* In Russian we say about a certain kind of man that he has nothing to show but his money."

"That's a great expression and true to life," I remarked, further convinced of the wisdom of the Russian soul, as I had recently discovered it in Dostoyevsky and Gogol.

"Thank you."

"You know, Natasha, I think you just made that up," Lenny said.

"So you're not such an idiot after all," she answered, giving him an approving smile that I did not like.

By eight we were sinking. We ate liverwurst sandwiches with wilted onion on stale rye to keep us from sinking more deeply.

"We should have pickles," I said. "They keep the alcohol from absorbing too quickly." We had a debate about this.

"Eat bread," Natasha said.

"Eat your mother," Lenny said.

"Is disgusting," Natasha slurred.

"Just drink. Who wants to slow down anything anyway?" Lenny said.

I had lead shoes tied with lead shoelaces. Lead head, lead hair, lead voice.

The lights switched on and off until Lenny paid and we filed out, Mike's voice behind us: "Come again, lassie."

We staggered to an empty Chinese restaurant on West 125th Street and ordered so much food that the waiter said, "Too much for three persons." Lenny laughed and ordered even more. The waiter hated us. When he returned with the first tray piled with steaming dishes, Lenny put a five in his palm. This did not buy him a smile.

"Big shot," Natasha said.

Halfway through the meal, Natasha rushed to the bathroom. A minute later we heard her throwing up. So did the waiter, smiling for the first time.

"The Romans knew how to banquet," she said, stumbling into her chair.

Lenny was stuffing himself with General Tso's spicy chicken and spare ribs and gulping tea. "What'ya want to do later?"

"I'm going home," Natasha said.

"I'll go with you, Natasha."

"Dream on."

"I'll take Fred with me," Lenny said.

I didn't want to go back to the Bronx. I wasn't even sure if I could make it all the way—the subway, the bus, the walk home, my mother. But I was pissed off by the way Lenny made me his second fiddle. "Go blow yourself up," I said, embarrassed that I had come up with such a childish line.

"Maybe," Natasha said, inching her face to his, like a challenge to a fight, "but you have to spring for a bottle of vodka because I have nothing in the fridge."

He did not need more encouragement and paid the bill, leaving a giant ten-dollar tip on the dish-packed table. The waiter pocketed it and turned his back on us.

"The Chinks are weird," Lenny said as we got into a gypsy cab with a busted headlight. We stopped at a liquor store on 116th Street with tall plastic shields housing the cashier and the cash register. Lenny bought two quart bottles of vodka that looked like the ones I remembered having in Mexico, made in America but with Russian-looking labels of bulb-topped buildings in a snowy night; it was the Cold War and we did not import vodka from the Soviets or their satellites. Lenny handed me two giant bags of pretzels and three smaller packets of potato chips.

"In case you get hungry again," he said, "and you can take them home."

"Fuck you," I managed to say through a mouth packed with wool.

We climbed up to Natasha's apartment and the three of us squeezed into her narrow bed, Natasha in the middle. I fell off twice but climbed back on and we all continued drinking from the bottle until I fell off again and passed out. I woke on the floor, which was layered with broken pretzels, with Lenny and Natasha on the bed spooned, naked.

Banishment

Manhattan, The City College of New York, Spring 1958

In the spring of 1958, I was standing at the entrance to Army Hall on the south campus with another student distributing the latest issue of *Promethean*. I was now an editor and sat more easily at the bohemian table. Two men in blue suits and crew cuts rushed up and said, "We are confiscating the magazines, and you are expelled. Go to the chairman's office." They scooped up the magazines and vanished.

Professor Edgar Johnson, the English department chairman, was a renowned Dickens biographer and a sweet, crisp man who looked like his bearded subject. The other editors and I and our faculty advisor for the magazine, Professor Marvin Magalaner, a young Joyce scholar, sat in the chair's office, worried.

"A mother called and complained that she does not want her daughter to go to a college that lets such filth be published. The dean has suspended you until further determination," Professor Johnson said.

He was not stern or admonishing, which was a relief. There was to be a hearing in the dean's office the following week, and until then we were not to attend classes or to show our faces on the campus. Our advisor was steadfast and supportive and gently raised the matter of academic freedom and censorship. The chairman asked, "Professor Magalaner, had you read the play before it went to press?"

Our senior editor, one of the star students in the department, and mature beyond her years, whom we all admired for her political savvy in the academic corridors, said, "We were late to the printers and overlooked showing the play to our advisor."

I was not sure this was true, but I was grateful that she got Professor Magalaner off the hook: we loved him and he made us admire *Ulysses* as he wove through its more elusive and allusive pages.

"I have read it in the magazine and I think it is a literary work without any hint of pornography or smut," Professor Magalaner said.

"I'm very glad to hear that," Professor Johnson said, "and let's hope we can soon get this all behind us."

We left with many thanks and apologies for the trouble, but not for the play that had caused it. I was stunned and fearful of being thrown out of my beloved college. We rushed to the cafeteria and to our table. The word was out, and we were greeted with applause. We were heroes. I enjoyed my first taste of fame and saw how exciting it is to be known and how one could want that all the time.

The following day the suspension was reported in the *New York Times* and some days after in the Soviet newspaper, *Pravda*, which lamented the lack of freedom in the United States. Now that the tempest had gone beyond the college's little teacup, we worried that the notoriety would further damage us and have us not just suspended but expelled.

The cause of the suspension was my one-act play, "Tea Party." It recounted in dramatic form and with painful sophomoric intensity and impassioned seriousness an event of several months earlier, the night when Lenny and Natasha and myself had ended up at Natasha's apartment drunk, a night of talk and sex.

Fame

I phoned John with the news of my suspension and perhaps eventual expulsion. He laughed and put Anita on the phone.

"My little rebel," she said. "John and I are proud of you."

"Find me a girlfriend like you if you are so proud of me," I said. I was still lusting for her and reprimanded myself—*Stop! She's like a mother!*—but it did me no good.

Maybe she'd read my thoughts, because she passed the phone back to John.

"Freddy, don't be a hero. Just apologize to the dean and be on your most polite and best behavior."

"Of course, meek and most humble," I said.

"Just be natural. He has all the power and you are a pain in his ass. He has to answer to his superiors and to the community and you want to be reinstated. Make him want to be on your side."

I understood better how John was able to work his way out of prison. He had made the warden and the governor and the whole prison administrative network believe that they could gain by releasing him. It brought them public credit for their role in his rehabilitation. An exchange: he goes free, they look good.

But what could I offer the dean in exchange for my rehabilitation?

My mother went to church for the first time in years, lit candles, and prayed for me, promising Jesus a novena for my reinstatement. Over dinner she cried, asking, "Can I go with you and tell them what a good son you are?"

The week passed slowly and miserably. Being banished from classes was terrible, because I missed the lectures, but being banned from the campus cafeteria was worse. Now there was no place to go to meet my friends, to talk, to be excited, to live. If they threw me out completely, I planned to get my seaman's papers, as John had done as a young man, and sail the world until I died, writing master-pieces of sea literature along the way. The problem was that I easily got seasick and turned green in mid-passage on the Staten Island Ferry, where I had taken some of my dates for glamorous voyages at night—five cents each way.

We sat in Dean Gotschall's giant office. He took his time shuf-fling papers and giving his eyeglasses a good cleaning with a spray and a cloth. But soon he started in with how upset he was that we had tarnished the college's good name. He pointed to a huge tap-estry behind him and addressed me. "This is a Renaissance hunting scene. Look at it closely." I studied it: men on horses with pikes and lances were spearing a wild boar held at bay by a pack of dogs.

"Have you noticed anything unusual, Mr. Tuten?"

"No, sir, but I'm sure I have missed something."

"Yes, you *have* missed something."

"Yes, sir."

"What is missing?"

I was baffled and frightened that I did not have an answer and said, "I'm sorry, sir, but I do not know."

"Excrement. Do you see excrement on the hunting grounds?"

"No, sir."

"If this were real life, there would be dog and horse and boar excrement. If this tapestry were copying nature faithfully, it would show the animals' excrement strewn around the ground."

"I see, sir."

"Yes, but this is art. Art selects and edits life and does not shower us with its filth and excrement. Do you get my point?"

"Yes, sir."

A sparrow circled outside the large naked window, then landed on the sill and puttered about. For a moment I was not thinking of the dean, of his lecture on art, of my suspension, but about my grandmother who, when I was a boy, used to put on our window ledge little bits of stale bread she had sprinkled with marsala to feed and revive the freezing sparrows in the winter. "*Povere creatura*—poor creatures," she would say. "They are so hungry and cold." Was I not myself hungry and cold? I wanted to ask her. Yes, but then again, so was she.

"Do you have anything more to say, Mr. Tuten?"

I had prepared myself for such a question, and I had rehearsed my speech.

"I'm very sorry that my thoughtlessness has caused so much trouble, and I promise to be more responsible in the future. I hope you will reinstate us because we all here love this college and wish to honor it and not disgrace it."

I had meant every word of my labored apology. And, strangely enough, I thought he was right about art and animal functions. All the writers I had loved did not need to shit on the page to have it smell like life.

He held us waiting for his verdict. Then, with great deliberation, he said, "The reports about all of you from your professors are good, and they recommend your reinstatement. So I will allow you to return to your classes and take your final exams."

I was suddenly seized with the crazy idea of asking, "What about the cafeteria: Can we go back there, too?"

We thanked him, declaring our gratitude to the point where abjectness and gratitude bordered on satire. Dean Gotschall did not crack a smile and did not rise from his cluttered desk or offer to shake hands. He gave our advisor, who was clearly in the academic doghouse because of us, a nod, the signal that we should all disappear, maybe even vanish permanently.

We rushed to the cafeteria to celebrate our victory. The word had already arrived, and once again we were met with applause. We were stars. I, the chief troublemaker, shone the brightest, but the brilliance did not last more than a week, and I was soon on the slide to the commonplace once again. Fame is power, and before long I was once again without both.

Jack

A week or two after my life had returned to lackluster normality at the college—that is to say, when I was once again a mere student and not a hero of revolt—I ran into Jack Micheline, a downtown poet friend of the Beats, whom I had met at a poetry reading a year earlier. He was a wild, fearless man just five or six years older than me but who lived to write and had managed to survive without any visible employment. Women were crazy for him, and he never went hungry or needed a place to crash.

Jack, a self-proclaimed anarchist, was a big, thick guy with a voice that announced a Brooklyn trucker or an old-time New York cabdriver from central casting. In fact he was from the Bronx, like me, but his accent was Yiddish-tinted, whereas mine was Sicilian-flavored. All the same, we spoke Bronx.

He was born Harold Silver in 1929, but was changed to Harvey Silver, and then to Jack Micheline. He was fun like no one I had known or would ever come to know. He loved life to his pores, and he loved, above all, being a poet, which was his life. Like so many exceptional people, he was an autodidact.

I found him once in the Strand bookstore reading at a stall. I did not want to interrupt him and started to turn away, but he saw me and called me over, excited: "Man, can you dig these old

Greeks?" He showed me the *Handbook of Greek Mythology* he had been reading. "You go to college. I suppose you already know all this stuff."

"Not at all, Jack, I just know what everyone picks up along the way." He was so endearing and earnest that I wanted to hug him.

"Well, then, you should have this book," he said, offering it to me as if it were his. In the end, I bought it for him—thirty cents—with his proviso that he would lend it to me whenever I wanted.

He said, "I just spoke to the people at *Evergreen Review* and they want to see your play. Send it right away."

It went to the editor with a note saying that Jack Micheline had suggested I send it. I wrote his name in capitals. I went to the post office to be sure I had the proper postage and to see that the envelope actually slid down the chute by my own hand.

I ran into Jack a week later at Café Figaro on Macdougal; the café was the closest thing to what I had imagined it was like being in Paris. I went as often as I could for the worldly European flavor: some of the patrons were leisurely reading books and foreign newspapers at their table, and some of the waitresses were actually French! Jack plunked himself down at my table. A waitress came over smiling the instant she saw him sit down.

"Laurita, this is Fred. He was busted for writing a great play. He's an outlaw, this guy."

She smiled. "Good, we need outlaws," she said.

I had seen Laurita before but I had been too shy to talk to her other than to order coffee. Also, she never smiled at me, although I saw she smiled at others.

"Laurita's from Argentina," Jack said. "She's teaching me about Spanish poetry."

"Jack thinks that the bedroom is the best place to study the poetry. Not me. So we do not have many lessons."

"Look," Jack said, "this is a great play, Fred, and you're going to get it published. I've got to take off. But I'll let you know about *Evergreen* as soon as I get any news."

"Great. Can you call me?"

"He has no phone," Laurita said. "Maybe he has a wife who does, huh, Jack?"

"I got a hundred wives, Laurita, but you're the only woman I'm *loco* about."

The café owner gave us sharp looks, and Laurita said, "I have to go back to work, boys."

"Me, too, I got to split. You can always leave me a message here at the café, Fred."

He gave me his meaty vise of a hand to shake and left me paying for his coffee.

I was ablaze with hope. To be in *Evergreen Review*, the avant-garde magazine that had published Beckett and Genet, meant everything. I dreamed of instant fame, a book contract, and the waitresses at the Figaro noticing me. Two weeks passed and nothing from the magazine. I imagined they were having heated discussions over my play, and that was why I had not yet heard. Then I went to the Figaro hoping there was a word from Jack. Laurita was there and waved the moment I walked in.

"Jack left me a note for you," she said.

I took a table by the window and waited for my coffee to arrive before unfolding the note, written with a thick pencil.

"They liked it, but it was not for them. They're all commies in publishing. Don't worry, Fred, you're a great writer."

Love in the Mountains

New York, the Catskills, 1958

I first noticed her sitting by the window with a morning light on her face. I was smitten. One day I planted myself, as if by chance, at the doorway before class began and, as she was walking in, I tried the intellectual approach. "Have you made any sense of Eliot's essay on *Hamlet*?" I asked.

She looked me over. "In what way do you mean?"

"I mean, why does he call it a failure?"

"Why don't you ask that in class?"

"Because I'm shy."

"Sure." She laughed, and I did, too.

"I know who you are," she said. "You're the one who got suspended for that play."

I was thrilled that my fame had cracked open the door to her. "That's me."

"I have a boyfriend," she said, not too aggressively.

"I have a girlfriend," I lied.

"Great, now we're even."

I was in a summer class in Literary Criticism; I had taken it because I had to make up a semester of credits for the time I had lost from my freshman academic suspension. I was glad that Eva was also there, but I sank a little on the few days that she did not show up. I was also pleased to be there, because I liked reading Matthew

Arnold, T. E. Hulme, Eliot, and the New Critics—all of whom took literature as the marrow of life and not merely its entertaining decoration. I liked the professor, Nat Berall, the most gentle man I had ever met and the most exacting. He read Eliot's *Hamlet* essay to us line by line, pausing to comment, to question, to point out the equivocation in the poet's frequent use of the word "perhaps."

"Eliot's 'perhaps' is a weaselly loophole," Berall said. "You stand by the sentence or you don't."

He, like Leonard Ehrlich, believed in the power and rigor of words, held them sacrosanct, and considered their misuse a slovenly, immoral violation. Together, they had led me to believe that the literary world was guided by such principled thinking.

One morning I was walking beside Eva after class, and invited her to go to lunch in the glamorous campus cafeteria. There, after I took her tray to the trash bin, I hinted that we might see each other sometime off campus.

"I'd like that," she said. "As friends."

"Of course," I said, wondering how long I could play this game before she saw that I had a crush on her and would like more than a peck on the cheek for our good-byes. She never spoke about her boyfriend, and I made a point of never asking: that would have cemented the idea that we were just friends. But one day she turned to me just as we were about to enter the subway station at 125th Street, each on our way home, and she said, "Sim's almost a Republican. Can you believe it?"

"He must be the only Republican at City College," I said.

I went home feeling the door had cracked a bit further, and that I had to be patient and wait for it to swing wide open.

We took long, companionable walks through the West Village, where she lived, and we talked about Kafka and his reactionary despair and agreed that Eliot was a crypto-fascist. We talked all the way from Washington Square to the Hudson River, where our little bohemian world ended and America began. By the end of June 1958, we were friends on the verge of being lovers.

"I like you," she said, "but I won't sleep with you until I break up with Sim."

I liked her even more for being loyal. "I can wait," I said.

"Maybe it won't be that long."

One afternoon, after our final class, at the iron gate entrance to the City College on Convent Avenue, Eva said, "You don't have to wait anymore."

Eva's mother, Magda, owned a small hotel, Apple Lodge, in the Catskills, and Eva took me there to work with her starting on the long July Fourth weekend. She had been a waitress at the hotel every summer since she was fifteen, and she knew the ropes. I did not know one end of the rope from the other and had never been to a hotel anywhere, let alone one with a large dining room packed with tables. Eva's mother was welcoming but not too pleased about my working there.

"Have you ever waited tables?" she asked. I did not lie. "Ever been a busboy?"

Eva jumped in. "I'll teach him, Mom, don't worry."

"You'll catch on," Eva said, giving me a great kiss. "Just think, we'll have the whole summer together."

I took to it right away. I bused her station of four tables, with eight chairs each. I set up the dishes and silverware and folded the napkins for each meal and cleared the dishes during and after each meal; I served the coffee and tea and the hot water with a side of quartered lemon for the older regulars, "So they should be regular," Eva quipped. I dressed the grapefruits, laid out individual pats of butter, sliced the two kinds of bread—rye and challah—by hand, arranged the slices in a basket, swept the dining room floor, and washed the silverware in two big tubs of hot water, one with soap

*Me on a break from serving dinner, summer 1958. I was the worst
waiter in the Catskills and often demoted to busboy.*

and one to rinse, after each meal. We worked seven days a week for
two dollars a day and tips. We had a Sunday off once a month. We
made love in between bouts of exhaustion.

Sometimes, when a waiter quit abruptly or was fired, I was given
his station. I was the worst waiter in the Catskills and maybe in the
cosmos. I could not remember the orders, especially in the morning
rush, when all four tables filled simultaneously with starved break-
fasters crazy to eat and to start their day of tennis or swimming, or
their painting class, or whatever it was they did to squeeze out the
most from their vacation.

Each table believed they had arrived first and grumbled when
another table was served before theirs. We were not allowed to write
down the orders. I suspected that the hotel did not want to be mistaken for a diner. I forgot an order as soon as I was given it, bewildered by choruses of "Soft-boiled eggs with bacon" or "Where's my

coffee?" or tea, or hot water with lemon, or "Where are my prunes? The other waiter always brings me my prunes!"—not realizing that the other waiter and I were the same person.

"You are adorable, but you're a mess," Eva said. "Also, it wouldn't hurt to smile when you take the orders. A lot is forgiven for a smile."

Sometimes I made up the orders in the kitchen because I had to shout them out to the breakfast chef quickly; if I hesitated or stumbled, he sent me to the back of the line behind the other desperate waiters. I was always late bringing the food and everyone was livid from having to wait. The other three tables, whose orders I had not even started to take, clinked their glasses with their spoons, and some even pounded on the table, as they did in prison movies, so that Eva's mother ran over and tried to calm everyone. As soon as they could find a real waiter, I was demoted to the busboy I was born to be.

"I'm sorry, Fred," Eva said. "I know how hard you've tried." I was sorry, too, for my diminished status, but at least I was Eva's busboy again, so I could brush against her from time to time and give a tug on her apron strings.

By the end of the summer we were spent. Our lovemaking had winnowed down to a few pecks on the cheek, a few tender caresses, before we fell into a dead sleep in our matchbox bed.

"We might as well be an old married couple," I said.

"Speak for yourself. I know plenty of marrieds who have sex into their nineties."

"Maybe," I said, "but not with each other." After Eva and I served our final Labor Day weekend meal, I said, "I'm dead."

"I'm deader," Eva said.

Ernest

Cuba, Havana, 1958

"Let's run away before we return to school. Eva, let's go wild and fly to Havana," I said. I had stopped there for two or three days on the way over to Mexico City, in '56.

I had loved Havana, so ripe with sex, so immensely seductive, if you never looked behind the façade. "All I want is a place where we can have breakfast in bed," Eva said, "and where we never have to go out." Eva and I were cash-rich with tips from two months of work, enough for us to live softly for our week in that passionate city.

We paid off-season rates at the Hotel Nacional overlooking the Malecón, the flat green bay of Havana. There, waiting for us, was a huge room with a slow-turning ceiling fan and an open window letting in the aroma of sea and cigars and a revolution brewing in the streets below.

I wanted that revolution. I wanted to see Batista's dirty world turned over, flipped to its clean side, and rebuilt from scratch. I believed that Castro, the young bearded man in the mountains, and his band of idealistic revolutionaries were coming to sweep away Cuba's gangsters and were going to build a true democracy.[14]

Gunfire crackled through the night. It was for us the music of revolt, and heightened our lovemaking. The revolution in the countryside had started to infiltrate the city, and the few times we left the hotel, we felt an electricity everywhere in the streets. The hotel bellhops and desk clerks and housekeepers seemed excited, as if in on a big cheerful secret. I was twenty-one, Eva twenty; for us, who believed in the revolution, what more was there to life?

"I love it here," she said.

"Havana?"

"Everything."

A few days after we arrived, and we finally thought it was time to leave our bed, I phoned Herman to show us around the city. Herman was an old German Jew who had fled the Nazis in time to save himself from the camps and death; his destination had been America, but his visa had gotten him no farther than Havana, where he remained alone but safe in the tropical heat. Herman chauffeured and guided tourists about the city in a worn-out Oldsmobile, but mostly he had a sideline in taking boys from the States, most still virgins, to the brothels.

Two summers earlier, Herman had driven me one night to my first and only brothel.

"Don't worry, it's a clean place. I've taken many boys like you from New York to get sex for the first time," Herman said, like an obstetrician who had proudly delivered a thousand babies.

I was excited to have this new experience; as a writer-to-be, wasn't experience everything? But I was so drunk and nervous and guilty with the thought that I was exploiting a woman's body that I was not able to get it up. I was wearing the Saint Christopher's medal my mother had given me to protect me on my travels, and, in a token of reparation for my failure, I gave it to the woman with whom I had gone so ineffectually to bed. She led me into a garden where women were sitting and sipping *cafecito* and she showed them the medal. They passed it around and kissed me and told me tender things and said I should come back soon, when I was not so tired.

But this time, as I was with Eva, it was not the brothel Herman offered.

"Ernest Hemingway. Do you know who he is?" he asked. "And would you like to meet him?"

Apart from Hemingway being the writer I admired most, and most imitated, his was the glamorous life I most dreamed of.

"Of course I want to meet Hemingway," I said.

"I'll come to the hotel in the morning and we'll get to him by lunchtime."

"Won't we be interrupting his lunch?" I asked.

"Don't worry. He's an old friend of mine, that Hemingway."

I hesitated, wondering how true all this was. Eva said, "Mr. Herman, we would like to meet him, as long as he knows we're coming."

"He will be happy to see you. He loves beautiful women."

"How much will this trip cost, Herman?" I asked.

"I want you should be happy. I could see you happy for thirty dollars."

That night in bed, I said, "You don't seem too excited about meeting Hemingway."

"Of course I want to meet him. But I don't glamorize him the way you do."

"I don't," I said. "I just admire him."

"For his work?"

"For everything. For the way he was a great antifascist and went to Spain to fight for the Republic."

"Well, many went to Spain."

"Yes, sure," I said, getting more and more defensive. "But he wrote a great novel about it."

"Freddy," she said, "he wrote one very good novel and several very good short stories. There are better writers than him, but you never fawn over them."

"I don't fawn."

"I think you like Hemingway's legend. The drinking and the bullfighting and the hunting. You don't like any of that, so I'm surprised you're attracted to him."

"Who's better than Hemingway?" I asked.

"Faulkner."

"Faulkner's unreadable. He's just a swamp of piled-up, boozy words."

"He's not glamorous enough for you, that's all."

"What's bothering you? Hemingway's created his own, original life, an exciting one, and that's more than most of us have done or will ever do."

Eva laughed. "OK. He may win in the excitement category. But then, so did John Dillinger when he robbed all those banks."

We arrived at San Francisco de Paula, a village of ugly dogs and mangy huts, at one o'clock in the heat of an already burning day. Within minutes we drove through it and were on a narrow dirt road ending at a low whitewashed wall with a large wooden gate.

Herman walked up to a small open shed where a hatless man was dozing, and he returned, smiling and holding up a large key. "To unlock the gate," he said, which he then opened to a path surrounded by wavy, lush trees.

"Aren't you coming with us?" Eva asked.

"Hemingway has seen enough of me these past weeks. Just go up," he said, pointing the way, as if we could miss the house and veranda standing on a small hill.

Eva and I started walking but stopped briefly to read a sign in French, German, Spanish, and English, advising us not to enter without an appointment. Obviously this did not apply to us, since our visit had been previously arranged, but I was uncomfortable that Herman had left us to make our own introductions. In only a few minutes we were standing on the veranda. I looked through the screen door and saw Hemingway seated with two younger men, clearly house servants. They were lunching, speaking softly in Spanish.

I called out, "Mr. Hemingway."

The giant in shorts, the shirtless giant with a barrel chest, the giant bigger than anything I could have imagined from his photographs, rose from the table and opened the screen door a crack.

"What're you doing here?" he said, in a voice packed with annoyance. It was a voice that told me what a mistake I had made and what a fool I was even before he added: "Didn't you read that sign?"

"I did," I said. "But we came to see you."

"You just can't walk into people's houses like that." He looked us over, focusing mostly on Eva.

"Herman said it would be all right," Eva said. "I guess we should have known better."

He laughed. "Oh! That Herman! Last week he brought over a van-load of Hassidic students." Then, looking us over again, he said in a warmer voice: "Well, I understand, but I can't have people barge in here every minute."

"I just wanted to see you," I said, ready to run and find a place to die. "I'm really sorry, Mr. Hemingway."

"We apologize," Eva said, in her beautiful voice, the one that stirred me at night even when I was exhausted. "Good-bye, Mr. Hemingway," she said, with the dignity of a beautiful woman saying to an indifferent man. "You don't know what you are missing."

"Good luck, you two," Hemingway said. Then he looked us over for a long moment and said very softly, "Would you like to come in for a few minutes?"

"We don't want to bother you, sir," I said.

"Only a few minutes"—he lowered his voice even more—"but don't talk too loudly. Miss Mary is upstairs and I don't want her to know I have people in the house who aren't expected."

I nodded.

"She gets angry when I do that."

The notion that Hemingway would be fearful of his wife's anger—that he would be fearful of anything—startled me. After all, wasn't a hero self-contained and invulnerable? Hemingway conducted us through a room full of hunting trophies. Looking down from the wall were the head of a long-horned impala and that of a lion with its mouth open, fangs bared. We soon came into his airy, sun-filled studio. He pointed to a tall table.

"Best to write standing up—not to get too comfortable," he said. Hemingway did not address Eva, only nodded her way.

He turned to me. "I suppose you're a writer."

"I want to be," I said, feeling embarrassed by my declaration. Was I a writer or did I merely want to be?

"You have to write every day," he said. "It is like being in the army: you have to get up every day and do the drill."

I nodded. Was I agreeing on the basis of my experience? Or was I agreeing to acknowledge the wisdom of his advice?[15]

"I'm studying writing at City College," I said. "The Proletarian Harvard," I wanted to add, but I assumed that, as a man of the world, he would know the college's proud epithet. "I'm working with Leonard Ehrlich," I said, wondering why I had, since I was sure that no one had ever heard of him.

"Oh!" Hemingway said. "How is Lenny?"

"Fine," I said, amazed. "He's a wonderful man."

"Did he ever write another novel?"

That was the question everyone who knew Ehrlich asked when his name came up.

"Not yet," I said. "But he's still writing," I added, feeling the need to defend my teacher and my friend—a man who, in the world's eyes, was a failure.

"Well, please send him my regards," Hemingway said.

"I will," I said. I wondered at that instant if I should not have said the more correct "I shall." But what young man says "shall" unless he is working hard, pretentiously, to wash away the patina of his Bronx childhood?

I grew more and more uncomfortable, fearing that the longer we stayed, the less I had to offer, and feeling smaller and smaller beside him. Finally I said, "We should probably be going, Mr. Hemingway. Herman is waiting for us."

"How do you commence working?" he asked.

"I don't know. I don't really have any special way," I said, thrown off by the question.

"I like to sharpen pencils," he said, laughing.

"Thanks. I'll try that," I said.

"Look, you can stay longer if you want. There are bathing trunks in the pool cabana, and you kids could take a swim," he said, walking us to the door.

It was hot, just after two o'clock in the wet heat of the semitropics. A plunge in the pool would have been a pleasure, and Hemingway was so welcoming and was so gentle, making leaving him all the harder for us. But something in me told me to leave and that any more time spent with him would strain his good mood.

We shook hands. "Your work means everything to me, Mr. Hemingway." He smiled.

I hated what I heard myself say. I hated my sugary adulation, which I knew he also must have disliked. Wasn't he the one who said it was bad form for writers to compliment one another to their faces, however sincerely the compliment had been meant? Somehow, hoping to redeem myself, I came up with a line fashioned after one of his hard-boiled characters: "You're looking pretty good, Mr. Hemingway."

He smiled and turned to Eva. "She's looking pretty good, too." He said that tenderly, and with sadness in his eyes.

Eva and I did not speak on the walk back. I was still amazed that I had met Ernest Hemingway and spoken to him. All that had really happened.

Herman was waiting for us, dozing in his car. "How did it go with Hemingway?"

"Very well," I said. "He was very kind."

"Did you mention me?"

"Of course."

"See? I told you not to worry," he said, beaming.

"Thank you for taking us, Herman," Eva said. She was silent all the way to the hotel, but no sooner had we arrived and were back in the world of our room than she said, "That was depressing, Fred."

"Was Hemingway depressing? I thought he was warm to us."

"He was, but didn't you see how lonely he is?"

"I wouldn't say lonely."

"He never wanted us to leave, and I'm sure his wife wasn't home. He had his servants for company for lunch."

"I like him for that," I said. "He's not a snob."

"I'm not attacking him, Fred. I'm just saying he's lonely—sad, too."

"It's not right to talk that way about him even if it's true."

"Why not?"

"It just isn't," I said.

"Oh, Fred, you're sweeter than he is."

That night we went to the dog races, where I lost four dollars on a greyhound that came in third. Eva won five on a race that was over in a few minutes. We had never been to a dog race or a horse race, and neither of us had ever placed a bet on anything before. We had been excited when we left the hotel, but we were both disappointed by how quickly the races were over, how silent the crowd remained throughout.

"It was more like a funeral parlor than a racetrack," I said in the cab back to the hotel.

"Try not to think about him, if that's what you're thinking," Eva said.

"I'm not."

That night was somber, and even the two cuba libre nightcaps and the exciting sporadic gunfire did not change that. The following morning, over breakfast in bed, we remained somber, and we stayed somber in the cab to the airport and on the plane back to New York.

"We should send him a thank-you note," Eva said.

"Yes, we should," I said.

On the plane I slept and dreamed of Hemingway beside a spongy, greenish pond on an African plain. He was in hunting gear, a rifle by his side, squatting among four old lions, their manes dusty and frayed, their heads heavy, their gazes directed far away to some distant place where they had once been young. They had seen too much, lived too fully, knowing that nothing ahead could match the pure force of the living they had left behind, all of them knowing that, the lions and the man.[16]

---

[14]REVOLUTION/REVELATION

At the time, we did not know that this was not just a revolution to overthrow a thuggish regime embedded with American Mafiosi who ran the country like a casino and a brothel. We thought that Castro would bring a fresh social democracy to Cuba. Only some while later would we learn that Castro's regime was to be socialist, and I welcomed that, thinking that the expropriation of vast areas of land and plantations owned by the Americans would be beneficial to the Cuban people. I believed that socialism in its most humanitarian form would now take root in the Americas—as it had not in the Soviet Union, its satellites, or China.

How predictable and how disillusioning to discover that slowly but surely, and under whatever pretext and justification, Castro's socialism was just another power play no different from that of the legions of other dictators in Latin and South America and, in fact, was based on a Soviet-style system of political and social oppression. That kind of humanist socialism—which purported to liberate humans, body and soul—was perverted into a system that hunted and imprisoned dissidents, homosexuals, and transgender people and alienated even its earliest and most ardent supporters.

[15]A FAILURE AT TWENTY-ONE

At twenty-one I had written only a few chapters of a novel about a young man in a tequila-drenched Mexico, based on guess whose true-life experiences? The young man bore some resemblance to the drunken consul in Malcolm Lowry's *Under the Volcano* but also to the Beat rebel Sal Paradise in *On the Road*.

If Hemingway had asked, I could have added to my résumé a few short stories, one praised by Paddy Chayefsky. Not to mention the one-act play "Tea Party," which was wildly famous throughout the City College student cafeteria and at select Greenwich Village cafés, including the renowned Café Figaro. I also wrote some poems that I had sent at fifteen to New Directions publishers in the faraway and magical land of light and art that was Manhattan.

There was so little to show for my six years of writing because I worked in a totally undisciplined, desultory fashion, in fits and starts, in moods exultant and despairing. When I was alive in the work, I would write day after day— nighttime, too—and in between and during meals and even in my sleep when I eavesdropped on my characters' conversations, which I reported in the morning with some coloration. I lived in the young man's luxury of time's seemingly endless bounty.

[16]HEMINGWAY AND DEATH

On July 2, 1961, in his home in Idaho. Hemingway put a shotgun in his mouth and blew off his head. I was shocked by the violence of what he had done to himself, not by the act of suicide. I commended him for that and wished that if I were in despair or painfully ill, I would have his courage. But the first thing I thought of was Eva remarking on the sadness in him, a sadness I, too, had witnessed but was loath to admit. I naïvely wondered how anyone with such fame and with a life so rich with adventure and creativity could ever feel lonely or sad or not want to live forever. Of course, I understand better now, so many years later, how one's public façade may just be covering a great internal despair.

How things change. The very things Hemingway was prized for—his super-macho hunting and fishing and drinking, his love of the bullfight, and his pared-down writing style—are now in some quarters regarded as a patriarchal old story.

The Eiffel Tower and the Tundra

Manhattan, The City College of New York, Fall 1958

That fall, in our senior year at City College, Eva and I lived glued together. We spent our evenings reading and making love, which cost us nothing, bed being the opera of the poor, as the old Italian saying goes.[17] We smoked unfiltered Gauloises, like the French intellectuals, and drank pots of coffee and stayed up until early dawn talking politics; we cried over the same injustice; the 1927 execution of the anarchists Sacco and Vanzetti was just over our shoulders an hour ago, and we were sure we would have gone to Spain in 1936 to save the Republic from Franco and the fascists. When we went out, we each paid for our own dinner and movie tickets because we were ardent believers in the equality of the sexes. How lucky for me, who sometimes skipped meals to save money to buy books.

"I don't like a man who invites me out to dinner," Eva once said on our first friendly walks though the Village. "It feels like I'm being bought."

Eva and I were in sweet harmony until she said, "Let's get married after graduation."

I did not want to marry and get a straight job—to do what? Teach high school, like my beloved Mr. Anderson, explaining poems to indifferent students, dreaming of the summer vacation to Mexico, and living a middle-of-the-road life only to die of a heart attack while grading papers over the weekend? Have kids and stay at home at night washing the dishes, changing the diapers, and getting ready to go to work the next morning? The writer Cyril Connolly had said, "There is no more enemy of good art than a pram in the hall." Marriage would also usher in the demise of erotic sex and the early death of my youth.

I was a writer and needed to see the planet and its wondrous doings. I wanted to be like Hemingway, who had invented himself and who wrote true sentences and who let the world come to him on his terms. I wanted to live intensely, as writers were supposed to, and one day arrive at a vision of life earned from experience and reflection. To come to some truth and to tell that truth in the form of an engaging, fresh story, I believed was the writer's task—if ever writers were to have tasks.

"Let's wait a year and get ourselves established first," I said, hoping to buy time.

"Oh. In that case, my mother has offered to send me to Paris for a year as a graduation present."

"I'd go with you if I had the money."

"When will you ever have money, Fred?"

Now, with graduation not far ahead, I wondered what to do with myself in the job department. Of course I would write novels and stories, but how would I support myself in the process?

A former City College student, Sy Migdal, who was studying at Syracuse University, suggested that I apply to graduate school there. I balked. Hemingway had barely finished high school before he set out for Europe and penned his way to fame; Melville had only a grade school education but wrote *Moby-Dick*, the greatest American novel. Djuna Barnes never finished grade school, and she went on to live in Paris and pen her wild *Nightwood*, obscure passages of which we, the bohemian elite, read aloud in the college cafeteria.

Why would I spend five years or more of my life of adventure and travel and creativity to earn a PhD—then strive for tenure in some middling university thousands of miles from New York, where I would die the slow death of complacency and convention and where I could not find an espresso?

"There are three reasons for teaching," Sy said. "June, July, and August. Also, you like to read."

I succumbed and applied to graduate schools, the last refuge of the English major without prospects. Harvard accepted me but without a scholarship. So that was out. Columbia rejected me. Syracuse University offered me a teaching assistant position that included nine credits of free classes and a stipend of two hundred forty dollars per month for ten months a year. I read the letter and felt sick: Syracuse was Siberia, removed from everything I loved and understood. I was to go into exile before I had the chance to live, to write my masterpiece.

I also applied for a job as an organizer for the International Ladies' Garment Workers' Union. I was hired sight unseen. I was to organize shops in Georgia, a right-to-work state, where many of the New York City garment factories had fled, secretly hauling machines and equipment into trucks on weekends and leaving the workers to arrive on Mondays to vacant lofts and no jobs. Runaway shops, they were called, running to where no union could follow them. My mother had worked all her life in the garment center, and there were several instances in which her union was able to protect her from being summarily dismissed or had fought for her to get unemployment benefits when her boss falsely claimed that she had quit. My sympathy with unions had started early.

To be a union organizer had appeal—some glamour, even. It fit into my idea of myself as a fighter against injustice and as a radical, though I had done very little to fill those roles except to read the leftist classics—Steinbeck's *Grapes of Wrath*, André Malraux's *Man's Fate*, and Trotsky's *Literature and Revolution*—and to argue politics with fellow lefties in the college cafeteria. In 1954 the United States engineered the overthrow of Jacobo Árbenz, Guatemala's democratically elected president, who was battling with the United Fruit Company. I was outraged and I joined a protest with five others in front of the United Nations. A photograph of me carrying a placard that said, "Get out of Guatemala" was on the front page of the communist *Daily Worker*, and I was sure that I was in the FBI files and that I would never have a job in the post office, as my mother had dreamed.

I soon learned that there was a reason I was hired so readily: the job was dangerous. Union organizers were not welcome in the fabled hospitable South, and they were greeted with clubs; some were dumped over the state line at gunpoint. I took Falstaff's advice that the better part of valor is discretion.

In 1959, after graduation and a summer spent working in the hotels in the Catskills, I saw Eva off at the end of August, on a liner bound for France. It occurred to me, as I was waving her good-bye from the dock, that, like Marilyn, she, too, was going to live in Paris before I ever set a foot there.

Instead of setting sail to Paris, I took the bus north to Syracuse and landed in the tundra.

---

[17]THE RESCUE

The problems with living with my mother that previous year had become so exacerbated that I began couch surfing in the homes of fellow students whose parents took pity on me. One of them called the Jewish Family Services and they came to my aid again. Mr. Stanley Diamond, the social worker and counselor there, said, "We will take care of you until you finish your senior year, because we think otherwise you might not finish."

I said, "You already know I'm not Jewish, right?"

"Yes, so what? In a traditional *shtetl*, if the family cannot afford it, the scholar receives full support for his studies from the community." He laughed. "Sometimes it is money, sometimes a meal, sometimes some small change, and sometimes a chicken."

They paid for my rent, utilities, a portion of a telephone, books, minimal clothes, and food. With their help I was able to share with two roommates a railroad flat on 112th Street between Amsterdam and Broadway. One was a student at City College, the other at Columbia. I was slowly able to organize my life and my studies with a much-needed calm and order.

Dostoevsky said sometimes three thousand rubles made the difference in a young man's life. The support from the Jewish Family Services was my three thousand rubles. There's no way to describe to this day, to this moment, my feeling of gratitude.

The Owl and the Bookworm

New York, Syracuse University, Fall 1959

It snowed the September week that I first set foot in Syracuse. That snow is still falling on my head all these years later, even in the hottest summer.

When it was not covered in an iron blanket of pelting snow, Syracuse was a cheerless pewter gray. The sky's complexion underscored my grim mood. Within a week I missed my friends back in New York City and their hunger to read and talk about books. I missed sitting with them in the college cafeteria and gabbing in the Emerald and in the all-night cafeteria on Sixth Avenue and Seventh Street, where the Abstract Expressionists had carried on after their Cedar Tavern hangout closed for the night. I missed Book Row, where I had spent so much rich time browsing and sometimes, when I could least afford it, even buying books. It was in one of those outdoor bookstalls that I had found a copy of Virginia Woolf's *Orlando*, charred at the edges but signed in violet ink, for just a dollar. That was almost as exciting as finding a pirate chest packed with the gold that would free me from worry forever.

Sy Migdal, my studious roommate, had already spent a year in Syracuse and had made no friends. My portion of the rent for the furnished apartment we shared—two bedrooms, a bathroom, and a living room with two wobbly desks—was a quarter of my monthly two hundred forty dollar teaching stipend; heat was included but not electricity. We could have found a cheaper place if we lived some miles away, but neither of us had a car and, like many New Yorkers, had not learned how to drive. The campus was a twenty-minute walk—much longer if it snowed, which it did continuously, leaving me to trudge through knee-high drifts.

There was a bar and a Greek luncheonette two blocks from my apartment, and then, farther down the street, nothing but rows of brown houses covered in darkness. Syracuse proper was in the distance and too far for me to walk, so my life was circumscribed by a few cheerless streets. I was a displaced, provincial New Yorker, a greenhorn landed not in the polyglot and ethnic mixes of turn-of-the-century Lower East Side but in the true, vanilla, monolingual white America.

I was lonely. Although that had always been my state, it felt worse in Syracuse because there was so little to do to offset it. I could not, on a whim, go to a coffeehouse or a movie or a museum, or hope to run into a friend on a park bench in Washington Square. It was so much easier to have little money in New York City, where the city itself made you rich. I was an in-between person: not an undergraduate who could mingle with the other undergraduates, and not a married man like many of my fellow graduate students who had no interest in lonely bachelors. I came to understand why Sy had made no friends.

Sy wrote his papers within days of receiving his assignments. I spent hours in the library reading both primary and secondary material and making long, handwritten notes on large yellow pads. My papers were overdue before I even started writing them, and I had to ask for extensions or incompletes.

"Sy, did you look like an owl when I knew you at City?" I was envious of his ability to concentrate and get his work done on time. "Because you look like one now. A studious owl, in fact."

"Did you look like a fool when I knew you at City? Because

you look like one now," he replied, without ever looking up from his Wordsworth.

I was a fool because of my dreamy approach to graduate school, to literature.

"I don't want to be brilliant, Fred, I just want to get my PhD and get a good teaching job," Sy said.

Where was his passion for literature? Why did he not become an engineer? Still, I took his point. Why was I so foolish, feeling that everything I wrote had to be brilliant, extraordinary? Did I think that I had infinite time to write my papers, infinite time for my life to come together?

After phone, laundry, food, and incidentals, I was left with about twenty dollars a week. I had two pairs of shoes, both always wet from the snow. I had only a thin spring topcoat, so I layered myself with old sweaters I bought from the local Salvation Army. Someone became ill in the third week of the semester, and I was offered his job teaching composition at night school, and that helped my finances. I bought long underwear and rubber boots and wool trousers that had the complexion and feel of Brillo. I had a bit more money, but now I had to read and correct compositions from both my morning and evening classes, fifty essays a week total, and I had to find time to study and write my own papers, that is to say, to forever prepare to write the papers.

I limped along, demoralized, and when the college closed for Christmas break and the students had fled for home—even Sy went home to his mother on the Lower East Side—or flown to warmer climes for vacation, I stayed behind. I spent days and evenings in the library doing research for my already-late final essays. One was on Melville's novella *Billy Budd*. I went deep into the secondary material and read the available biographies, going back even to the earlier ones like Raymond Weaver's 1921 *Herman Melville: Mariner and*

Mystic. My yellow-lined note-filled pads resembled schizophrenic pencil drawings.

I did not simply want to master the bibliography; I was searching for the yet-unfound key to Melville's art, to his soul. My love for Hemingway now seemed naïve. He was a lightweight and, in his vaunted brevity and concision, limited in the range and richness of language, shallow in experience, lacking in what great fiction offers and what Melville possessed, wisdom.

The first and only page of my essay was unoriginal, a bland digest of the already published and worse, stiffly written. Each sentence seemed a tortured translation from German. I had wanted to be considered serious, subtle, scholarly. Somehow I believed, with the example of T. S. Eliot's critical essays, that the drier and creakier the sentence, the more profound the work. Also, I yearned to be more than a competent graduate student. What new and brilliant and penetrating and astounding thing could I say about Melville's dark, complex story that would make me shine?

By the end of the Christmas break, I was not much further in my essay than when I had begun; the same was true of my essays for two other classes. By the end of the first academic year that spring, I had successfully finished only one class of the six I had taken; the others were incompletes, with papers due before the semester's end, a deadline I had surpassed. My drive to perfection had only led me to nullity.

Perfume and Work Boots

New York, Syracuse University, Fall 1960

Eva returned from her sojourn in Paris looking like another woman. Gone was her peasant skirt and her embroidered blouses, her open sandals made in Greenwich Village. Her hair was cut short, showing her beautiful bare neck, and her chic, tight-fitting Parisian clothes and elegant shoes made her a woman you'd turn twice to see. And now she was also perfumed with a scent that meant sex. She had transformed herself from a bohemian girl into a glamorous Parisian woman. I was still a boy dressed in denim work shirts, work boots, jeans—like the clichéd bohemian rebel of City College and Greenwich Village.

Eva was now a woman with a past: Paris. She was Eva, but then again she wasn't. Clearly she had learned exciting new things about bed and I was jealous—more, I was worried that I did not measure up against the skill of a Frenchman who was born to make love and to know wine. There was a new and unfamiliar erotic tension in our lovemaking, and I strained to win Eva away from this phantom Frenchman or Frenchmen. I suddenly felt that I could not let her go away again, that I could not lose her. I said, in the last hours before she took the train back to New York, "Wait for me until I finish the master's degree at least. Only a year more. Then I can get a teaching job in a high school and we'll marry."

"You will never marry me, and if you did, it would be a disaster."
She was silent for a long moment, then added, "Let's think about it."

A few hours after she left, I wrote her saying how much I loved
her and wanted a family, as she had always wanted. We would start a
fresh and vibrant life in just a year. I meant it: I imagined us walking
hand in hand into the conjugal dawn. But I did not believe it.

I would not marry in a year, or in the following year or the years
after. I had not yet met the open road, had not yet written a complete, full, extraordinary novel, or any kind of novel, or any kind of
anything. I had not yet lived life to its hilt or had ever been to Paris.
When would all that life start? When, in fact, would my life start?

Rebecca and Sandra

New York, Syracuse University, Fall 1960

My second year at Syracuse University was grayer than my first. I found a dank, barely affordable furnished apartment on the top floor, under a leaky roof that the wind went through and sometimes let in the rain and snow. A single window generously gave view to a brick wall with runny mortar, its white lime leaving mysterious streaks for me to decipher when I was bored with my ceiling.

Rebecca, my neighbor across the hall, was an artist getting her MFA; her husband was a law student in faraway New York. On his

few visits they spent their time arguing, then fighting, then making quickly finished love. He moaned. She didn't. She was beautiful, with large and sad eyes. In fact, she was sad and beautiful. I thought, in one of my more profound meditations, that sadness was a kind of beauty and a way of life.

Me, exiled in Syracuse, 1961.

Sometimes Rebecca and I had coffee in her place and we smoked strong, expensive Balkan Sobranies she bought in a fancy shop in Manhattan, and we talked—the stuff of life, books and art. I even enjoyed the line that divided our taste: she was for Cézanne; I was for Van Gogh. I liked that she smelled of turpentine and that her jeans were paint flecked, reminding me of my Art Students League days, and our conversations brought me back to the talkfests at the arty table in the City College cafeteria. Rebecca was Brooklyn born and pronounced, as did I, "courfee" for "coffee" and "laur" for "law." I found these familiar sounds comforting, taking some of the edge off my homesickness. Sometimes she left a pot of vegetarian lentil soup at my door. I did the same for her, but my lentil soup had hot dogs in it. Because men need protein, I explained. Of course I had a crush on her, mostly for her warmth and the mystery of her sadness.

Autumn, with its bright days, endearing in their brevity, quickly took leave, and what seemed like winter came crashing down early in late October. Snow made the sidewalks impassible, and snow shrouded the parked cars like rows of frozen baby white whales. Silence, whiteness, more snow. They had to close the university. I was housebound, the fridge empty as usual. I ate the last of the huge pot of lentil soup I had made three days earlier, and by four, when it was black outside, I trudged to the bar, its window lights mellow, like a monk's snowbound hut in the Alps.

Halfway to the bar and knee-deep in snow, I looked for a Saint Bernard with his little barrel of brandy sent to rescue me but saw only a sparrow drunk with cold and reeling on a tree branch far overhead.

I walked into the bar like a snowman minus the pipe and the porkpie hat.

"Shake off the snow before you come in," Malcolm, the barman, said. I removed my coat and flounced it like a matador's cape. I was shivering. I had been to the bar several times for a quiet beer but had not gone often enough to be counted as a regular; nonetheless, Malcolm brought me, without my asking, a snifter of brandy. Had he read my thoughts? He had become to me what my grandmother had been to the freezing sparrows. I felt a warming glow from the brandy and a surge of affection for him.

"Hungry?"

"Very," I said.

He disappeared and came back a minute later with a soggy liverwurst sandwich.

Malcolm was bearded like a romantic pirate captain in B films; his whiskers masked his age, which I guessed was near forty. He spoke little and moved with studied care, positioning himself aloofly at the end of the bar, away from the action. But he *was* the action. He was famous. Married women were his specialty, and he theirs. Rebellious undergraduates with a poetical bent also flocked to him. He was their ideal of the outsider. It was said he wrote poetry, and the rumor alone made girls' heads spin. Only jazz musicians had more cachet than a poet.

I nursed my brandy, wondering how I would get back home. For economy's sake, I had left my lights off, and now I childishly imagined I would never be able to see my house in the dark and in the falling wall of snow. How could anyone ever leave his home to travel to faraway jungles and deserts and vast arctic wastes? How could I? Maybe, in spite of my adventurous dreams, marriage, home, and adoring children suited me after all.

There were only two patrons in the bar: a young woman in her twenties who was nursing a tall drink, and Collins, a fellow graduate student with whom I had exchanged only a few words and had never wished to go further. He was a negative being; even his hellos sounded like a fuck-you. He nodded to me and sank into his beer. The young woman gave me a look of no meaning.

Collins suddenly took the stool beside me and went right to it.

"This town is shit. The school, too."

"So why are you here?"

"It's this or being a cop like my father."

"Your father's a cop?"

"My brothers, too."

"That's great."

"You think so? You should try it. You wouldn't last a day."

"Probably so."

"Anyway, it's not the kind of job for a Jew. And you're a Jew, right? I nailed you from the start."

"What gave me away?"

"You read all the time and always have something to say in class, like you want everyone to know how smart you are, like a smart Jewish cookie."

Malcolm was chatting up the woman. She was not smiling. He said, "If you read Dylan Thomas, you wouldn't feel that way about poetry."

I thought not to answer and went to the door to leave but changed my mind and returned to the bar and to Collins. "I'm not Jewish, Collins, but now I wish I were."

"The fancy conditional. Why couldn't you say 'was' like everyone else?"

"It's the subjunctive," she called out, not looking at anyone.

She was in a hacking jacket and gray flannel trousers. Her face was a lion's, her hair its tawny mane. Malcolm brought her another tall glass even though she had not finished the first. He whispered as if he were praying.

"Do you have anything else to eat?" I asked.

"I can give you a can of tomato soup to take home," Malcolm said.

"What about me?" Collins called out.

"I only have one."

I lingered too long. Couldn't bear to stay, couldn't bear to leave. An old story.

The young woman came over and, without looking at Collins, said, "I'll drive you home."

"Bad idea, Sandra," Malcolm said. "You'll never get beyond ten feet. I'll fix up a cot for you upstairs."

She led me by the hand out into the snow, then a few feet farther to her car, where we slept side by side with the motor running and the heat on, the window opened just a sliver for air. I slept in fits and starts.

The snow trucks had cleared some of the road by morning. We dug our way out of the car, and finally she was able to pull away in second gear. She waved and left me to negotiate the snow-clogged streets.

No sooner had I opened my door than the phone rang. It was Eva.

"I'm married," she said.

I laughed. "When did we get the license?"

"I married Mark, from City, the guy you never liked."

"Stop kidding."

"You knew I always wanted children," she said, "and you don't, and you'll never have any money." She was right. I had long ago said to Money: You walk on your side of the street. I'll walk on mine, with your rival, Time.

"I wish you great happiness." Of course, I didn't, even though she was right in deciding for a life that she wanted rather than waiting for one that might never happen. That she was right didn't matter and did not soothe my heart.

"I love you and will always love you," she said before ringing off. I was sure she believed that. So did I, who still looked up for the little boy in the moon. Eva and I were taking separate trains. I imagined that one day, having forgotten by what means we had gotten there, we would meet again at the same station. And we would be the same: young, hopeful—and as in love as when we were first together. There is nothing so wishful and credulous as youth. Even a baby amoeba has more savvy.

For days I was at war. Half of me was angry at Eva and her betrayal: Had she been cuckolding me behind my back in cozy Manhattan while I was suffering for literature in the intellectual Siberia of Syracuse? The other half of me regretted not winning her when she had wanted to be won. What kind of man was I to run from what most men desired: a wife and a family, a home? I answered: the hero of independence, the lonely loner for Art, the soon-to-be World Traveler, that's who! But for the moment the hero was a confused, self-deluding, aging young man.

I knocked on Rebecca's door and remembered she had taken a week off to be with her husband in New York. I was sad, but somewhere I felt a strange relief that Eva had made the decision for me.

This mood carried me again to the bar, where I planted myself at the window booth for the next days and weeks. My teaching and seminars ended by midday, and my twice-a-week evening composition class started at eight and ended by ten, so there was much time in the day for nursing a few beers and watching snow-drowned trees, dreaming of the sun. And time to reread *Under the Volcano* and live again in Mexico alongside the drunken consul, whose self-destruction I understood: he was a broken man and a failed writer, his head in a tequila bottle, his soul drifting among the stars. What could be more noble?

I was drawn to failure, so much more worthy and dignified than a success earned by mere uninspired hard work and dogged application, or by the sheer chicanery and unscrupulousness that sometimes was needed to achieve it. All great literature was the literature of rebels and failures—Ahab, Raskolnikov, Don Quixote, Milton's Satan. There was a beauty in defiance, a dignity in lost causes. Was I not one of those pure of heart, choosing failure rather than conformity, mediocrity, and success?

I wanted to write my master's thesis on *Under the Volcano*, and by some strange miracle I found Lowry's widow's address in the American Northwest and wrote her. No answer. Then, toward the final weeks of the semester, when I had almost forgotten that I had written her, a letter came from Margerie saying that the plane carrying my mail had crashed and burned and that only a fragment of my letter and the envelope with my return address had survived. Why, she asked, had I written her?

The fate of my letter jibed with Lowry and his misfortunes: his cabin in Vancouver burning down along with his manuscripts; his alcoholism. The real thing, not just heavy drinking but the kind of drinking that has no end except tremors and a painful death.

I did not answer Margerie immediately because by that time I was removed from Lowry and all thoughts of my thesis. My life was being lived in a woman's bed.

Ulysses and Riding Crops

New York, Syracuse University, 1961

One bleak afternoon at three, I was in the bar reading.

"That's a very boring book," Sandra said. She was standing over me in the same riding habit in which I had last seen her, but now she was wearing a fierce red lipstick.

"Sometimes what seems boring isn't."

"Maybe, but I doubt it in this case. People read it or pretend to because they're told it is important, special, and they want to be thought special," she said.

"Maybe. Have you read it?"

"I threw up on the first page."

"Threw up?"

"I mean threw it away."

"Thanks for the car ride in the snow."

"Aren't you going to ask me to sit down? It's impolite to keep a woman standing while you sit."

"Yes, I've heard that."

She took a stool at the bar. It was a different bartender, one who took her order without flirting.

I returned to *Ulysses* and to Leopold Bloom's voyeuristic adventure on the beach. He was besotted by the sight of a girl's bare ankle as she lifted her skirt against an incoming wave. Bloom was masturbating at the sight and about to explode into a fireworks-scale orgasm when Sandra slid in beside me. She looked at the page and read some lines aloud.

"That's a good passage," she said. "One of the few."

"I thought you threw the book away."

"So? I picked it up again. Anyway, don't be so serious."

"I'm not," I said, like a kid.

"Anyway, what's the difference? Let's go."

She lived in a two-story Victorian house, thirty minutes from the bar. We went directly to her bedroom. A giant iron four-poster bed stood in the center; the windows were shuttered and shaded, the walls bare except for a whip and a riding crop hanging on wooden pegs. She undressed to her bra and panties, black. She had been wearing a garter belt and stockings under her trousers.

"Have you ever had a slave before?"

"No."

"Do you know what to do with one?"

I did not answer because for the moment I was dizzy, like Leopold Bloom at the sight of a girl's ankle. Sandra had hidden her beautiful body under the armor of horsey riding clothes, and I now could see she was from another sphere of womanhood, the one from the soft-porn films I had shamefully devoured in Broadway's dumpy movie houses—the one where women undressed to their underwear and left me to ride the subway home in a haze of longing and fantasy.

"I'm sure I do," I said, not sure of anything but my crazy excitement.

She took the whip from the wall and handed it to me. The crop she tossed on the bed.

"All right," she said, her voice at once defiant and humble. She slowly took off her bra and went down to her hands and knees on the bed, spreading her legs wide. "Let's start with this."

We met every three days, enough time to build up the appetite and the desire and, for me, the stamina. I would have shortened the interval, but our time together exhausted us both. So small a stage, so few props, but the theater lived large in my thoughts: images of what we had done, images of what we would do next. Tying her blindfolded to a chair for a half hour grew to forty-five minutes or until she begged to be released and whipped. An afternoon of a few hours turned into an evening and then into a night.

The belt, the crop, her back, her ass, the narrow braided whip, and the spread-open thighs. Her standing in the chilly room spread-eagle against the bare wall until she begged to lie down. Each new episode became longer, darker, more cruel.

She lived in my morning coffee and all the hours after. She lived in my sleep. She lived deep in my guts, where no reason sounded. I had no idea where or if at all I lived in her or was an occasional, necessary visitor who embodied, enacted her fantasies. I did not care. I worried only that I had sometimes gone too far and hurt her so much that she would rebel and leave me and I would dissolve. Where would I ever find her again? Who would grant me this wild, consuming, uncivilized power again? One evening, before she was to drive me home, she spoke flatly, as if in answer to a question she had supposed I was about to ask.

"It's not pain I want," she said, "it's the humiliation. And it always needs to escalate. *Tu voir?* Do you have the imagination for that?"

One afternoon I was in the bar at my usual booth by the window, glancing up into the sky, which was gray with threat. I was reading Norman Mailer's *Barbary Shore*, but I stopped every few pages to think of the thin welts on Sandra's back and ass, of her open mouth. The sky was suggesting a snowstorm. After all this time in Syracuse, I could forecast the weather: the gray cold, the gray sky, the gray silence threatening a snowstorm. What if I were snowed in? How long could I stand without her?

"I see you're hanging out with Sandra," Malcolm said, putting a stein of an unasked-for beer on my table. He had been buying me drinks and making small talk, which I tried to keep as small as possible because, for all of his reserved, strong, silent-man posturing, he was a run-of-the-mill gossip.

"We run into each other sometimes," I said.

He waited a long time before saying, "Sure."

"Thanks for the drink," I said, opening my book and hoping he could take the hint.

"She's a bitch, you know. A crazy bitch." He stroked his beard, the man who had navigated the world solo in a rowboat with a spoon for an oar.

"I wouldn't know."

The bar was empty. It smelled of sawdust, brine, beer, and undistinguished failure.

"And she's rich, too. Her parents own half the buildings around here."

"You sound angry with her, Malcolm. Did she take a pass?"

He laughed. "I wouldn't touch her. She's a cock teaser."

"Then why do you flirt with her?"

"For the game of it." Then he got cagey and said, "You're not in love with her or anything, are you?"

"Not anything, just an acquaintance."

I went back to my book, but it was a pretense—for Malcolm, for me. I was seeing her blindfolded on her knees, waiting and wondering what would come next.

I wondered, who was the slave? She who crawled to me with my belt between her teeth and begged to be punished, or was it me, whose every minute was tied to her without a single string?

Sometimes Sandra and I sat in the bar facing each other without speaking. What was the point of conversation when no words could penetrate as deeply as a few simple commands? Sometimes, after our erotic theatrics were over, if we cared to eat at all, we drove to some local joint for burgers and fries and ice-choked Cokes or we went to a formal French restaurant, where she took charge and ordered cold lobster and a vintage Montrachet. She ordered in French. I finally understood why people raved about the greatness of this or that wine.

"Remind me to buy a case of this," Sandra said. "And one for you, too."

She always signed the bill, never writing a check or producing a credit card. But she would leave cash for a tip, sometimes half the cost of the meal. I loved her for that, for the excess and the politely arrogant show of power, which at other times she thrillingly yielded to me.

Food, drink, work—these were the dreams I walked through. The vivid, the vibrant, the only real life was with her. There was only her, until one morning I opened my eyes and it was spring, my last semester of teaching and taking classes, and the road had opened to summer.

Waterfalls and Rubbers

New York, Syracuse University, Spring 1961

Sandra picked me up in her red MG with the top down, although it was still chilly in the bright May sun. Large sunglasses and a red silk scarf covered her head, and a black sweater was wrapped about her shoulders. She looked like a teenager with a graduation car; she looked like the first light of day.

She took the curves easily and then sped away so fast that I saw a blur of trees and clouds above. She smiled and caressed my face, her eyes never off the road.

"What are your plans for the summer?"

"To stay here in Syracuse with you and make up my incompletes," I said as she took a turn to a side road that led to a waterfall.

We kissed. "I like you," she said. "I wish you were crueler, more indifferent."

"That can be managed."

"It's not in your nature."

"I think about it, about you, all the time."

"Because it's new and you like the power. But it's not authentic to you or you would have started this life long ago."

"What difference does it make?"

"Let's walk to the waterfall. I always go there when I want to get away from myself."

We sat on a large flat stone and held hands. It was not a high fall, and the water cascaded with a gurgle into a torpid stream. Beer cans and broken bottles and condoms flowered along its soggy banks.

"My parents have rented a little villa in Saint-Tropez for the summer. Up in the hills. Away from the noise."

"That's good."

"I'm going to spend some time with them. I owe them."

"I'm sure it's not all obligation."

"Look at this. Completely trashed. No, I like it there."

"Will I see you?"

"Sure, I'll be back and forth a few times."

"I suppose there's no point, then, in my staying in Syracuse for the summer."

"Well, of course, if you can get your work done here."

"Won't you miss me?" I wanted to ask? "Won't you miss what we do and what for me and I believed for you as well was at the center of our lives, all else merely existing at the periphery?" A great wave of self-pity swept over me: she would leave and I would be empty and left to fend for myself in the ordinary day—the empty day, to be filled with tasks like finishing my incompletes. "They would have been done but for you," I wanted to say, like a wounded child. Of course, it was not her fault that I never finished the essays: we had been living in different dreams. I would have found another excuse for leaving my work unfinished.

"It will be lonely here without you," I said, feeling the same burning in my throat I'd felt when my father left, when Elizabeth said good-bye.

"Oh, Fred, don't you know yet that things don't last forever?"

"Not even the snow," I said, having no idea what I meant.

We sped back at the speed of light, trees and clouds blurring by, and the sun blinked on and off until I got home. We kissed good-bye. I felt my heart tighten. She drove off without a toot of her horn.

I put my winter clothes in the two cheapest cardboard suitcases

I could buy and stored them in the landlord's musty basement—no charge. I left my apartment with the understanding that I could have it back in the fall if he had not found another tenant. My plan was to spend the summer in the Bronx at my mother's and think of nothing, not even Sandra, and to write my papers and make up the incompletes and return to Syracuse with a clean slate. I packed five of my favorite books and took the Greyhound bus back to New York.

I slept intermittently. As much as I wanted not to, Sandra came into my dreams. She stepped off the bus with me at the Port Authority Bus Terminal on Thirty-Fourth Street and sat with me on the subway all the way back to the Bronx.

Gutted Hares and the Library

Manhattan, Alphabet City, East Eighth Street, Fall 1961

I was back to where I had started: my fragile mother, my cot in the living room, the subway stop—Pelham Parkway, the Bronx. Two weeks after I settled in, a letter arrived from the English department chair of Syracuse University: my incompletes had turned to grades of F. I was terminated as a student at the university. I had had prior warnings but I had brushed them aside. Still, I was shocked. I later learned that the same thing had happened to a fellow student, who immediately got a lawyer to protest and perhaps sue the university, but I never heard the results. I did not think to protest or beg to be reinstated. Maybe I thought I deserved the expulsion for letting everything slide; maybe, at heart, I had just had enough of Syracuse and was glad that someone else had ended it for me, taken it out of my hands. I was hurt but glad it was over.

Two years had vanished with nothing to show for my reading, my course work, my pages and pages of notes and the starts of what were to be essays altering the course of conventional literary criticism. Worse, with my stained record, I had forever ruined my chances of getting a PhD anywhere else; that meant that unless I became famous, there would never be a job for me at any university or college of any repute—or any college at all. High school teaching, with its Monday-to-Friday weeks, loomed large on the horizon.

I applied for a part-time job teaching English at a yeshiva in

Brooklyn; it was a two-hour bus and subway ride there, four hours round-trip, for an eight-minute interview with the principal.

"I like that you went to City College," the interviewer said. "My father went there, and me, too. I liked you at first sight, but pardon me for asking: Which of your parents is Jewish?"

"Neither," I said, wanting to add, "But I've met with anti-Semitism."

"Thank you for coming all this way," he said, giving me his hand.

I reasoned that I was lucky. Brooklyn was so huge that if I turned down the wrong street or got off on the wrong subway stop, I'd be forever adrift in its strange vastness. "Only the Dead Know Brooklyn," the novelist Thomas Wolfe once titled a story. How well I now understood that. Lucky or not, I rode the subway back to the Bronx jobless.

I applied for a proofreader's position with Prentice-Hall, a giant publisher of educational books based in New Jersey, starting at a fortune of five dollars per hour, three days a week. I went to their New York office, where a kindly-looking man gave me five pages to proof and return the following day. I rushed home and sat at the same kitchen table where I did—or didn't do—my homework but this time striving for a high grade. I brought the test back the next day; he read it in less than a minute and asked very sweetly: "Are you sure you went to college?"

I had missed half of what I should have noticed: punctuation, spelling, and the distinction between such words as "discrete" and "discreet," "pore" and "pour." I consoled myself that I would never have been able to work in an office. I would not last two weeks under the fluorescent lights and amid the sterile rows of desks. Had I not known that life when I worked in the Sperry and Hutchinson mailroom? But I was a mere boy then! I would never be able to shower and shave every day before dawn and get dressed—tie and jacket required—and cross over the Hudson on the PATH train to

New Jersey and clock in at nine, even if it was only three days a week.

Of course, being glad at not being hired was a cover for the truth: I had no skill to sell. For all my fancy thoughts of myself, I was unemployable. I was not a good waiter or even a busboy—a dishwasher, maybe. I had written one story in the last two years: a story about a young man who prowled the lowest movies houses on Broadway and went home to masturbate, hoping his mother, sleeping in the next room, did not hear him groan as he came into a hand towel.

That story, like my graduate school essays, was left unfinished. I still felt everything had to be perfect, stunningly original, publishable in the best literary journals, and so brilliant that a major university would seek me out and offer me a professorship—better yet, a distinguished writer-in-residence position, maybe at Princeton or Harvard or Oxford or even the Sorbonne, where I'd magically lecture in exquisite French. Did any of the great literary critics of the day have a PhD? Did R. P. Blackmur, Irving Howe, William Empson, Alfred Kazin, John Berryman, or Howard Nemerov have one? Kenneth Burke did not even have an undergraduate degree, and he wrote like a god—a smart one who went to the core of poetry and fiction by mining the work's key images and bringing to the surface its occult meaning.

I had left my short story unfinished for fear of what it revealed me to be: not the artist with Plato as his friend but a lonely boy with low thoughts, with filthy thoughts, with no thoughts at all.

I left the interview and wandered about the streets until I walked into a paperback bookstore opposite the New York Public Library on Fifth and Forty-Second Street. I was wondering if I could afford to buy a book, when I heard: "Freddy, is that you?"

I didn't recognize the man behind the cash register. He laughed. "It's me, Richie!" He came into focus: he was one of the kids from my Bronx neighborhood, a few years older than the rest of us but always ready to build a fort in the park or take a side in a snowball fight. He quickly filled me in on the years we had not seen each other. He owned a small chain of paperback bookstores called Book Masters and was married and had a child. Richie was all grown up.

"And whataya doing, Freddy?" he asked.

"I'm taking a break from graduate school. I'm looking for a job," I said, as if having a job was a vacation.

"I need someone to work here, but I don't suppose that would be a job for you?"

Of course it was, and I started the following day. Book Masters sold bestselling hardcovers but mostly dealt with paperbacks. I shelved the new arrivals, tried to keep track of what we needed to reorder, and took charge of the register when Richie was off to his other store on Broadway and Forty-Fourth. I worked six days a week from eight to six, with a half hour for lunch. The minimum wage then was a dollar and fifteen cents an hour, and I made sixty-nine dollars a week before taxes. For now, I was saved.

After work, I went directly to Café Figaro, the old haunt of my City College days. In the two years I had been away, there were few changes; the new crew of younger waitresses was as beautiful and cosmopolitan and cool as ever. One, Silvi, the only American, took me under her wing, making certain that I understood she had a serious boyfriend so that I did not mistake her smiles and friendship for an invitation to further developments. Another, Luce, was so beautiful that I had to avoid looking at her. She was from Rome, maybe twenty-two, and married to an American artist. I imagined her as Audrey Hepburn in the film *Roman Holiday*, smiling, riding a Vespa on café-lined streets under an open blue sky.

Luce liked that I spoke to her in an Italian larded with Sicilian words that threw her off. "What is a *jadrool*?" she asked. I was surprised, thinking every Italian knew the word for a shabby, poor devil of a loser. She forgave my grammatical mistakes and comical pronunciation, correcting them sweetly.

"Luce, do you have a girlfriend for me?"

"In Rome," she said. "But improve your Italian first."

"I will start tomorrow," I said, imagining myself on a Vespa, riding behind a beautiful woman with long hair and a laugh to make me always happy.

I would sit alone in the café, and after I finally left, then move on to a basement-level bar on Houston Street where I heard girls came to meet men, before I took, not having met or spoken to anyone, the long subway ride back to the Bronx. The world—for others—was made of friends and lovers.

All my City College friends were gone. One had moved all the way to San Francisco with a Mexican woman he had fallen in love with at a brothel in Mexico; one saved enough driving a cab to put a down payment on a taxi medallion, then spent his days and nights driving to pay off the balance. Others disappeared into conventional careers of school teaching and marriages, and moved to Westchester or New Jersey, which to me were just other versions of Siberia or Syracuse or Brooklyn. I had lost contact with those friends anyway.

One evening when I was lounging at the Figaro, Luce asked if I knew anyone looking for an apartment; she and her husband were moving back to Rome.

"Me," I said. "If it's affordable." I needed to add that. The rent was fine, twenty-eight dollars a month, but I had to pay them three hundred dollars key money for the apartment—money they wanted right away, as they were leaving right away. And another one hundred dollars for the bed and chairs and kitchen table and lamps. The apartment was rent-controlled and the key money was Luce's fee for introducing me to the building agent and for having him put my name on the new lease. This was the way it was always done. I asked Richie for the money and offered to work on Sundays until the loan was paid off. Without a word, he peeled off thirty tens fresh from the bank. I scrounged up the other hundred from who knows where.

My first apartment in New York was on the top of a six-floor tenement at 394 East Eighth Street between Avenues C and D, with a bathtub in the kitchen but with a separate toilet and shower in the small back room. There was plenty of heat and hot water, and sunlight from the two windows that faced north, uptown, where the men wore jackets and ties and the women lipstick and high heels, and everyone took taxis—the adult world to which I could not belong, and perhaps, for that reason, had never wished to.

From those two windows I could see, by stretching myself out on the sill, a slice of the East River and the freighters and tugs plying it. I loved the soft, melancholy hooting of the tugs at night as I was falling to sleep. It comforted me to feel a part of the river's strong flow, carrying me out into the Narrows and out to the far edge of night. I did not see but imagined Tompkins Square Park to my west with its little monument to those who, in 1904, on a beautiful June day trip, had drowned in the burning of the steamship *General Slocum*. A thousand people, mostly women and their children from the Lower East Side, drowned in the very river where the tugs I loved to hear now did their watery work. Sometimes I imagined the hoots of the tugs were mourning wails for those who had drowned. The river, the park, the drowning were forever packaged into my new life.

I was close to everything I loved. The park on the East River, filled every Sunday with families from the whole of the Lower East Side, and where Jamaicans in their impeccable whites came to play soccer. The library on Tenth between A and B, with its solid oak tables, was filled with luxurious silence, except for readers turning pages.

But there was a nether side of this urban pastoral: muggings and break-ins galore. That was one of the reasons not to live in the neighborhood. But the low rent was more than compensation, and thus the neighborhood was a draw for artists and writers from everywhere. My building, aside from a few leftover old Polish and

Jewish tenants, was filled with them. I was in love with the whole area: the tiny shops that sold pickles floating in huge wooden barrels on the sidewalk and the fish markets with their window displays of porgies and ling sleeping on beds of crushed ice. I was fascinated and repulsed by the gutted hares suspended on hooks in the butcher shop windows.

I even liked the cold. It was a familiar Lower East Side cold, one that had clung to my grandmother and mother not far from where I was now living, a cold that had frozen them in the tenements, in the streets—frozen them everywhere but in church on Sunday. They never defrosted, not even later in the warmth of the Bronx.

No one in my building had escaped a burglary. A neighbor on a lower floor pinned a note on her door: *You have taken everything.* I had to illegally double-gate the fire escape window. A neighbor down the hall, Samuel, a carpenter in his late eighties from Kraców, built me a new reinforced door with a police lock after the first time the apartment was broken into. For some reason my radio was taken but not my sweet red Olivetti. Some books had disappeared, too, but only the few hardcovers. The second time around, I came home to find the door almost broken from its frame, but it had held, thanks to Samuel's Old World skill. He accepted no money for his work but asked me to take in his gray cat when he infrequently visited his daughter for a weekend in Westchester. Samuel said, "Gustav is happy with you. Will you take him when I die?"

"Of course," I said. I loved this man, who wished never to leave our building, our streets, never to live with his children, who promised him comfort in the suburbs. "Who wants to die up there with all that grass?" Samuel said. I loved Gustav, or the gray pelt of whatever there was left of him dragging himself from room to room behind me.

Sometimes I saw Samuel walking with his carpenter's toolbox on his way to repair another old-timer's broken chair or table leg. He was hatless on the coldest days, and his black overcoat had holes in the elbows and was missing two buttons. But he walked erectly and strongly, like a man of twenty going to see his love. Every morning before I left for work, I made a point of stopping at his apartment down the hall and listening at the door just to be sure he was still alive. I was relieved when I heard him talking to his cat in Polish or his radio playing, or if I could smell that he was frying sausage from the butcher on First Avenue and boiling up a pot of mushroom soup.

I had girlfriends, but none who stayed in my heart. I sometimes went to Stanley's, a bar on Twelfth and B, the East Side mecca for artists and other wannabes like myself. I had no friends there, either, but once a young woman my age took me to her apartment close by and we listened to Puccini's *Turandot* on LPs, playing over and over the "Nessun dorma" aria. "*Vincerò! Vincerò*" ("I will win! I will win!"), the singer cried, risking death for the chance of love. I heard it for the first time, and it buoyed me up with the feeling that I, too, could win in life and not grow old and die a loveless old man stacking books in a small bookstore. The eyes of the woman I was with were teary; mine, too. Maybe she was thinking the same about her life. She took my hand: "It will all be OK, right, Fred?" she said with forced brightness.

We sat drinking wine and playing the aria until dawn, when I left to open the store at eight and she went off to teach in a high school in Queens. I did not see her in Stanley's in the following days and weeks. I asked Stanley about her; he had no idea who I meant, and I had no memory of the building she had taken me to. I never saw her again, but she lives in me.

Sliced Tomatoes and High Fever

Manhattan, Greenwich Village, 1961

I was happy to run into Jack Micheline at the Café Figaro. He wanted to meet me again soon and read me his poems. I had a phone, finally, and gave him my number. He, as always, had no permanent address and no phone, but there were plenty of phone booths in the streets and drugstores, and it was easy to call someone if you had the right change.

I got sick one week and had to stay home from work. I had a high fever and was too weak to leave my bed and go up and down the six long flights to the grocery on the corner. Samuel brought me a pot of his homemade mushroom soup and a loaf of thick black bread from a shop on First Avenue that sold day-old loaves, leftovers from the restaurants. The loaves tasted just baked from the oven. Samuel wouldn't take a penny for the food. I offered him a glass of vodka, which he swiftly downed in one swallow and went to rinse the glass.

"Go back to bed," he said.

I had to walk him back to my door so I could fasten the police lock. I was very weak after we said our good-byes and I slept for an hour. I was feverish when I woke, and I was not sure if Samuel had been there or I had just dreamed him.

On my third day in bed Jack phoned saying he had passed by the bookstore and was told I was sick.

"Got anything to eat?"

"Can you bring me something? Maybe a liverwurst sandwich with mustard?"

"I'm in the West Forties by the docks. I'll be right over, man."

I got dressed except for my shoes and went back to bed and back to sleep. I woke over an hour and a half later when Jack knocked and came in with a large brown paper bag. He had walked all the way to save the fifteen cents bus fare.

We sat at the kitchen table, where he poured from his paper bag the tomatoes he had bought from a street cart by the docks. They had kept the cold that always blew in from the Hudson. I managed to bring out some plates and a knife for him to slice the tomatoes into quarters, and we seasoned the whole mound with pepper and salt and drank tap water. "We can live on this," he said. "Who needs steak or a pork chop?"

We finished eating and sat by the window on two old chairs that I had found on the sidewalk. You could sit on them, but the seats needed caning. Jack read to me, in the fall afternoon light, some of his new poems, written in thick pencil in a softcover notebook. I thought they were naïve, crude, but I said I liked them. I compared them to Kenneth Patchen, whose poems, with their sentimentality dripping from the page, I had loved when I was fifteen, the very reason I disliked them now.

"I'm my own poet," he said, a bit miffed. "I'm not even a Beat, you know? Although Kerouac digs my work."

"Of course, Jack, you're your own poet," I said, trying to redeem myself.

"What's the difference," he said. "Everything's OK, right, Fred? As long as we can eat some tomatoes and drink cold water from the tap, right?"

"More than right, Jack. It's everything."

I was feeling tired and it was obvious, although I tried hard to hide it.

"Hey! Go crash, man. I'm splitting," he said. "I'll call you to see how you're doing and if you need anything."

I was feeling so weak, I couldn't last another minute. I got into bed and fussed about with getting the blankets and pillows right, fretting whether or not I should get up to pee, and finally, just when I was about ready to go to sleep, a knock at the door stopped me: it was Jack with a shopping bag with four cans of Campbell's chicken noodle soup and a loaf of Wonder Bread, whose wrapper promised to help "build strong bodies 12 ways."

"So long," he said, racing down the stairs.

There are kindnesses that live in you, live even in your ashes after you're dead.

I returned to the Figaro a week or so after my recovery, hoping to see Jack and thank him again for his visit and for cheering me up with his tomatoes and chicken soup. He was not there, but Laurita, the Argentinian waitress Jack had introduced me to what seemed a lifetime ago, was. "I haven't seen him for over a week," she said. "But I'll let him know you came by when he's in again."

"Where could he be?" I said.

She laughed. "Where could he be? On his mother's couch in the Bronx, or maybe in Mexico with Kerouac."

I sat there by the window and in the light from outside I resumed reading *The Magic Mountain*. I was with Hans Castorp as he slowly fell in love with the rude, loud Russian, Clavdia Chauchat; I was starting to fall for her, too, and that she made bread pills and flicked them at the others sitting at her breakfast table. I joined the other men crazy for her in the sanitarium, high in the Alps, where she made them forget that their lungs were slowly rotting away with consumption.

Finally, it was evening, and I wondered where I would go to eat. Maybe Il Tacchino, a few blocks away, where the food was terrible but cheap. There was a bocce-ball alley in the middle of the restaurant where some of the old neighborhood Italians played, seemingly oblivious to the diners being served.

I was still deciding where to go when Laurita walked over and said, "I'm off work now, and if you like, we can go." We went to a spaghetti joint off Sheridan Square and finished off a flask of raw chianti and soon we walked to her apartment close by in a prewar art deco building off Sheridan Square. A man in an olive green uniform with baggy pants greeted us with a sleepy nod.

"I liked you from time we meets," she said in the elevator. There was not a scratch on the wood paneling.

"I liked you, too, Laurita, but I never thought you would like me."

"I like you OK," she said. "But I like you more when Jack said you are a great writer."

She saw me stare at the paintings in an otherwise bare living room. I went up close to one, a green river with a yellow barge and red sky. It was signed "Derain."

"Yes, yes. It's for real," she said.

"Is it yours?"

"Of course, Federico. Well, my father's, I should say."

I was about to let out an unsophisticated "Wow" but saved myself in time, and said, "Very beautiful."

I went to look at the others. A Vlaminck, a Picabia, two by Juan Gris, and a small pastel study of greenish-red apples on a blue plate by Gauguin.

"Did you come to see paintings?"

Her bed was strewn with skirts and jeans and paperbacks that she swept off before undressing. She was skinny with clothes on, but bones and honeyed flesh without them. I was afraid I would crush her with a hug or splinter her skeleton once I was on top of her. She saw but mistook my apprehension.

"Do you dislike thin women?"

"The opposite," I said, which was not too true, but I was no longer thinking about her body, because I was struck with the paintings in the other room and wondering why a woman with a rich father and rich apartment and immaculate elevator was a waitress. But what did I know about life? What did I know about anything?

I left her apartment before the crosstown bus had started its normal morning schedule. I never considered paying all that money for a cab, so I walked across town and got home in time to shower and change. I was so happy; I thought I did not need to even change or shower. I only needed to stay awake forever.

A few weeks later, with a giant grin, Jack appeared in the bookstore. He took me aside, pretending he needed my help so that my boss wouldn't think he'd come to socialize while I was on the clock. "Man, you left a big impression on Laurita. She said you were *muy hombre* and she'd leave her boyfriend for you if he wasn't in jail."

"Jail?"

"Yeah, he's a boom-boom man: knocks you on the head with a blackjack and lifts your wallet. I think he does it just for fun, because she gives him all the money he ever wants."

I was ready to run to Mexico before Boom-Boom was released and cracked my head open.

"That's really great," I said.

"There's nothing to worry about. Laurita's not gonna leave him while he's still in jail. It's a point of honor. She feels guilty that she slept with you. So she's fixing you up with a belly dancer friend who saw you at the Figaro and digs you, too."

"Jack, is she the one with long black hair and flared nostrils?"

"And big tits," Jack added. "Susan, she's the one."

"Wow! I've seen her at the Figaro a lot and was dying to meet her."

"You should never make a move with a woman. They'll come to you if they like you. Haven't you ever noticed that? And it's always better for you when it works that way."

A belly dancer, like the one in Bowles's *The Sheltering Sky* or in

Lawrence Durrell's *The Alexandria Quartet*, the burning, most famous books of the day that I had read every night in bed, volume after volume, until I went blind and forced myself to turn off the light.

A belly dancer, like the one I would sometimes go to see on Friday nights at a Greek dive on Thirty-Eighth and Ninth, near the General Post Office. For days after, I would dream of her and her slow work up from a hip shimmy to a full-body frenzy and her smile and quick exit at the end. Faria, the Turkish Delight, the goddess was called on the poster, and the night-shift post office guys on their break packed the bar, where I nursed a tall, watery drink and waited for her eleven o'clock set.

Susan, aka Jasmine, danced at a club off Sheridan Square in the West Village. She was as good as Faria, and she had all her teeth. She reserved a table up front for me. After her first set, she came over, ordered drinks, smiled, and said, "Jack says you're a great writer."

I went to see her every Tuesday and Wednesday night for a month, and I became a fixture: the bartenders called out a friendly hello and the tubby manager smiled when I appeared and even walked me to my reserved table. The weekends were out, because the place was packed to the ceiling then and they needed my table, even if I paid for my drinks. Sometimes on Saturday nights, drink in hand, I hugged the bar with the other guys who were wild for her. I felt sorry for them and superior to them as well, in the most primitive way. The poor saps could just fantasize about her, jerk off at home dreaming of her, as I would have done. But at the end of the night, when she was done dancing, she'd come over to the bar where I was waiting and plant a few kisses on me. "Let's go home," she said. The guys sank with envy.

I was so glad that I had not married Eva or anyone else. I couldn't endure the monotony of monogamy and cohabitation: the morning, noon, and night closeness that would eventually turn into a bad smell.

Susan loved Blake and Whitman and Pablo Neruda. She read to me first in English and then in Spanish from his *Twenty Love Poems*.

"You should write poetry," she said. "You're more romantic than Neruda."

"I will write a poem for you," I said. I did and read it one night in bed.

"That's very sweet, Fred. You should get into yoga."

She made hissing sounds when we made love, and it frightened me that she would turn into a snake just as we were coming. I liked the fear; it made me come harder.

She brewed coffee for me before I left for the bookstore in the morning, and I kissed and fondled her and tucked her into bed, where she would stay until late afternoon. We never said "I love you." We never said "I'm in love with you." Sometimes it is better that way; the moments are richer and less filled with disappointment.

With Susan, I was not an hourly-wage bookstore clerk or a failed graduate student or a poor boy from the Bronx: I was an intense young writer—soon to write something astounding—living a glamorous writer's life with a belly dancer for a girlfriend.

One early evening I went to the Figaro and fell into a reverie. Susan: the naked curve of her hip; her full, beautiful breasts; her small, tight ass; her flared nostrils and long black hair; the inverted isosceles triangle of her pubic hair. I thought: There are women more beautiful than Susan—Sandra, for example—but when Susan danced, she made me and the world dizzy. As I was engaged in this profound meditation, Jack walked in.

"Susan told me to tell you she liked you very much, Fred. Don't be hurt—she even loved you a little—but she's gone to Mexico to become a vegetarian." Jack sniffled. "She was far out, man, wasn't she?"[18]

[18]JACK AND HIS HIPPIE GIRLS
Jack Micheline (1929–1998)

I did not see Jack again for five years, not until maybe 1967, this time in Golden Gate Park in San Francisco. He was tossing a Frisbee with four young girls with flowers in their hair and laughing like a goat. He ran over to give me a giant hug.

"Come meet the ladies," he said, bringing me into their circle, but I was too shy to dance and stayed stiffly behind watching, needing, as always, to be drawn into life by others.

Thirty years later I saw that dancing circle again, in a painting by Poussin, *A Dance to the Music of Time*: the sybaritic man playing the lyre is Jack, and he is whirling the beautiful young women and himself to a joy in time never ending. I later learned Jack had died of a heart attack on the BART in 1998 in San Francisco.

I wonder to this day why I never thought of trying to find him or find out where he had gone. He just seemed to vanish, and I seemed to let him. To think I had all those years before he died to be his friend. I don't ever believe that people die, imagining instead that they just go away for a while, and that one day or another I will run into them again.

Rebecca

Manhattan, Alphabet City, East Eighth Street, circa 1961.

Rebecca called one rainy fall evening. "Can we meet?"

"Of course."

"I mean soon, like tonight."

"Tonight?" I repeated, taken aback. "Where?"

Meeting her anywhere seemed too far, now that it was nine and I had settled in after a day's work and a sandwich at Stanley's bar.

"I could come to you," she said.

"Where are you?"

"Home, where else?"

She was on the Upper West Side in the Eighties. It would be at least an hour before she arrived: I figured the A train to West Fourth Street, then the crosstown bus that ran every so often, then the walk from Tenth and D—dangerous, especially for a woman alone. I could wait for her at the bus stop so we could be mugged together.

"I'll take a cab," she said, as if understanding my apprehension. I was a bit shocked. A cab? It was about seven dollars from where she lived; no one in my world took a cab, unless, I supposed, it was to a hospital.

"I don't have much of a place," I said. But then I thought: *So what?* My pad in Syracuse was much worse, and she had seen that.

Rebecca arrived in a half hour, calling out from the street below, as I had told her to. I bundled up the outer door key in an old sock and sailed it down to her, then I ran down the stairs to be sure that no one mugged her on the climb up: sometimes muggers found their way into the building and waited.

"When I told the driver where I was going, he almost didn't take me," she said. "I had to promise him a five-dollar tip above the meter."

She was more beautiful, more soulful than ever, but all I could think about was how she would get back from this neighborhood, where taxis feared to travel.

I made tea. For the past several weeks I had tried not to drink alcohol, marking off forty dry days on a calendar from the De-Robertis pastry shop on First Avenue between Tenth and Eleventh, my second home after Café Figaro. We sat in the kitchen and were cheerful for the first few minutes—saying how glad we were to be back in New York, how glad we were to see each other—but soon the cheer was gone, and Rebecca broke into tears.

"Have you and your husband split?"

"Yes, but that's not why I'm crying. My father was shot a week ago."

I had met her father on his visit to Syracuse: a thin, nervous man who spoke very little. He had taken us to dinner in a steak-and-chops place with a red plastic tablecloth and a twelve-page plastic menu. He left a twenty as a tip.

"He owed some people money. He didn't pay. He *couldn't* pay. And finally, when he was alone on a Saturday catching up on his paperwork, someone came into his office and shot him."

I blurted the first thing that came to my mind: "He was doing paperwork?"

Rebecca gave me a cold stare. "He was the best father he knew how to be," she said.

That left me stumped. That may have been true of my own

father, if I chose to picture it that way. She stopped crying and eyed the bathtub.

"I have it there for convenience," I said. "Also, it's a conversation piece."

"Do you have much company?"

"Like a girlfriend, you mean?"

"That's what I mean."

She rose and stood over me, her hair longer than before, now straight down to her buttocks. I stood and felt the tension that could convert a friend into a lover. But I was not yet sure. Not sure if she was sure. We wavered in a kind of electrified silence. And in silence we undressed and went to bed.

The shoulders of a woman who is your friend are not the shoulders of a woman who has become your lover. Nor is her face or hair or any part of her. Her beauty may be the same, but an alchemy has taken place, and she becomes another being, another person, the one whose eyes you kiss and whose shoulders you kiss, the one whose hair you stroke, the one whose thighs open to you.

"Your breasts are beautiful," I said, outlining the curves with my finger.

She caressed my face. "Why did we wait so long, Fred?"

Kim's Laundry

Manhattan, Alphabet City, East Eighth Street, 1961–1962

Every Tuesday morning at half past eight sharp, a middle-aged man came into the bookstore, bought a book, and left with a simple nod. He chose gems: a recent translation of Plato or the collected plays of Georg Büchner or a new edition of Yeats's poems. He was spry and lean, with steel-gray hair, and he always carried with him a black satchel, like a doctor's bag for house calls. He had an accent I couldn't place. One day, after he paid for Joseph Campbell's *The Hero with a Thousand Faces*, he said, "The best books go begging on the shelves."

"I've noticed that," I said.

He nodded, left, returning a moment later.

"Thank you."

Each week he added more words, until one morning he asked, "What are you doing here?"

I was taken aback. "What do you mean, what am I doing here? I work here."

"Of course, but I feel you are very intelligent, and you should be doing something else. May I ask what that something else might be?"

"I want to be a writer." I disliked myself for saying that: it was so lame, so clichéd, and so self-defensively boastful at the same time. Like a galley slave, chained to his oar, who says that he's just rowing part-time but aims to be a navigator.

"Writers need a great deal of time. Good-bye," he said, offering his hand for me to shake.

Time. I was back to working six days a week, now that I had paid off the key money. I got to the store at seven thirty a.m. and opened it to the public at eight. Sometimes Richie asked me to stay until eight or nine at night. I did, especially on Saturdays when there was much business from tourists wanting guidebooks and city maps. By the time I was finished talking to customers, stacking new arrivals, and working the register, I was half-dead, the other half comatose. Rather than go home and try to write, I would run down to Café Figaro, have a sandwich, flirt with the waitresses, and melt into the scene with a book until it was too late to do anything but take the crosstown bus and hope I didn't get mugged on the two-block walk home.

Every other Sunday I brought my laundry to Kim, the portly, old Chinese man whose shop lay across from my building. He worked all day until late and slept in the curtained rear, where he lived illegally. I saw through his window a faint light at midnight, meaning he had stopped working and was listening to the radio and reading his Chinese dream interpretation books and manuals on what days to engage with the world.

I had given him my birth date and he checked my sign in his book. Sometimes he waved me into the shop to caution me when to stay home and when not to answer the phone. If the forecast was bad, he was not shy about saying, "No go work." Of course, I went anyway, although I was looking over my shoulder all the time and was doubly cautious getting on and off the bus. I took the steps up to my apartment like a fearful snail without a shell and paused on the landings to listen in case anyone was coming up behind me. Not that that would have done me much good if someone pulled a knife or a pistol or a blackjack to splinter my head.

Kim liked me because I had brought him food after he was

robbed and beaten in his shop—beaten so badly that he could not walk for more than two weeks. The two kids that did it kept shouting at him, "Where's the gold? You Chinks always have gold." He laughed as he told me this, saying, "Maybe they no see this," pointing to the two gold teeth in his mouth.

He had been left weak from the beating, and was fearful of slipping on the ice that always seemed to be glazing our streets well into spring.

I went behind the counter and took his snow shovel and a box of raw salt that he kept under the bathroom sink. I tried not to look too closely at his room, but I saw he slept on a mattress with a wooden block for his pillow. There was no shower or bath. For a stove, he had two hot plates: one for his teakettle and one for cooking rice. There was only one chair, where he was sitting, hand on his bandaged head. I shoveled away the snow and sprinkled the pavement with the salt. "Thank you," he said, taking out his wallet.

"Don't be silly, Kim," I said. The next time he did my laundry, he refused to take payment.

He promised to take me to a restaurant in Chinatown where, he said, Chinese were served delicacies that the tourists—meaning anyone who was not Chinese—never saw. He had to consult his books to find the propitious day.

A day in spring came when all the stars and planets agreed that it was favorable to travel. Kim told me to meet him the coming Sunday at the bus stop on Avenue B and Ninth Street at twelve thirty. I offered to come collect him. He said, "No, bus stop." I suspected that he did not want to be seen walking with me for fear that his other clients would be jealous. He was already at the bus stop when I arrived, but I hardly recognized him. He was in a beige tropical suit and beige shoes with woven straw uppers. He was wearing an understated green tie with a pearl stickpin. And his hat, which he had rakishly cocked to the side, looked like the finest panama. He also carried a cane, which I had never seen him use even when he hobbled around the shop. He greeted me and remained silent until the bus arrived packed with people.

In Chinatown he brought me into a restaurant filled with Caucasian families eating heaping bowls of food that looked brown and mushy and all the same. I saw a free table and moved toward it. Kim shook his head and gently took me by my sleeve, leading me down a staircase into a room with Chinese at every table. Some looked up at us; some nodded to him and continued eating. He and I sat alone at a corner table. He ordered in Chinese, and I had no idea what was to come.

Five or six dishes were brought to us at the same time. Fish pieces? Chicken shreds? Tasty, but too delicate for me. I started for the soy sauce and chili peppers, but there were none at the table. Kim ate with chopsticks, and seeing what a mess I was making with mine, he barked at the waiter, who went up the stairs and grudgingly returned with a fork and spoon.

All through the meal we drank scalding tea. I calculated Kim had downed about a gallon, and he broke into a sweat, which he patted away with a very fine white handkerchief. I realized we had not spoken fifteen words between us, but I also realized I didn't know what to talk about with him. To rescue me, he produced a photograph from his jacket pocket, a picture of a two- or three-year-old in black pajamas whose fly was open, exposing the genitals. Kim said, "Grandson. A boy."

I said, "Oh, Kim, I'm so happy for you. A grandson."

He smiled. "Thank you. My country strong now."

I didn't know if Kim was aware or cared that his country was now being ruled by one of the most ruthless dictators, Mao, and that his homeland was a man-made catastrophe of mass starvation and deaths and countless imprisonments. If so, it didn't seem to matter to him, because what was important was that China was being restored to international prominence. I said nothing, but he gave me a bigger smile and added, "Very strong now."

He motioned to the waiter, who brought the check. I offered to pay, but he refused. "My day," he said. We went back into the streets. I stood on a corner with him, and three or four Chinese men on the opposite corner called out. He answered quickly and turned to me, saying, "Time you go home now." He seemed embarrassed to be in my company and could see that I felt slighted. Then he added, "My friends ask if you policeman."

"Oh," I said. "Aren't you coming back with me?"

"No," he said, and then very shyly added, "Time to play fan-tan."

He crossed the street and joined his friends, who kept looking over at me. I didn't wave or shout my good-bye. I walked all the way back home, wishing I could have joined Kim and his suspicious friends and feeling that I was part of nothing and no one. I wondered if I should get a cat and some plants to look after and to greet me when I stepped through my door.

A few years later I moved not too far away, to an apartment on Tompkins Square Park. I continued to visit Kim periodically and brought him cartons of Camels, which he chain-smoked. One day I found the shop closed, and I could see through the window that it was empty except for a snow shovel leaning against the bare wall.

Around that time, I also went to Sam's door and heard no voice or radio. I knocked, but there was no answer. Taped to the door was an index card. *T. Simpson*, it said, with a flourish. I asked one of the old neighbors if he knew where Sam was.

"Gone," he said.

"Gone where?"

"To the cemetery. Where else?"

Rodin and Vagabonds

Manhattan, Tompkins Square Park, 1961–1962

Sometimes on my free Sundays I tried to write, but when the weather was good I longed to be outside, having spent most of the entire week in the bookstore. I strolled through Tompkins Square Park like an explorer without a mission. There was a hobo meeting ground on the benches on the Avenue B side of the park off Eighth Street; wayfarers and loners from everywhere in America traded stories and smokes and info on good soup kitchens and the best place in the Bowery to crash for a quarter.

Sometimes I brought over a pint of rye from Winarski's liquor store on First between Eighth and Ninth and passed it around the hobo benches, taking the first swig before it vanished among all the thirsty men. I was always politely thanked and maybe asked for a cigarette, but that ended their interest in me. Once I asked why they always came to this end of the park, and a man in his seventies said, "It's where we birds come every year. No one knows why, but it's always been that way."

"I see," I said. "It's like a tradition."

He laughed. "If that's what you want to call it. You got a cigarette, sonny?"

Later, I saw a whole band of hobos enter Saint Brigid's Church on Eighth and B. It featured a soup kitchen, always a magnet.

Old Poles, Ukrainians, and Jews, and the few Italians still living on

First Avenue from Ninth to Thirteenth Street took up the benches on the north side of park. They turned to the sun while talking, taking in every last minute of it before returning to the tenements where we all lived. They would all be dead in a few years, but for now they had their languages and memories to share. Some of the old Jews lived with their children and grandchildren in the suburbs but came back to visit friends while their daughters or sons shopped for creamed herring or pickles soaking in barrels on Avenue C. Some of the grown children waited in cars parked along Avenue B to bring their nostalgic parents back to Riverdale or to some tidy house with clean windows in Westchester.

Young people embracing and smooching had no set territory and sat or walked at all points of the park, indifferent to the junkies and the junkie muggers and fences who sold shoes and sports jackets and hair dryers and typewriters laid out on blankets, all hot goods. You might have found your own stolen radio there and then bought it back, no questions asked. It was like a tax for living there, so there was no use for hard feelings, no point in running to the police. They would do nothing in any case, their problems much larger than a few stolen items on a blanket.

I was not on the benches with the old or the hobos or the junkies or the thieves; I was not there strolling among the coupled young. I was a species alone, wishing I were not, wishing that by some magic I would be walking through the park with a woman I loved and buying her an ice cream cone from the Good Humor truck stationed on Avenue A since the beginning of time.

"What will you do when you really have trouble, Fred?" asked a sparrow perched on a bench.

Rebecca came downtown to see me, but Tompkins Square Park, or even the folksinging farther west in Washington Square Park, was not for her. The whole of lower Manhattan was not for her. I had no hope, at least in the near future, of ever leaving my pad on Eighth

Street, and I actually never wanted to leave unless it was for a larger, more sunny place in the neighborhood, on Tompkins Square Park itself, say, facing south.

"I'm never going to greatly improve my financial circumstances," I said to Rebecca one night in Lanza's, the neighborhood Italian restaurant with frescoes of old Sicilian villas and their lush gardens.

"Or your creative circumstances," she said. "I'm not chiding you, but with the way you're working at the bookstore, you're not going to get any serious writing done. Or any writing at all."

She was right, but for the moment my thoughts were on the restaurant's frescoes. A green garden baking in the Sicilian sun, two tall palm trees standing guard by a fountain as dry as the scorched blue day. I saw my grandmother walking there, dreaming of her escape to America. The frescoes were fading, along with the once-Italian neighborhood, where my grandmother and her family had lived when they first arrived—off the boat and into a cold-water flat with a bathtub in the kitchen and a toilet down the hall. Now I was walking the same streets and, except for having an in-house toilet, living in the same kind of walk-up flat, inhaling their immigrant shadow.

"Can't you work fewer hours and give the time to writing?" Rebecca asked.

"You don't understand about money," I said. "People who have it never understand people who don't."

I was mean to her because I was upset by what she had said, wondering if, in fact, by working all those hours at the bookstore I was giving myself an excuse for not writing. At least Ehrlich had written one novel before he went into pained silence.

Sometimes on Sundays Rebecca and I would go to the Metropolitan Museum of Art, where we often made a stop at Cézanne's painting of a table with apples. "How can he have done that?" Rebecca said, her voice thick with awe. I loved this painting, but her lavish appreciation made me wonder whether my love for it was honestly felt or filtered through my reading Rilke's *Letters on Cézanne* and finding there, in the old painter's devotion to his art despite critical indifference or scorn, a message of courage for me. Did I love Cézanne's work, or did I love him? My doubt made me wonder about Rebecca, too, and whether she believed in her love for Cézanne, for anything not officially sanctioned and housed in the pantheon of art.

In good weather we'd walk from the Met on Eighty-Second Street all the way down to Fifty-Third and Fifth Avenue to drink coffee in the sculpture garden at MoMA, with Rodin's statue of Balzac as our bronze chaperone. It elevated us to be there, in the noble world of Art. In this quiet garden, the buses and subways, the spilled-over garbage pails and the noisy trucks that came to empty them, the monthly rent and unlit staircases with bandits waiting on the landings, the murder of her father, were no longer concerns—or, better, had never existed.

After the museum excursions, Rebecca came back to my place, but we no longer shared the hope-filled mood of a new romance. As for sex, we were still in the fresh beginning. While not exciting, it was comforting—except for the afterward and the staying overnight in a small bed and the leaving with me in the early morning and getting packed in the bus, crushed in the subway. All that dampened our romance, and we were not old enough or wise enough to be grateful that we had each other for the night or for a whole Sunday. I didn't want to end with her, because there was really nothing to end, since we had hardly begun, and because we each had exactly no one else.

Expensive Watches and *Martin Eden*

Manhattan, Around Forty-Second Street, Spring 1962

One Tuesday morning at eight fifteen sharp, the man with the doctor's bag appeared. He did not come to buy a book. "I want to show you something," he said. I came from behind the register and faced him. He removed his jacket and rolled up his shirtsleeve to reveal blue numbers tattooed on his arm.

"Do you know what this is?"

"Yes." I had seen such tattooed numbers before on the arm of Solomon, a counterman at the Second Avenue Deli, New York City's mecca for Eastern European Jewish food. Solomon had been in Auschwitz as a teenager. He had survived, but his eyes seemed always fixed on the crematoriums where his mother and father had been turned from flesh into ashes.

"Then you understand that there is nothing more precious than freedom. Nothing." Had John Resko not said the same thing to my friend, the Francophile Elizabeth Charon, before she left her husband and two sons to live with a man in Paris?

"I believe you."

"You don't, or you would not still be here."

I was dazed by his directness, by his blunt fist at my heart.

Like a child, I said, "What should I do?"

"Find a way to make a living that gives you the most time possible. Learn a skill that pays well for little work."

I didn't want to seem ungrateful, but what he had said was obvious, useless. What such skill could I learn?

"What do you suggest?"

"Work you can do at home. A proofreader, for example."

"I have already tried that."

"A diamond cutter! You can work anywhere in the world."

"I have butterfingers. And it takes years to learn."

"A poor excuse. Have you read *Walden*?"

"Of course," I said, becoming defensive.

"Then you remember how Thoreau made his living?"

"He was a surveyor."

"Yes, and he had to work only a few days a week, then he was free to write or stroll in the woods."

"That was then," I said, annoyed. For all his good intentions, I didn't like being hectored like an errant schoolboy. I also didn't like the truth he had implied about my lack of courage, my taking the cowardly way out of struggle. I asked, rather sharply, "What's your profession?"

"I repair very expensive watches. I work at home, not more than two days a week. I bring in the fixed watches and pick up the broken ones. I'm going to the jeweler now, right up here on Fifth Avenue."

"That's great for you," I said.

He stayed silent and gave me a sympathetic look. He extended his hand. I felt stupid for being so stupid.

"Thank you. You've given me golden advice, I know it."

At the door he called out, "Don't look back with regrets."

It had never occurred to me to ask what he did with his free time, and I made a mental note to ask when I saw him again.

But he did not show up the next week or any week after. Had he died? Was he bringing his watches elsewhere? Or had he had enough of advising me, with my stubborn ignorance and fragile pride?

All the same, his words spurred me to model myself after the protagonist in Jack London's *Martin Eden*, an aspiring young writer who rose in the black hours before dawn and wrote stories before he left for work boiling shirts at the laundry. His situation was worse than mine but he willed himself to stream words onto a page—and by hand. And this without one friend to phone when lonely, no woman to wake beside him from time to time and say that she loved him.

I followed Martin's example: no Café Figaro, no chasing girls, no lingering over beer at Stanley's bar. I went to bed at nine and woke at five. No breakfast, only a roll and coffee and then to my kitchen table and my waiting Olivetti, bright red and cheerful like a kid's first fire engine. I started my adventure with hope and excitement.

It was easy at first, and there was something glamorous about being at my table so early in the morning. I saw myself as a hero in my struggle to be a writer. But after my fifth day I woke later, and then later still, until, by the tenth day, I turned off the alarm and returned to sleep until my usual hour. The chilly darkness had depressed me, the blank pages had taunted me. I had sat and stared at the blankness and known I was lost.

Simona

Manhattan, Fifth Avenue, Spring 1962

I was in the bookstore opening boxes of newly arrived paperbacks and daydreaming. Richie was on the phone. "Of course," he said. "We would be honored. At your convenience."

When he hung up he asked, "Do you know this Italian guy who comes in every week or so and buys a half a dozen books by writers no one else has heard of?"

"Like who?"

"Like Ronald Firbank." Richie was right, I had never heard of him.

"Who's the guy?"

"The Italian guy; you're always talking to him."

"Oh, him! Marcello, the journalist."

"What journalist? He runs the whole of the Rizzoli office in America."

I had always found Marcello a bit formal and distant, and he wanted to know too much about me and what it was like to be raised an Italian-American: Why did I work in a bookstore? Did I own it?

"I know him. What about him?"

"He wants to open an account with us. Because of you, he says."

That was good news, but what did it do for me? I still made a dollar fifteen an hour, and a promised raise stayed a promise.

"Good," I said, both glad and sour.

"I have to make up a package of books for him, and he wants you to bring it up. Nothing heavy, just five or six books."

The Rizzoli office was around the corner at 500 Fifth Avenue in a stately building that housed the no-fooling-around nine-to-five jacket-and-tie world. The elevator soon exalted me up into that world. A woman opened the door without even bothering to ask why I was there and I followed her into a large windowless room with three desks stacked with newspapers, magazines, and red telephones and then into another bright room facing Fifth Avenue, where Marcello was on the phone and motioning me to sit on a red ottoman. Books and magazines sat in four-foot-high piles on the floor on either side of a giant leather couch.

The woman took my parcel of books and said, "I'm Simona. I'm a Roman. Would you like a coffee?"

"Thank you," I said, taking in that she was shoeless in stockings and smoking a clay pipe.

Marcello ended the call with a flourish—"No, don't call again when I'm at work"—and he let the phone down like a hot potato.

He composed himself, gave me a long look, then said: "The women. I'm sure you understand."

"Of course," I said with a worldly nod.

Simona came in with a tray of three demitasse cups and an espresso maker. She poured, puffed on her pipe, and smiled at me. Marcello seemed in a trance.

"Have you met Dr. Morini?"

"No," I said. "Where is he?"

He looked at me, baffled. "What do you mean? She's right here: Simona." Then, in Italian, he said, "Forgive me, but it's not right you should be working in a place inferior to you. A good boy like you. I will find you a job."

I thanked him, more for his kind words than for the prospect of a new job.

Simona, without looking at me, said, "What makes him a good boy?"

"He reads Pavese and Ungaretti and has good manners, polite. And look! He's even presentable."

We drank. It was bitter. But I did not ask for sugar, as there was none on the tray.

"It lacks sugar," Simona said, turning to me. "I see you are too polite to ask."

Her English was accented, but not Italian or anything that I knew; it was charming, and her voice had a sweet lilt to it as if it rode on flowers. I thought how beautiful it would be to hear her say "*Buona notte*" before we turned off the light.

The Teletype machine went wild with clicks and clacks, and two men entered the room, filling it with cigarette smoke. They looked at me and nodded and spoke so quickly in Italian that I caught only the message and not the flourishes. The gist: one of the two was ready to fly to Texas to write about a giant rodeo and political rally; the other said that the assignment had been given to him.

Simona said, "Neither of you should go. Your English is terrible, Texans won't understand a word, and they'll make fun of you."

"Settled," Marcello said. "I will go."

"Who will translate for you?" Simona said.

Marcello threw a paper clip at her, which she tossed back, missing his ear.

They continued to argue, ignoring me. I stood to leave; no one but Simona noticed, and she walked me to the door. "Good luck," she said. Marcello called out from far away, "Bye-bye."

Soon I was back to the humorless street and the charmless store.

I would have loved to work with them in any capacity, but mostly I would have loved to be able to see Simona all day.

Sandra and Baby Ice Cubes

Manhattan, King Cole Bar, 1962

Sandra phoned me at the store as I was leaving work. She was in New York and wanted to see me.

"I'll go home and change," I said.

"Don't bother, and don't bother to shower. Just come over for drinks."

I rushed to the King Cole Bar, the glory of the St. Regis Hotel. The maître d' at the bar entrance flashed me a dirty look. "You need a jacket to come in here."

Sandra waved and he let me in, minus a smile.

Tailored jacket and skirt, both black. Man's white shirt, buttoned to the top. Nails painted a murderous red. Lips to match. Where were her tweed hacking jacket and gray wool slacks?

I had imagined she had booked a room in the hotel, where she would open a suitcase of whips and restraints and we would recommence our dramas. I had missed the dramas, dreamed of them.

Sandra, without asking, had ordered a double-malt Scotch for me; it came with a little silver pail of baby ice cubes. The Scotch was an amber flame with a hint of peat, kilts, bagpipes, and a charred briar pipe bowl. This was a Scotch that never had seen a shelf at Stanley's sawdust-and-liverwurst sandwich-palace, or anyplace east of First Avenue and below Fourteenth Street.

Behind the long, venerable wood bar glowed Maxfield Parrish's mural of the merry old soul, Old King Cole in his court. It was a timeless world of infinite merriment and mellow sunsets. It took only a minute for the Scotch to mellow me, too, and carry me into the courtly scene and hold me there in its ever-golden serenity.

"I thought you were still in France," I said.

"Came back to settle things in Syracuse before I leave for good."

"For good?"

"Yes, I wanted to say good-bye."

"Leaving soon?"

"Early tomorrow, for Paris."

Paris, where I still had not been. Ten years had passed since I dropped out of high school with the plan of living in Paris and becoming an artist, and at twenty-five I was no closer to that city of light, of art and sex.

"Take me with you," I said jokingly, but with my heart heavy at the thought of its impossibility, heavy with envy.

"Fred, I met the man of my life. I know how banal that sounds, but it's true. I'm going there to be with him, and live for him."

"I see. Is he French?"

"Of course! Do you think I'd go there to be with an *American*?"

What do these Frenchmen have, I wondered, that beautiful, intelligent, independent, sexy women like Elizabeth and now Sandra would leave family and country to join them? Even Eva had come back a changed woman after only a year under France's erotic spell. It frightened me to think of the power that Frenchmen had over women. Were we American men so anemic? Was I?

"I'm glad you're happy," I said, not glad at all. I seemed always to have to pretend pleasure at another's good fortune or impending marriage.

"It's not happiness, Fred. It's a wonderful dread. No one has ever made me feel so afraid."

I finished my Scotch and considered another. But it arrived without my asking. The waiter made a slight bow to her.

"Are you going to live together?"

She studied me as if to see if I was a real fool or just pretending to be one: "He lives with his wife. But I have an apartment nearby where I wait for him."

I started to imagine her in a bare room with a bed and a whip and a telephone, waiting for it to ring. The Eiffel Tower leering in the window, the Seine flowing beneath it with barges tooting in French. I was dizzy with wanting her. I hoped she would ask me to go to her room for one last steamy night. She waved for the bill. She signed and put a twenty-dollar bill on top of the check.

"Must get up very early," she said.

"I'll miss you," I said, too upset to say anything more.

"Well, come over one day. You'll love Paris."

I took the Fifth Avenue bus with the idea that before going home I would get off at Eighth Street and walk across Washington Square Park and over to Café Figaro and there, under its warm protection, nurse my humiliation and my anger at being dumped again. The bus made every other stop and gave me time to brood. I ran the gamut from disappointment at not having another one-act with Sandra to a kind of bitter jealousy and resentment. She was rich, never had to have a job or take a bus or subway or worry about the price of a taxi ride. Anyway, she owned her own car; she owned her own house; she could dine out wherever and order whatever she wanted and never had to figure the cost. She spoke French and was going to live in Paris, where she had found her ultimate sexual heaven. I was back in the Bronx, alone in my cot.

By the time my first espresso arrived and the cheering smile that Claudine, the French waitress, brought with it, my thoughts had run to this: All the time I knew her, Sandra had always had the control and power. I only had the whip—and that she had lent me. I wrote on a napkin: *Beware of power given you. It is only on loan.*

Fucking profound, I thought, impressed with my insight and its imperishable phrasing on the paper napkin. But in bed that night, the insight was not enough to keep me from imagining us in her Syracuse bedroom.

The Interview

Manhattan, City Hall Area, 1962

Simona walked into the empty bookstore at eight thirty. She smiled and started to browse the bookshelves.

"Do you remember me?" I asked. "We met at your office last week."

"Of course I remember you; we all remember you because we made such fools of ourselves in front of you."

"Not at all. It was fun. I would have stayed all day," I said. "Stayed all day and looked at you," I wanted to say. "Watched you pouring coffee like precious drops of water in the desert. Looked at your legs." But she was the older, sophisticated woman I dared not speak to like that. In fact, what *woman* would I speak to like that?

"Come by again, then. I know Marcello would be glad to see you."

She saluted, leaving a trail of worldliness behind her. Had she been pretending to look for a book as a pretext to see me again? Was it at all possible she was interested in me—was flirting with me? *Don't flatter yourself, fool,* I told myself, and went to shelve some new arrivals.

In the afternoon my mother phoned. There was an envelope with a New York City seal. She was afraid to open it.

"Is it a summons of some kind?" I asked, worried I was being called to jury duty—maybe to a federal case that would last three years, one where they stashed away the jurors in a hotel in New

Jersey. I asked her to read it to me. She pieced it out: I was to appear for an interview regarding my application for a job at the welfare department. I had forgotten all about that application, and the job itself. I had learned about it from my friend Eli from City College, the one who went to Mexico City to live a Beat life and write a novel. He came back a married man and soon-to-be father, and had to support a family. He had found a job in the city welfare department.

"It's a cool gig, Fred. You'd be surprised how many writers dig the job, because it gives you lots of time to write." Of course, this was the kind of job I had dreamed of.

The interview took place a week later at eight thirty in a building near City Hall. The minute I saw it, I felt overwhelmed by its size and its crushing official weight. I went right up to the assigned room, wondering where the other applicants were. A man with a sweet expression greeted me with a smile. He sat behind a narrow desk with a rubberized gray top. He glanced at some official-looking papers.

"Hi, Fred, I'm Dr. Z. I'm a psychologist with the city."

He was Dr. Z and I was Fred. The power was his. I extended my hand but he quickly looked down at the papers.

"Fred, why do you want to work for the welfare department? And if we hire you, do you expect to stay, or do you see it as just a temporary move?"

I sensed that the best way was to play it straight: no quips, no jokes. Tell him what he would like to hear.

"I want to help people, Doctor. I was raised in poverty and know the problems that come with it." (*So what?* my inner voice said.) "And, yes, sir, I do see this as a long-term career, one with growth potential. I'm thinking of getting a master's in social work." (*How do you come up with this bullshit?* the voice asked.) I hated myself for this fiction, but as Céline advised, "In life either you lie or you die."

Then the smiling and bonhomie stopped, and he said curtly, "Why are you an Army 4-F?"

"I don't know why."

"I have a note here saying you were having trouble at home and you went to see the City College psychologist."

I was shocked. So my private meeting with the shrink at City was on record and made available to the powers at large?

"I was having problems with my mother," I said, "and I needed advice."

"And the 4-F?"

"I don't know the reason. I was surprised when I got the 4-F notice."[19]

There was a long pause before he asked: "What do you do in your free time?"

Without thinking I said: "Do you mean after I go out with girls?"

A slight smile, and he extended his hand. "Thank you for coming, Mr. Tuten," he said.

I heard the welfare department door shut behind me. I smiled, left, sank with the elevator.

Then I was back in the street again, back in the world of courts and the city's administration offices, with their machinery of serious matters and the serious people who ran them. I had avoided that world all my life, and now I felt bounced from it, and very small.

---

[19] I had worked to get my 4-F. Some of my friends had used the pretext of being homosexual to avoid being drafted, but then, as their claim was on record, they would have trouble finding employment in any government agency—or maybe anywhere.

I did not want to spend two years of my life subjected to Army discipline, to be drilled, squeezed, crushed into becoming a robot with a crew cut. I did not want to be shipped anyplace, especially not Alabama or Georgia, somewhere in the South, the Great Dark Place, where Yankees were routinely mistreated on principle and for sport.

I had thought myself a rebel against any institution that I had not willingly joined. The test of my commitment to independence was the Army physical.

I stayed up all night, drank coffee until my eyes popped, having been told by older boys that by looking frenzied and disoriented, many had escaped service. I got to the physical exam frazzled and frightened. The line was long. Boys like myself stood in shorts, moving along from one inspection post to another. I kept getting out of line and going to the end; the point was to seem different—odd.

At the end of the physical, I mustered up my courage to ask to see the psychiatrist. The man at the desk looked up and said, "Don't worry, you're going."

My interview was brief: "Do you want to serve your country?"

"Yes, sir, if I'm needed."

"Do you ever have thoughts of killing your mother?"

I was taken aback, but then I realized he had been given the report from the City College psychologist that I had seen twice during my troubled senior year. John Resko had once told me, "Trust no one, not even me."

"Sometimes I wish she were dead."

He wrote on a sheet and looked up at me, saying, "Thank you."

Then, some weeks later, a card arrived in the mail: 4-F. I wasn't sure I was happy. I wondered why I was exempted. Maybe there was something really wrong with me after all.

Simona. The Sociology of Flirtation

Manhattan, Café Figaro, 1962

Simona appeared in the bookstore twice more, glancing at the books, buying nothing, giving me a cheerful smile and a polite hello and good-bye. On the last visit she said, "Hello, Frederico, don't you ever stop working?"

I summoned the courage and said, "Dr. Morini, would you like to have coffee with me?"

"That would be nice. When?"

I was so surprised that I said the first thing that came to mind: "Tonight, after work?"

"I have to stay late tonight," she said, "and won't be finished until eight."

"Me, too. So this is perfect, then. By the way, may I ask what you're a doctor of?"

"Oh, that's nothing," she said. "It's a doctorate in classical philology."

I went blank.

And she added, "You don't know what that means, do you, Frederico?"

"I'm afraid not."

"Nobody does."

"I see. So I can't come to see you when I have a sore throat?"

"Only if it's sore because of a linguistic complication."

I stumbled for at least a halfway clever answer and finally, lamely said: "I'll try to have such a complication."

She gave me a big smile and said, "Bravo, Federico."

After she left, I started to fret. What was I doing? What was I thinking? Where on earth could I take this sophisticated, elegant, international woman who wore knitted skirts and jackets and stockings and high heels and had a doctorate in classical philology, whatever that meant? First I thought of the Oak Room at the Plaza hotel; it was within walking distance, only fourteen blocks. The Oak Room was a worldly bar with solid tables, some facing Central Park; maybe Simona had never been there and I could show off a bit of old New York, in a place where I was clearly at home, although I'd only been there twice. I was bounced the first time because I was not wearing a jacket and tie when I strolled in to take a look. The other time I was brought there by Rebecca for my first, life-changing martini—sophistication in a glass of chilled gin and vermouth and a stuffed olive—before we went to see *Last Year at Marienbad* at the chic Paris Theater across the street.

Simona was at the door at five after eight. I closed up. On the corner of Forty-Second Street and Fifth Avenue and in the growing chill of a fall night, she asked, "Where shall we go? Show me what you like."

In a flash it came to me: "A little café in the Village."

"Greenwich Village? I have never been there."

"Wonderful," I said, feeling relieved and in grown-up command of the situation. We were going where I was known and where I thought she would feel at ease, as it had a European flavor and thus also hinted at my cosmopolitan savvy.

Simona suggested we take a taxi. "Of course," I said. Then I stepped into the traffic and hailed a cab as if it were something I did every day, even twice a day. Once in, I checked the running meter and saw my money vanishing with every click. But when we arrived at the Figaro, Simona said, "Let me charge this to my office."

The meter rang to twice my hourly wage, not including the tip. I made some feeble protests, but finally and gratefully I surrendered. "On the condition that the coffee is on me," I said.

Cynthia, one of the waitresses, greeted me with a kiss on the cheek. Simona's smile froze. After coffee had arrived, she said, "So we come to a place to meet your girlfriends?"

"I have no girlfriend."

She defrosted after that, and we entered into the realm of biography. Not that hers flowed freely. "I'm not used to talking about myself so soon," she said. "It's what you Americans do."

"Don't Italians do it?"

"Between a man and a woman? Do you think an Italian man cares what a woman thinks?"

"I don't know," I said. This turn in the conversation bewildered me. It proved again how inexperienced I was.

"And the English are not better," she continued. "The men chat you up, as they say, and try to charm you with talk and talk about books and the BBC, but they don't give a fig what you think, only to go on about themselves."

"I see."

"That's the English idea of flirtation: chatting you up."

"And the Italian men?"

"They can spend a hour praising your eyes. That's their way to flatter you into bed."

"Simona, your English is excellent. How is that?"

"Ha-ha! Is this the American technique?"

"I never used it before, so I don't know. But I just wanted to compliment you."

"I've lived some years in London, among literary people."

"Do you miss Italy?"

"I miss my mother and sister. I miss my street in Roma. I don't miss the Italians. I hate the Italians."

"Hate all the Italians, Simona?"

"Of course not all. But let me tell you a story. When I got my doctorate, I went to my professor and said that I wanted to teach in the university: Could he help me? He tapped me on the shoulder several times with a kind of fatherly pat. He said, 'Oh, Simona, Simona. Why would you want to take a job away from a man? Get married. Have children.' I have never been treated like this in America, and that's why I love it."

"And your father, is he alive?"

"Unfortunately. And what about yours?"

"He left us when I was ten. He was a communist and went out to save the world." I faked a laugh.

"Maybe he just left for another woman."

"I don't think so," I said, hurt by the idea. It stripped away his glamour and left him an ordinary adulterer.

"So how did you and your mother survive?"

"Barely," I said. "We were poor."

"Before I came to New York, I never heard of poor Americans," she said. "During the war, we were hungry, but we were not poor." She excused herself to search for the bathroom. I rose. She smiled. I rose when she returned.

"Who taught you such good manners in the Bronx?"

"My father's only gift."

"Some fathers leave you only poison."

I let that pass and added, "My father was from Savannah, Georgia; he was a bad boy but with Southern-style aristocratic manners. I had to say 'Yes, sir' and 'No, sir' and 'May I leave the table, sir?'"

"Sounds terrible."

"At fifteen, he was sent to one of those military academies to break his wildness. I suppose he wasn't 'Yes, sir'–ing and 'No, sir'–ing enough for his father. He ran away and joined a relative who ran rum between the Florida Keys and Cuba."

"I don't know what it means, 'ran rum,' but it sounds romantic. I think I would have liked him."

"I'm sure," I said.

We were hungry and settled on provolone sandwiches from the thin list. "This is fine," she said. "Maybe also a glass of wine?"

But there was no wine; the café had no liquor license. I made my apologies. Simona was sweet about it.

"It's a little late for wine anyway," she said, "and I would rather stay clearheaded to form my impression of you."

"What idea have you formed already?"

"That you are a good boy, maybe even a sincere one."

"I hope both are true, but I'm a little too old to be a boy." I laughed lightly to show that I was not offended, but I *was* offended. I felt called out for the boy I was, the boy trying to seem grown-up.

"I like you, Frederico. I like that you read Pavese because I love Pavese and that he understands the sadness of women. I like that you are still sweet and do not flatter yourself, although I'm sure the girls chase you."

At that moment Cynthia came by and gave me a check and a long look and a warm smile and said, "I'm going off work now, Fred."

"Okay, thanks," I said, in the most neutral way I could without seeming cold.

"She's very beautiful," Simona said. "Don't let me stop you if you want to go home with her."

"I'm with you, Simona, and you are more beautiful."

"Finally, the Italian in you comes out."

"Anyone can see that you are beautiful, even an American."

"Better and better," she said. "Soon you will be the perfect Italian charmer. Anyway, it's getting late, my dear Frederico."

We walked along Sixth Avenue to look for a cab. I wanted to take her hand but dared not. I was a boy before a serious woman, and I was in awe of her.

"It is wonderful, your New York," she said.

I opened the door to her cab and kissed her on both cheeks, as I had seen done in the French movies. She gave me a look whose meaning I could not fathom. She smiled, but not completely—it was on the way to a smile.

I walked home in a pleasant daze and with the still-fresh aroma of her jasmine perfume. Wasn't that the same aroma that had clung to me when I left Miss Middleton's office so many years ago, and only moments ago? It seemed to take longer than ever to get home. It started to get dicey after Avenue A, and I checked who was behind me, slowing up to let the hoodlum-looking ones go by. If I saw any thuggish guys lingering on a corner, I took another street; it was longer but safer that way. I got to my building and stood in the hallway, listening. Maybe someone was on a landing waiting to mug me. It had happened to others. But my thoughts of Simona made me brave. She was greater than any bad that could happen to me.

I finally arrived at my landing and was glad to find the door still intact and the double gates to my fire escape window still fixed in place. I tried to read for a bit, but the words danced away, and soon Simona visited me in my dreams.

Tugboats and Clouds

Manhattan, Alphabet City, circa 1963–1964

The next morning I started again to practice Martin Eden's writing schedule and got to my typewriter at five a.m., skipping everything but a cup of coffee. I thought the discipline would see me through; it had worked for Martin Eden and, after all, it had worked for Jack London, his creator. Somehow I knew that Simona had spurred my return to writing. She was a serious person; could I not, in knowing her, become a serious person, serious to myself? Simona: *una vita nuova*.[20]

I was writing a book about a young man on the Lower East Side who made his meager living by collecting bottles in the trash bins at night and turning them into cash. My hero was an urban Thoreau who lived close to the bone and had a waitress girlfriend, an aspiring painter, who lived with him and pressed him to get a paying job. Her dream was to leave the city and live in rural Vermont, to have a home and three children. His was to live as he was and to read and write and one day see the world, maybe even Paris.

He borrowed books from the Tompkins Square Library and read them, weather permitting, on a bench in the park on the East River. There he wrote his impressions of all the passing freighters and tugs making their watery passages, and of the seagulls and the sounds of the engines swirling in the river. He noted the changes in the sky and the clouds, too. Some clouds were heavy and fiercely gray and hinted at rain and storms that flooded rivers and took away houses.

Some were feathery and high and would cross mountains and cover them in chilly shadow. He would fill his notebooks with such impressions and imaginings. His idea was to write a novel—or an anti-novel—without a character or a story or a plot, an impersonal book that breathed personality.

My novel was intercut with newspaper items both found and invented, and with quotes from American literature, mostly from Emerson and Thoreau and Melville and Poe. The intercut passages provided ironic comment or a parallel light on the narrative and my hero. If the book was a mess, it didn't matter: it was *my* mess, imitative of no other and reading like no other. And hadn't the novelist Albert Halper, years earlier when I was a student at City College, advised me, "Kid, when you're writing your first novel, no one is looking over your shoulder, so throw everything in it, even the kitchen sink"?

I had written thirty pages of this book and was hopeful for its future. A future with rewarding work ahead, with travel, maybe, finally, to Paris. "Time, Strength, Cash, and Patience" was what was needed, Melville wrote in *Moby-Dick*. I would have added "Love." What was all the rest without that?

Simona phoned me at the store ten minutes after I had opened the door. A friendly good morning and a thank-you for showing her the Village. Then: "Do you think I'm your aunt?"

"Of course not."

"Then why did you kiss me like I am?"

"Next time I won't."

"Good. *Ciao*, Federico. By the way, do you like opera?"

"Of course."

"Why of course? Some people hate opera."

"Like who?"

"Like my father. So, do you want to go or no?"

"Yes, very much."

"I have two tickets to *La Bohème* for next week. You are a bohemian, so you must love it."

"I love *Tristan und Isolde*, so what does that make me?"

"A man who can sit through noise."

Richie came in and gave me looks as if to say, "You are on my time."

"I have to get off. I'm sorry, Simona."

"Me, too. Meet me in the opera house lobby next Tuesday. *Ciao, buon lavoro.*"

I had listened to opera on the radio but had never been to one live. I had no idea where the opera house was. I had no idea what I was required to wear. In the thirties black-and-white movies men wore tuxedos to the opera and women wore gloves and gowns and jewelry. I wondered if I had to rent a tux, and where, and how much it would cost.

"I have to talk to you about something," Richie said.

"I never get calls here. It was just a fluke today."

"No, no, Freddy, I have good news. I'm opening another store on Broadway. A big one."

He wanted me to manage the new store, with a raise to a hundred dollars a week, and I could hire someone to work with me. Seven days a week, but I could close at six on Sundays.

I said that I would think about it. But what was there to think about? If I didn't do it, he would hire someone else, and I would work under a stranger. I could use the money, but I would have to get up at four thirty every morning if I expected to write a book. By the evening I said yes and asked for a hundred and twenty-five a week. We agreed to a hundred and fifteen. I would be able to open a checking account.

My newfound wealth emboldened me, and as soon as Richie stepped out, I phoned Simona to invite her to dinner. Her boss, Marcello, answered, and when I asked for her, his voice got cold.

"She's not here."

"Oh. Can I leave her a message?"

"If I can remember."

"Please ask her to call me. I'm at the store all day."

"I doubt she'll call you today. She left for London."

"When will she be back?"

"In time for the opera," he said. "Don't worry."

It was ten when the phone rang. I hoped it was Simona stuck at the airport in New York or maybe calling me from London, having just arrived. I was sure she had gotten my message or that she had already felt, as I imagined and wished, our deepening connection and wanted to hear my voice.

"I've missed you," Rebecca said.

"Me, too," I said, although it was not true. I missed Simona. Rebecca was starting to vanish from my mind, and what was left of her I found fault with. A painter who didn't paint. A woman without fire or a singular passion or a mission that she pursued with fervor. When did I start to think that beauty was not enough, that there was no beauty without flair, without spirit?

"Can I come over?"

"Yes, that would be great, but I'm really tired tonight."

"I'll be very nice to you," she said.

"You are always nice to me."

"You know what I mean. If you're too tired tonight, OK," Rebecca added. "But I want us to move ahead in our relationship."

The last times with her had been boring. Conversation circled the reasons she could not paint: "My studio is too small and I want to make large-scale paintings like Frankenthaler or Hartigan, or even Jackson Pollock himself."

"So find a big studio," I said. "You have the money."

"Am I a painter, Fred?"

"Of course, as long as you like doing it."

Boring also was the sex. The only position she allowed was missionary; everything else made her feel like a bad girl.

"I'm not that kind of girl," she said when I asked her to go on all fours.

"What kind of girl is that?"

"A girl dog."

"And I'm not a missionary." I loved myself for what I thought was my witty answer, but I also felt like a jerk for being so mean.

We hung up the phone. I got into bed. Bach's Cantata 140, "Sleepers Awake," played on WQXR. I was reading *The Magic Mountain*. Hans Castorp was sitting in a darkened room, listening to *Aida* on the gramophone, and suffering from unrequited love. Then the phone rang again. I was sure it was Rebecca with new thoughts on our relationship. Finally, I couldn't stand it; the ringing won.

It was my mother. She had received another official-looking letter from the welfare department. She nervously read it. I asked her to read it again. I had been hired for the investigator's position, a job that would give me time to dream, to write, if that was in me to do.

---

[20]SIMONA: THE AFTERMATH

Simona and I continued seeing each other for a year, and eventually we moved in together. Many of her friends wondered why she had anything to do with me, a guy who clerked in a bookstore and who, maybe, was soon to work in the welfare department. It was a mystery to me, too. All the same, we enjoyed each other in a happy, relaxed, moneyless way. We were close, affectionate friends who had sex.

From 1962 to 1964 we lived near the East River in my sixth-floor walk-up with my famous bathtub in the kitchen. The rent: twenty-eight dollars a month. Simona—who was a journalist for Italian magazines, had come from a middle-class family of journalists, and been raised in a spacious apartment with her own room and a terrace overlooking Rome—pronounced our little tenement charming.

"A bathtub in the kitchen. That's so convenient," she said. "And wood floors, too. My parents' floors are marble, which is less expensive than wood in Italy. Italians hate nature. They chopped down all the trees. And they'd cut them down in the parks if they had the chance."

She never complained about the dangerous neighborhood, the fear of muggings, the break-ins, the broiling heat under the tar roof, or sunning ourselves on that same roof-tar beach, as we called it.

In 1964 we found a place facing trees and sky on Tompkins Square Park, and we thought ourselves blessed. And we *were* blessed, although we were worried how to come up with the one hundred and sixteen dollars a month rent every month. We managed.

One late snowy afternoon we got married in Brooklyn in a justice of the peace's no-frills office. The wedding music cost five dollars extra.

Simona said, "Thank you, but we will not need the music."

"I like you, kids," the justice said. "I'll throw it in free."

We said our "I do's" to the accompaniment of Dvořák's *New World Symphony*.

We had gone to Brooklyn by subway and returned to Manhattan the same unceremonious way. We stayed happy for several years.

Acknowledgments

There are no precise words to say how grateful I am to the many who have helped me in the making of this memoir.

I want to thank, first of all, Gloria Loomis, my long-standing agent and dearest friend, for her willingness to stand by me and help find a home for the memoir. And with the same measure and spirit, I want to thank Gloria's colleague Julia Masnik.

Anne Stringfield read the memoir with a magnifying glass. She ordered the chronology and located places, people, and dates in a way that Sherlock Holmes could never have imagined. I am at once grateful and awed.

A thanks to Rebecca Jewett, coordinator of public services for the Thompson Library Special Collections at The Ohio State University, for the photographic research in the book. I am indebted to Iris Smyles for her most focused reading, as well as her astute editorial suggestions.

There were several people who read the book in various stages and were kind enough to offer both encouragement and insights that were very helpful in its fruition. They are Diane Keaton, Wayne Koestenbaum, Dorothy Lichtenstein, Steve Martin, Tom McCarthy, Edward Mendelson, and David Salle.

I want to thank Angela Dilella, Joanna Goldberg, Anton Haugen,

Jamie McPartland, and Rebecca Steever for their research and careful preparation of the manuscript. I never could have seen it through without their support. I am grateful to Karen Marta who patiently and wisely saw this memoir through from its conception to its completion.

No writer could wish for a more sympathetic and brilliant editor than Ira Silverberg.

About the Author

FREDERIC TUTEN grew up in the Bronx during the Great Depression. At fifteen, he dropped out of high school to become a painter, taking odd jobs and briefly attending the Art Students League of New York. He later traveled through Latin America, where he studied pre-Columbian art and Mexican mural painting.

While touring through South America, he wrote about Brazilian Cinema Novo and joined the circle of such filmmakers as Nelson Pereira dos Santos and Glauber Rocha. He taught film and literature at the Université Paris 8, acted in a short film by Alain Resnais, cowrote the cult film *Possession,* and conducted summer writing workshops with Paul Bowles in Tangiers.

Tuten has published five novels and a book of interrelated short stories. He is the recipient of a Guggenheim Fellowship for Fiction and was given the Award for Distinguished Writing from the American Academy of Arts and Letters.